# WATCH OFFICER'S GUIDE

*Fourteenth Edition*

# WATCH OFFICER'S GUIDE

## A Handbook for All Deck Watch Officers

Capt. James Stavridis, USN

NAVAL INSTITUTE PRESS/ANNAPOLIS, MARYLAND

Naval Institute Press
291 Wood Road
Annapolis, MD 21402

First edition 1911
Fourteenth edition 2000

Library of Congress Cataloging-in-Publication Data
Watch officer's guide : a handbook for all deck watch officers. —
   14th ed. / rev. by James Stavridis.
      p. cm.
   Includes bibliographical references and index.
   ISBN 1-55750-813-5
   1. United States.   Navy—Watch duty Handbooks, manuals, etc.   2. United States.
Navy Officers' handbooks.   I. Stavridis, James.
   V133.W37   1999
   359—dc21                              99-26570

Printed in the United States of America on acid-free paper ∞
06 05 04          9 8 7 6 5 4

# Contents

Appendixes

# Preface

The sea is eternally demanding, presenting myriad challenges to the watchstander: shiphandling, weather, the rules of the nautical road, engineering, formation and convoy steaming, communications, navigation, and underway safety, to name just a few. In port, the watch officer faces other challenges, including safety, the management of boats and vehicles, the rendering of honors, and the execution of ceremonies. Both at sea and in port, the watch officer must stand a taut watch, exhibit forehandedness, remain ever vigilant and alert, and maintain a scrupulously accurate deck log.

These are challenging duties, not learned in a day or exclusively from reading books like the *Watch Officer's Guide*. In fact, honing the classic skills of a watch officer requires a combination of study, education, training, review, and above all, experience. This slim volume serves two purposes. First, it provides the watch officer beginning his or her course of study and training a great deal of useful information in a single volume. Second, for the more experienced watch officer, it is a compendium of information handy both for review and during the actual standing of watch.

Nothing remains the same; this classic of the profession has now been through fourteen editions since its initial publication in 1911. Its wisdom is the result of the contributions of hundreds of naval officers and mariners who have worked to modernize and improve it during the eighty-eight years since it first appeared on the bridge and quarterdeck of many ships.

This edition offers important new material, including sections on the rules of the road and standing watch in the combat information center. Much of the other material in the volume has been reviewed, brought into line with current practice, and improved.

This edition is strictly the product of officers who have served at sea in U.S. Navy ships. In particular, I would like to thank three great Navy captains who taught me much of what I know of ships, the sea, and shiphandling: Captain R. F. Gaylord (Ret.), Rear Admiral T. C. Lockhart, and Captain L. E. Eddingfield (Ret.). I would also like to thank the many other naval officers who took the time to teach me about the sea and the standing of watches. Above all, I owe a great debt to my family, especially my wife, Laura, herself a Navy junior and the inspiration for all that I have been fortunate enough to accomplish in my career.

The successful watch officer is one who is willing to learn, to grow, to adapt. Failure to adapt is a sure precursor to danger, even disaster, at sea. Be flexible and forehanded as a watch officer and you will do a great job and stand a safe watch indeed.

# 1

# INTRODUCTION

The OOD reports directly to the Commanding Officer for the safe navigation and general operation of the ship; to the Executive Officer (and CDO if appointed) for carrying out the ship's routine; and to the Navigator on sighting navigational landmarks, and on making course/speed changes.

OpNavInst 3120.32C

## THE OFFICER OF THE DECK

The officer of the deck (OOD) occupies a unique position in a naval ship. Nowhere in military or civilian life is there a parallel to the range and degree of responsibility that is placed in the hands of the OOD. As direct representative of the captain, he or she acts with all the authority of command and, next to the captain and the executive officer, is the most important person in the ship. Modern technology has given the OOD sophisticated tools but, at the same time, has added to the scope of traditional duties and responsibilities. Qualification as OOD is the cornerstone of professional growth for a surface line officer and the most critical milestone of the surface-warfare qualification.

A junior officer must devote every possible moment to learning the skills to qualify as an OOD and, while doing so, must expect to be closely and critically observed. Mistakes will be corrected on the spot because, in the fast-paced atmosphere of modern fleet operations, there often is no time for lengthy critiques and explanations. As demanding as this learning process may be, its rewards are superbly satisfying. There is no feeling quite like that of standing watch for the first time as a fully qualified OOD knowing that you are in control of the ship. Whether that ship is a fleet tug or an aircraft carrier, the trust given to the OOD carries with it a time-honored and unique distinction.

## RESPONSIBILITY AND AUTHORITY

The duties, responsibilities, and authority of the OOD are delineated in OpNavInst 3120.32C Standard Organization and Regulations of the U.S. Navy. These regulations have legal status under Title 10 of the U.S. Code. They prescribe *minimum* duties and responsibilities. Factors such as the special mission of a ship, command policy, and guidance for a particular situation may add to these duties and responsibilities but not reduce them. Even more important than the letter of the regulations is the unwritten but traditional requirement that an OOD apply good judgment, intelligence, and initiative to his or her duties and exercise authority fully. This can be difficult. Given the diverse and often complex activities that take place aboard a ship at sea, it is easy for a watch officer to unwittingly allow authority to be delegated to a subordinate, particularly where specialized operations are concerned. There is nothing wrong with delegating authority, but the OOD must clearly understand that, regardless of who carries out duties, the responsibility for their being carried out is always his or hers. It is good practice, for example, to allow the quartermaster or the junior officer of the deck (JOOD) to take and plot navigational fixes. This does not, however, relieve the OOD of responsibility for the safe navigation of the ship. "Experts" who perform some of the many tasks required on a watch are assistants, never surrogates.

## ACCOUNTABILITY

On the sea there is a tradition older even than the traditions of the country itself and wiser in its age. . . . It is the tradition that with responsibility goes authority and with them both goes accountability.

"Hobson's Choice," *The Wall Street Journal,* 14 May 1952

Accountability is a subtle responsibility that is often misunderstood. A naval officer is accountable for the outcome of his or her duties, good or bad. Just as the commanding officer is inescapably accountable to a superior for everything that happens aboard the ship, so the OOD is accountable to the commanding officer for everything that happens during his or her watch. The only exceptions are those laid down by law or regulation. As the captain's direct representative, the OOD is the only person on board who can make decisions that affect the safety of the ship and the lives of her crew. The captain cannot be on the bridge at all times, and as history has repeatedly demonstrated, the OOD sometimes has to take actions that determine whether shipmates live or die. Accountability is one of the reasons why the OOD holds a unique position. No OOD should ever forget that.

## PRIORITIES

There is nothing that indicates which of the watch officer's duties are most important, for the simple reason that they are all equally important. It is necessary, however, to establish priorities, because the OOD can expect to be constantly confronted with the need to decide without delay where to focus his or her attention. Training a watch, for example, is always important, yet there will be times when training must be skipped to carry out other duties. The safety of the ship and the fulfillment of her mission always come first and must never be neglected. On the other hand, there will be times when the ship's activities allow the OOD to delegate many responsibilities and to become, for a while, a teacher and observer. At such times, the JOOD should run the watch. Not only does this give the junior officer self-confidence, but it gives the OOD a chance to step back and observe just how well he or she has performed.

Although theoretically responsible for all the things that go on during a watch, the OOD obviously cannot exercise personal control over everything. Total control would hopelessly enmesh the OOD in detail, drawing attention away from those aspects of the ship's operation over which he or she *must* have control.

Making a distinction between what is of direct concern and what is not requires a well-developed sense of judgment, and acquiring that sense is a vital part of a watch officer's training. The OOD should not become involved, for example, in how a petty officer on the fo'c'sle assigns a paint-chipping job. However, if the OOD sees one of the crew using a power tool without regard for safety, the situation must be corrected immediately. This sort of action can cause conflict. A department head or a senior officer may want to take an action that is in itself proper but will interfere with more important tactical operations being controlled by the watch. Here again, the duty of the OOD is to keep priorities straight, even if it means referring the matter to the executive officer or the captain for resolution.

## COMMAND RELATIONSHIPS

The OOD's command relationship with the commanding officer of the ship is clear and fixed. His or her other command relationships are equally important but much less clearly defined. Although regulations imply that the executive officer has authority over the OOD only on matters pertaining to the ship's routine, in most ships the executive officer is empowered to correct or modify any action taken by the watch officer. Because the extent of the executive officer's authority is a matter of individual command policy, the OOD must be familiar with the ship's regulations and with standing orders and directives that deal with this subject. The executive officer is second only to the captain as the most senior and experienced surface-warfare officer on board. Therefore, that person's advice and authority should be carefully weighed by the OOD. In addition, the OOD has a responsibility to the executive officer for the complete and accurate execution of the ship's routine. The OOD must keep the executive officer informed of changes that may affect the ship's routine, just as he or she must keep the commanding officer informed of changes that may affect the operational picture.

The relationship between the OOD and the engineering officer of the watch (EOOW) must be clearly understood by both officers. All regulations are very specific in stating that the EOOW reports to the OOD. However, each captain must outline in writing the policy regarding any automatic actions by the EOOW. For example, it may be a captain's policy that in the event of an engineering casualty, the EOOW is to automatically take whatever action is required and to keep the

OOD informed of the status of the propulsion plant. Another captain may require that the EOOW get the permission of the OOD before altering any propulsion plant condition, regardless of the casualty. Another possibility is a policy directing automatic actions by the EOOW except under certain conditions when the permission of the OOD is required. The OOD and the EOOW must each have a clear understanding of the captain's policy. It is a good idea for the OOD, upon relieving the watch, to review with the EOOW ship's policy regarding automatic actions by the latter.

In the rapidly changing world of modern warfare, a ship must be capable of the quickest possible reaction to a threat. Often there is not sufficient time to move from a routine underway condition to general quarters with weapons systems ready. To enhance weapons system readiness, the tactical action officer (TAO) concept has evolved. The TAO is a qualified OOD who also knows weapons systems capabilities as well as potential enemy threat and capabilities. The TAO normally stands watch in the combat information center (CIC) and has the authority to release the ship's weapons systems.

The relationship between the OOD and the TAO is especially important, because it involves a significant exception to the concept that the OOD is the final decision maker during a watch. Tactical control of the ship, particularly in the areas of threat analysis and reaction, belongs to the TAO in the CIC. This officer is normally a department head and is often senior in rank and experience to the OOD. In the CIC, the TAO has direct access to sensor information and weapons control as well as the means to evaluate enemy threats quickly and to take immediate action against them. OpNavInst 3120.32C and the ship's tactical doctrine may authorize him or her to direct the OOD in the tactical handling of the ship and, depending on circumstances and readiness, to fire weapons without permission from the OOD. Even when a TAO watch is set, however, the OOD remains responsible for the safety of the ship. If, in his or her judgment, a course of action directed by the TAO would put the ship in immediate danger, he or she may decline to follow it but must immediately inform the commanding officer of the situation. Assignment of decision-making responsibilities must be clearly understood by both watch officers at all times. In the fast-paced environment of modern warfare, there is not likely to be time to discuss a decision or to debate who should make it.

Specifically, control of the ship may be shifted, by positive command, to the TAO in the CIC or, in some cases, to other watch station officers; but the safety of the ship remains the responsibility of the OOD.

A TAO is stationed when the threat or the tactical situation requires that the ship be capable of assessing and reacting to a rapidly changing environment. The OOD must know the source of the TAO's authority and understand his or her relationship to the TAO.

The OOD has a unique relationship with the navigator. While on watch, the OOD is responsible for the safe navigation of the ship. This is a dual responsibility, shared with the navigator, who is at all times responsible for the safe navigation of the ship. It is quite clear, therefore, that the OOD must understand the navigation plan, the intended track, potential dangers to navigation, and the quality of fix available. The navigator may be authorized by the captain to relieve the OOD if in his or her judgment the OOD is endangering the ship from a navigation standpoint. Such a policy, established in writing, would only be executed in rare situations.

Normally, the quartermaster of the watch (QMOW) maintains the navigation picture for the OOD and is the navigator's representative while the navigator is away from the bridge.

Many large ships are organized to provide for the assignment of a command duty officer (CDO) at sea. He or she is required to keep informed of the tactical situation and the status of equipment and must be prepared to assume operational direction of the ship. The CDO's position relative to the OOD is similar to that of the executive officer to the OOD. The CDO may be, and usually is, authorized by the commanding officer to relieve the OOD if necessary. When a ship under way has a CDO assigned, the OOD should make all the reports to that person that he or she would normally make to the executive officer and the commanding officer.

These brief comments show that, although the OOD's relationships with other key watchstanders are regulated, there is latitude for each command to supplement, and to some extent modify, the various regulations. This is a prerogative of the commanding officer, whose duty it is to see that his or her watch organization is the best one possible to meet the needs of the ship. This might mean that in wartime the captain would order the TAO to direct combat. When a TAO watch does not seem necessary, the captain might decide not to set one, in order to use the crew to better advantage. These are command decisions that will, in all cases, be communicated either orally or in writing to the watch officers concerned. It then becomes the duty of the watch officer to understand clearly and without any doubt what his or her position in the organization is.

## CHARACTERISTICS OF THE OOD

### Forehandedness

The watch officer should be ready for any situation. For that reason, the most important faculty for the watch officer to cultivate is forehandedness. If there is reason to think that there will be fog during a watch, he or she should check over the fog procedure before taking the deck. If the ship is to take part in fleet exercises, the watch officer should arrange to look over the orders before going on watch. If the ship is to enter New York Harbor, for example, the watch officer should review the inland rules of the road. If there are to be ceremonies during the watch, the watch officer should be letter-perfect in the honors required and put a little extra snap in his or her own appearance. The watch officer must always look ahead, a minute, an hour, or a day, and make it a matter of pride never to be caught unprepared.

The wise watch officer will mentally rehearse the action to take in the event of a fire, a man overboard, a steering failure, or any other serious casualty. This habit is not difficult to acquire and is certain to pay large dividends. Forehandedness is the mark of the successful watch officer.

### Vigilance

Next to forehandedness, the most important quality for the OOD is vigilance. Vigilance is essential to safety. The OOD must, of course, observe intelligently all that comes within his or her vision, both outside and inside the ship, but vigilance extends beyond the visible. The OOD should also encourage vigilance on the part of all others on watch.

### Judgment

A third important quality for the OOD is judgment, which means a sense of proportion and of the fitness of things. Watches vary all the way from extreme tenseness, when the OOD must be alert every instant, as in high-speed work at night in a darkened ship, down to the calm of a Sunday afternoon at anchor, when the OOD is just keeping ship. On a darkened ship, only essentials count and the OOD must key his or her mind to its keenest pitch. On a quiet Sunday afternoon, it may be that the most immediate responsibility is to be affable to visitors.

## Intuition

Most officers who have spent some time at sea have a special sense for what is going on around them. An experienced chief engineer will awaken immediately if the sound of a blower or a pump is not right, just as a good navigator will go to the bridge to check the weather at even the smallest change in the ship's motion. There is nothing magic about this ability and it requires no special talent. It is the product of experience and of the carefully cultivated habit of close and continuous observation. To a new officer, so many things seem to be happening at once that concentration on one detail is almost impossible. With experience, however, things begin to sort themselves out, and before long what seemed like a confusing and impossibly complex environment becomes understandable. At this point the learning process that makes a good watch officer begins. Once the basics of the watch become second nature, he or she can turn attention to developing an ability to observe and evaluate everything that is going on during the watch.

## Leadership

The fifth important quality is leadership, which the Navy officially defines as "the sum of those qualities of intellect, of human understanding, and of moral character that enable a man to inspire and to manage a group of people successfully." Every watch officer should cultivate dignity, forcefulness, confidence, and precision in his or her manner and should exact similar qualities from assistants. Striving to avoid any indication of confusion or peevishness and to perform quietly, the watch officer should always act the part of what he or she really is—next to the captain and the executive officer, the most important person in the ship.

## Technical Knowledge

The OOD, no matter how well endowed with forehandedness, vigilance, judgment, and leadership, must also know the technical aspects of the job, know the relative importance of his or her many responsibilities, and have experience. This book cannot cover all the technical knowledge that the OOD requires, nor can it furnish experience; it attempts, however, to indicate:

1. The kind of technical knowledge with which a watch officer must be familiar.

2. The relative importance of the watch officer's many responsibilities.

3. The lessons of accumulated experience, so far as they can be reproduced on the printed page.

4. Certain useful information that otherwise might not be readily available when wanted.

## Energy

A seventh quality that marks a superb watch officer is a high energy level. It can become tedious standing watch on the bridge. Many long midwatches and 0400–0800 watches seem to go on forever, and even the best watch officers can feel fatigue and a certain sense of complacency. On exciting watches, the level of effort required to keep track of everything that's going on can likewise begin to wear down the watch officer.

There are several things a watch officer can do to enhance his or her level of energy while on watch. Getting the proper amount of rest is critical, as is eating a balanced diet. Watching a movie until 2230 and gulping down a soda and hot dog for dinner is bound to reduce the energy of an officer on the midwatch. Additionally, attitude is important. Maintain an upbeat approach to watchstanding. To pass the time on long, slow watches, train the watch section. Stay enthusiastic and your energy level will remain high.

## CONCLUSION

We have talked about some of the bedrock qualities that lead to the standing of a good and competent watch. But there are some intangibles as well. What are some of these intangible but important qualities a captain looks for in a good officer of the deck?

Confidence comes first—a serene inner sense of assurance that will quickly radiate to the entire bridge team. Enjoyment of responsibility is certainly an important component as well. Another key attribute is a sense of humor. Don't take *yourself* too seriously, but always take your responsibility as OOD very seriously. There is a big difference.

Finally, you should always, always stay calm. You will not be able to control many things on the bridge of a ship—the wind, the seas, the equipment casualties, the requirements and missions—but there is one thing you can always control: your own temperament. Stay calm and focused, work hard to learn what you must, admit your mistakes when they occur, and all will be well.

# 2

# THE WATCH IN GENERAL

DUTIES, RESPONSIBILITIES, AND AUTHORITY. The OOD under way shall:

(1) Be aware of the tactical situation and geographic factors which may affect safe navigation and take action to avoid the danger of grounding or collision following tactical doctrine, the U.S. Coast Guard Navigation Rules of the Road, and the orders of the Commanding Officer or other proper authority.

(2) Be informed of current operation plans and orders, intentions of the OTC and the Commanding Officer, and other matters of ship or force operations.

(3) Issue necessary orders to the helm and main engine control to avoid danger, to take or keep an assigned station, and to change course and speed following orders of proper authority.

(4) Make all required reports to the Commanding Officer.

(5) Ensure that required reports to the OOD concerning tests and inspections and the routine reports of patrols, watches, and lifeboat crews are made promptly and that the bridge watch and lookouts are posted and alert.

(6) Supervise the personnel on watch on the bridge, ensure that all required deck log entries are made, and sign the log at the end of the watch.

(7) Issue orders for rendering honors to passing ships as required by regulations and custom.

(8) Ensure that the Executive Officer, CDO (when assigned), and department heads concerned remain informed of changes in the tactical situation, operation schedule, the approach of heavy weather, and other circumstances which may require a change in the ship's routine or other actions.

(9) Be aware of the status of the engineering plant, and keep the Engineering Officer of the Watch advised of power requirements and the operational situation so he/she may operate the engineering plant effectively.

(10) Carry out the routine of the ship as published in the plan of the day and other ship directives. Keep the Executive Officer advised of any changes in routine.

(11) Supervise usage of the general announcing system; the general, chemical, collision, sonar, and steering casualty alarms; and the whistle following the orders of the Commanding Officer, tactical doctrine, and the U.S. Coast Guard Navigation Rules of the Road.

(12) Permit no person to go aloft on the masts or stacks or to work over the side except when wind and sea conditions permit and then only when all applicable safety precautions are observed.

(13) Supervise transmissions and acknowledgements on the primary and secondary tactical voice radio circuits, and ensure that proper phraseology and procedures are used in all transmissions.

(14) Supervise and conduct on-the-job training for the Junior Officer of the Watch (JOOW), the Junior Officer of the Deck (JOOD), and enlisted personnel of the bridge watch.

(15) Assume other responsibilities as assigned by the Commanding Officer.

OpNavInst 3120.32C

## PREPARATION

The more thorough the preparation before going on watch, the more likely the OOD is to perform duties efficiently.

A newly commissioned officer reporting to his or her first ship, or an experienced officer ordered to one that is unfamiliar, will be required to quickly learn about the ship, her organization, and the people who run her. To get this information there are some helpful references available. OpNavInst 3120.32C, supplemented by instructions for the particular type and class of ship concerned, constitutes the Standard Ship's Organization and Regulations Manual, familiarly known by its acronym SORM. At first, the sheer bulk of all this material may be dismaying, but most of the chapters of SORM contain material that can be absorbed gradually, as the newly reported officer becomes acquainted with the ship's operation. A watch officer should immediately begin familiarizing himself or herself with the ship's watch organization. The SORM chapter on this subject contains the most important regulations of the watch and details precisely the duties and responsibilities of, and relationships among, watchstanders. Particular attention must be paid to the italicized sections, because these are regulatory and have the force of law. The sections in bold-face type provide guidance on the organization of the command. There are a number of ship's instructions that detail the specific duties of the various watchstanders, such as sounding-and-security and roving patrol. Because the first duties of a junior officer of the deck (JOOD) are likely to involve checking in some way on the performance of these watchstanders, it is important to know what their duties are, especially if the ship has special watch requirements.

Although a warship's organization for damage control is quite complex, the basics of that organization—including the location of repair lockers, the number and composition of repair parties, and the essential components of installed firefighting and drainage systems—should be learned as soon as possible.

Today's fleet operations require a watch officer to be familiar with a wide range of tactical and operational situations on any given watch. It is therefore foolish for an oncoming OOD or tactical action officer (TAO) to assume the watch after only a ten- or fifteen-minute rundown of what is happening. Preparation must be longer than that. Operation orders, concepts of operations, and operational tasks (OpTasks) should be studied carefully, well before the information is needed, and not in the corner of a darkened bridge on a rough night. Essentially, preparation for the underway watch begins before the ship gets under way. The OOD must participate in pre-exercise briefings and be familiar with the battle group commander's standing orders. However, the immediate situation must be absorbed and reviewed just prior to the watch. The best place to do this sort of preparation is usually the combat information center (CIC), where formation disposition, tactical data, and communications plans are all displayed. However, the CIC is not the only place the OOD should stop before relieving the watch. It is a good idea to visit the engineering officer of the watch (EOOW) and find out the details of plant status as well as any possible extra drills, maintenance, or repairs that are being planned. A tour of topside spaces will give firsthand knowledge of readiness for heavy weather and send a signal to the lookouts that the officer will be in charge for the next watch.

The OOD should be physically prepared, fresh, and well rested before assuming the watch. He or she should be dressed for the weather and take along his or her own equipment—flashlight with red filter, notebook, etc.; the OOD should not expect to borrow them from the officer being relieved. On a night watch, the OOD should allow at least twenty minutes to become night-adapted before even considering taking over. It is most important to be psychologically prepared. For the four hours or so of a watch, the OOD's mind should be on nothing else. In a fast-moving tactical situation, only a few seconds of inattention can cause an OOD to become confused, sometimes with disastrous results.

## RELIEVING THE WATCH

The process of relieving the watch should not be undertaken until the relief is absolutely familiar with the general situation. It used to be that the oncoming OOD would appear on deck fifteen minutes before the hour, but modern operations at sea usually demand more discussion between the offgoing and the oncoming watch than is possible in the traditional fifteen-minute turnover. Unless the oncoming officer is prepared, the information the offgoing officer passes on during the turnover will make little sense. The new OOD will then be in the unpleasant position of either having to ask for information or, worse, taking over without really understanding what is going on and then spending the rest of the watch trying to catch up.

No matter how thoroughly the relieving officer has prepared before reporting ready to relieve, the oral turnover is still important. This is the last chance to clear up anything that may seem vague or confusing, and it is the on-watch officer's opportunity to pass on to the relief any necessary miscellaneous information. For example, there might have been some last-minute changes to the watch team. Perhaps the officer in tactical command (OTC) has a weak transmitter on a tactical circuit and can barely be heard. This is the sort of information the relieving OOD needs to run a smooth watch.

The oral turnover should be formal and businesslike. The officer coming on duty should step up to the officer being relieved, salute, and say, "I am ready to relieve you, sir (or ma'am)." The officer being relieved returns the salute and says, "I am ready to be relieved." Aside from setting an example of smartness and military courtesy and observing a time-honored custom of the service, there are very sound reasons for this procedure. The key word is "ready." By declaring himself or herself ready to relieve the watch, the officer is stating that he or she has made all reasonable preparations, gathered all available information, and needs but an oral turnover to assume duties. A mumbled "What's going on?" is not an acceptable substitute. The officer being relieved describes the operational situation, being sure to cover everything about other ships in the formation and other contacts. He or she should outline all known events scheduled to take place during the upcoming watch, then give a rundown on the propulsion plant status, highlighting any limitations.

While receiving information about the watch, the incoming OOD has an opportunity to observe what is going on, both on board and outside the ship. When the OOD thoroughly understands the situation, has heard all the outgoing OOD has to say, and has asked any necessary questions, it is his or her duty to salute again and say, "I relieve you, sir (or ma'am)." It must be stressed that this is an obligation, not to be dispensed with a sloppy "Okay, I've got it." The officer being relieved returns the salute and replies with "I stand relieved." Both officers then inform the bridge watch and report to the captain that the watch has been relieved.

## DECLINING TO RELIEVE THE WATCH

Some junior officers feel they may be considered timid if they exercise their option and decline to relieve the watch. However, it is an officer's duty to do so if, for example, the ship is out of position in the formation or a busy watch in port has become confused, with boats astray or out of fuel. Of course, a ship may be out of position for good reason and be headed back for her station, in which case it would be proper to relieve the watch.

A meticulous approach to this question is recommended. As the saying goes, "Relieve in haste, repent at leisure." A reputation for being detailed in taking over a watch is not a bad thing to acquire. It will keep the preceding watch officer on his or her toes, ready to turn over the watch without leaving embarrassing loose ends. The oncoming watch officer must remember that once the relieving officer has said, "I relieve you, sir (or ma'am)," the full responsibility of the watch is his or hers. If difficulties arise, he or she cannot then try to pass the blame back to the officer just relieved.

It is usually best not to relieve in the midst of a complex operation. Rather, it is better to stand back and observe the situation and, when feasible, step forward to relieve.

## LEADERSHIP RESPONSIBILITIES

In addition to responsibilities for the operation of the ship, the watch officer has an important role as leader of a watch team. No matter how competent or well prepared the OOD may be, he or she cannot hope to perform well without positive control of the watchstanders. In all likelihood, some of the people on the watch will be experienced, others inexperienced. Some will be fully qualified, some will be in the process of qualifying, and some may be standing watch for the first time. Their performance will be no better than the leadership given them by the watch officer. Consciously or unconsciously, they will take their lead from what they see the watch officer doing. The OOD is the center of action and the most visible person on the watch team. His or her manner must therefore convey an attitude of seriousness, concentration, and self-discipline. The OOD should insist that officers on his or her watch continually check, inspect, and train their subordinates, and should not hesitate to relieve a person on watch who is clearly incompetent or not trained to perform a job.

The high rate of turnover that most ships experience means that a watch officer can expect the training of new people to be a major and continuing duty. In addition, depending on command policy, he or she may be authorized to sign off on certain portions of a junior officer's surface-warfare personnel qualification standards. Not only does the training of watchstanders bring about obvious improvements in the readiness of the ship, but it also does a great deal for the morale and enthusiasm of watchstanders. A watch officer who shows a sincere interest in improving the skills of subordinates almost always gets a good response and builds a team he or she can be proud of. The quality of a watch helps significantly to determine a watch officer's professional reputation. He or she must exercise leadership by insisting on high standards of performance and appearance. He or she should take care that in the relieving process not all key watchstanders are relieved at once. One other point should be noted: All of the ship's resources are available to the OOD. He or she must never hesitate to use these resources when necessary.

**ROUTINE**

An intelligently conceived and punctiliously executed routine is essential to good shipboard organization. It is the OOD's job to supervise and closely control the manner in which this routine is carried out. If the plan of the day calls for "turn to" at 1300, he or she must be sure that, as far as can be determined, the crew does "turn to" at that time. If reveille is scheduled for 0600, he or she must see that all hands are turned out at that time. If something about the plan of the day does not seem right, the OOD should consult the executive officer, but until the routine is changed, he or she must see that it is carried out. The plan of the day is a directive. All hands must follow it, whether or not the word is passed over the general announcing system.

The boatswain's mate of the watch is the OOD's most important enlisted assistant and handles much of the detail of carrying out the daily routine. That person should be made to feel responsible for the watch routine and for the instruction, behavior, and appearance of the deck watch. It is his or her duty to see that all stations are manned and that the previous watch has been relieved. Like the OOD, the boatswain's mate of the watch exercises all the attributes of leadership required of a naval officer. One of the boatswain's mate's major duties is to carry out the plan of the day. He or she must know what is happening on board ship and must pass the word in accordance with the prescribed routine. The OOD should supervise the boatswain's mate in carrying out the watch routine rather than deal directly with the people on watch. The standard routine is usually written into the ship's organization book and is varied only by specific instructions in the plan of the day. When it seems advisable to change the routine because of unusual and unforeseen circumstances, the OOD must obtain permission for such change from the executive officer or the command duty officer.

**PASSING THE WORD**

For the ship's routine to be carried out as planned, the word must be passed. Few daily evolutions are more basic, or more abused, than the passing of the word. The amount of control the watch has over the general announcing system, designated the 1MC, is one of the best indicators of how well the ship is being run and how much attention the watch officer is paying to what is happening in the ship. Except in unusual or urgent situations, the 1MC should not be used as a means of communicating with individuals, nor should it be used as a paging system. The habit of passing the word for individuals (in most cases, simply because it is the easiest way to contact people) is one that is easy to get into and hard to break. Unless watch officers monitor what goes out over the 1MC, its abuse will quickly become part of accepted shipboard procedure. People will become so accustomed to hearing the 1MC every five minutes that when something really important is passed, no one will listen. By controlling the system, the OOD can prevent this from happening but also can avert problems in the carrying out of the ship's routine. If, for example, a ten-hand working party has been called away and fifteen minutes later the quarterdeck is asked to pass the word to "bear a hand in mustering the ten-hand working party," the proper reaction should be to turn down the request and instead find out why the party was not properly mustered.

When the word is passed, standard phraseology should always be used. This is not only the mark of a smart, seamanlike ship, it is the best way to ensure that the message gets out with maximum clarity and brevity. Standard phraseology (see chapter 4) will be found in SORM. A copy of the word to be passed for ship's routine and other standard announcements should be available on the bridge and at the quarterdeck station.

### Things to Be Avoided in Passing the Word

1. Use of clumsy or redundant language such as "All personnel not actually on watch," "Now payday is being held on the mess decks at this time," "Now bear a hand . . . ," or "That is all."

2. Improper use of circuits. SOPA (senior officer present afloat) regulations and regulations in many foreign ports prohibit the use of topside speakers except in emergencies.

3. Passing word that is not of concern to officers on the officers' circuit.

4. Use of the 1MC during church services or ceremonies, except in emergencies.

5. Addressing a long list of people.

6. Asking officers or chief petty officers to "muster" or "lay to." Courtesy demands the phrase "please assemble."

7. Pauses, hesitations, and breaks in the course of a message. If the watch is not sure what to say, the message should be written down and read.

## APPEARANCE OF THE WATCH

The OOD, circumstances permitting, must see that the men and women on watch are in clean regulation uniform. The OOD sets an example, at all times, for the whole ship. At sea, particularly in bad weather, he or she should be dressed to keep warm and dry and should see that the watchstanders are similarly protected. In port, when visitors are coming aboard, the maximum spit and polish is expected; uniforms should be in good condition, shoes polished, and personal appearance neat.

The boatswain's mate of the watch is responsible for the appearance of the watch, and the OOD should not hesitate to have him or her order any person who does not come up to standard to change. Wrinkled, ill-fitting, or dirty uniforms and work shoes may be worn about the deck when a clean uniform might get soiled, but they are not good enough for a messenger of the watch on the quarterdeck.

Similarly, the appearance of the bridge or quarterdeck should be a matter of interest to the OOD. He or she should have the boatswain's mate of the watch keep the area clean and tidy. Sweeping the deck, emptying trash buckets and ashtrays, and keeping empty coffee cups out of sight are all details to which an alert boatswain's mate of the watch attends.

## CONDUCT ON WATCH

There is need for a certain formality on watch. This does not require pomposity; on the contrary, often a touch of humor is appropriate. But watchstanders must never be permitted to forget that they are on duty and that what they are doing is important. This formality adds to the professionalism of the watch and to the reputation of the OOD. It is usually the small things that count most. For example, it is inappropriate for officers on watch to address each other by first names, even if they are roommates. Officers should address crew members by formal title, and crew members on watch should similarly address each other.

A ship is always subject to emergency or disaster; fire, man overboard, and dozens of other events can disrupt the dullest watch. The OOD should make it a practice to run a taut watch and to prevent noisy and idle chatter; he or she should use common sense and not be arbitrary or harsh in dealing with subordinates.

## RELATIONS WITH THE STAFF

The OOD of a flagship has the additional responsibilities of keeping the embarked staff informed as to what is going on, handling additional boats and vehicles, and of course, rendering honors.

The staff duty officer is usually the person who receives special reports. In general, the events and sightings normally reported to the commanding officer should also be reported to the staff duty officer. He or she bears approximately the same relation to the admiral and squadron or division commander as an OOD does to the commanding officer.

The flag lieutenant is generally responsible to the admiral for the scheduling of honors and advises the OOD what honors are to take place. In return, the OOD advises the flag lieutenant, as well as the staff duty officer, of unscheduled visits that may require honors.

Staff officers take care to preserve the flagship's unity of command and do not give orders directly to the OOD. Routine requests may be made to the ship's officers, but in matters of any importance the chief of staff usually deals with the commanding officer of the flagship. An OOD will not be inconvenienced by an embarked staff as long as he or she remembers to consider their needs and to keep them informed.

## TURNING OVER THE WATCH

As a watch draws to a close, the OOD gives the relief all available information for maximum continuity. Both the relieved and the relieving officer must see that this is done. It may be necessary to make notes or to keep a checklist; in any event, the relieved officer should remember, even while turning over the watch, to be alert and on the job. The task of turning over the watch must not divert attention from maintaining a proper watch. If the OOD feels that the pace of operations makes the scheduled turnover inappropriate or even unsafe, he or she should so inform the relief, and a delay or change should be arranged. The oncoming relief must be flexible in this regard.

When the commanding officer is on the bridge, the oncoming watch officer should say, "Request permission to relieve the officer of the deck," and the offgoing OOD should report, "I have been properly relieved as officer of the deck by _____."

## KNOWING THE SHIP

Listed below are some of the basic facts that an officer should begin learning about a ship as soon as he or she reports on board. The "OOD under way" part of the surface-warfare officer's personnel qualification standards contains other things that he or she will be required to know as part of the qualification process. The surface-warfare officer's qualification process is designed to lead to various watch officer qualifications, and following that process is the best way to qualify as OOD. However, by going through the following list, a few items at a time, during a quiet watch or in-port duty day, an officer will soon improve his or her feel for the ship and how she operates:

1. Principal dimensions (beam, draft, length, displacement, etc.).
2. Fuel and water capacity, fuel consumption at various speeds, most economical speed.
3. Maximum speed available under different boiler combinations (steam plants).
4. Engine lineup and combination or turbine lineup and combination (gas-turbine and diesel ships).
5. Capabilities and limitations of weapon systems.
6. Capabilities and limitations of sensors.
7. Angles for standard, full, and hard rudder.
8. Steering-engine controls and steering-engine combinations; emergency steering procedures.

9. Location, sound, appearance, and meaning of all alarm systems on the bridge.

10. Location of and normal use for all radio and internal communications stations.

11. Procedures and safety precautions for raising and lowering boats.

12. Preparations for underway replenishment.

13. Preparations for entering and leaving port.

14. Operation of radar repeaters.

15. Operation of bearing circles, alidades, and stadimeters.

16. Publications kept on the bridge, where they are to be found, and how they are accounted for.

17. Procedure for manning watch and battle stations.

18. Make-up and check-in requirements for various security watches.

19. Regulations concerning disposal of trash and garbage.

20. Regulations concerning pumping bilges, oil spills, and environmental protection.

21. Characteristics and limitations of onboard aircraft or helicopters.

22. Operational, administrative, and task organizations that affect the OOD, and where his or her ship is in the organization.

23. Required reports to the OOD.

24. Location and use of emergency signals.

25. Precautions to be taken in heavy weather.

26. Basic ship's tactical information, such as turning-circle diameters under various conditions and limitations on acceleration and deceleration.

27. Thumb rules and quick procedures for "measuring the situation."

## A SEQUENCE FOR RELIEVING

A reasonable sequence should be established for the process of relieving. While this is generally a matter of personal preference, a reasonable guideline is for the outgoing OOD to inform the oncoming OOD about:

1. The quartermaster and navigation plot.

2. The bridge naval tactical data system (NTDS) terminal if installed.

3. Bridge status boards.

4. Helm/lee helm.

The following is the minimum amount of information the watch officer should know before relieving the watch:

1. Course, speed, position, and intended track of the ship.

2. Water depth, predicted set and drift, and navigational aids.

3. Rocks, shoals, shipping, and other dangers to navigation in the vicinity or on the proposed track.

4. Gyro error, magnetic variation, and magnetic heading on the present course.

5. Weather conditions, the force and direction of the wind, temperature, barometer reading, and the rate of change.

6. Ability of lifeboats and lifeboat crew to respond instantly.

7. Status of fathometer, SatNav, OMEGA, WSN-5, and radar navigation information as applicable.

8. General tactical situation, including assigned position in the formation, location of the guide, and the ship's actual position in the formation.

9. Major equipment in use and out of commission, and the readiness of the armament, engineering plant, and damage-control closure.

10. Any recent course and speed changes required by the previous watch to maintain station.

11. All unexecuted orders (the OOD reads and signs the captain's book and staff night orders if the ship is embarked).

12. Location and voice call of the OTC, the tactical voice nets in use, and the location and disposition information of other ships.

13. Identification of all ships in the formation visually and on the radarscope.

14. Status of shipping and current closest points of approach (CPAS).

15. Turbines/engines/boilers in use and maximum speed possible; status of off-line equipment and respective power train.

16. Watch status in the CIC; aircraft under control.

17. Emissions-control condition and specific restrictions placed on electronic emissions.

18. Radar guard assignments, air defense sector assignments, and nets utilized for reporting.

19. Authentication and challenging information.

20. Status of all electronic equipment.

21. Status of the towed array: scope of the cable, depth of the array, and minimum depth associated with that scope (if applicable).

22. Status of embarked helicopters (if applicable), time of flight quarters, ceiling, visibility, dew point spread, and the best course to place the ship in the envelope.

23. Lighting measures in effect.

24. Generators in use and status of off-line generators.

25. Steering cables and units in use.

26. Contents of the plan of the day, including any special events that may occur during the watch and preparations.

27. The location of the captain!

## RELIEVING ANY WATCH

This excerpt, taken from OpNavInst 3120.32C, is an excellent summary of the protocol for taking *any* watch on board a U.S. Navy warship. You should be very familiar with the process and use it in all your relieving processes.

RULES FOR RELIEVING THE WATCH. Relieving the watch will be controlled and precise. The ability to handle casualties and tactical decisions is significantly reduced during the transition period between watches. Accordingly, the following rules will apply:

(1) The relieving watch will be on station in sufficient time to become familiar with equipment conditions and the overall situation and still relieve on time.

(2) The relieving watch will inspect all spaces and equipment as required by the Commanding Officer before relieving the watch.

(3) If practical, the relieving watch will examine all applicable equipment log readings on the station since he/she last had the watch, noting any unusual variations such as voltages, pressures, and

temperatures. Such variations will be discussed and resolved prior to watch relief. (Check that the preceding watch has completed the log sheets as required.)

(4) The relieving watch will read the remarks sections of applicable logs from the last time that he/she was on watch (or from the time of getting underway, plant start-up, equipment light-off; or for the preceding three watches if continuity of watches has been interrupted), carefully noting and discussing unusual conditions, deviations, or other matters of importance.

(5) Both the relieved watch and the relieving watch are responsible for ensuring that the relieving watch is completely aware of all unusual conditions. These include tactical situations, equipment out of commission or in repair, personnel working aloft, outstanding orders, deviations from normal plant or equipment line-up, forthcoming evolutions (if known), and any other matters pertinent to the watch.

(6) The relief will be executed smartly under the following guidelines:

   (a) Permission is obtained from the appropriate watch supervisor to relieve the watch.

   (b) Relief reports, "Ready to relieve."

   (c) Person being relieved gives a status report of the watch section.

   (d) Relief tours the watch station.

   (e) Person being relieved completes briefing of relief (including unexecuted orders and anticipated evolutions) and answers any questions.

   (f) When the relief is fully satisfied that he/she is completely informed regarding the watch, he/she relieves the watch by saying, "I relieve you."

   (g) Responsibility for the watch station then shifts to the oncoming watchstander, and the person being relieved states "I stand relieved."

## TRAINING THE WATCH

A good watch officer is always in the mood for training. Particularly when a watch is long and dull, it is important to keep the watch team occupied and interested in being on the bridge. The best way to do this is to conduct training. A few ideas:

1. Set up a competition between the bridge and the CIC in solving various problems: maneuvering boards, looking up answers to questions in publications, communications procedures, tactical signals, and the like.

2. Have a question-and-answer competition among bridge watchstanders—who can locate the flight-deck crash alarm, the fog signal switch, the various radio circuits on the bridge, and so forth.

3. Show the lookouts profiles of various air and surface contacts operating in the theater.

4. Have an engineer come to the bridge to cover damage-control or engineering training on station.

5. Have a corpsman come up to conduct first-aid training.

6. Cross-train the boatswain's mate in navigation or the quartermaster in tactical communications.

# 3

# THE SHIP'S DECK LOG

All U.S. Navy ships in commission shall maintain a ship's deck log.

OpNavInst 3100.7B

The deck log shall be a complete daily record, by watches, which shall describe every occurrence of importance concerning the crew and the operation and safety of the ship or items of historical value.

OpNavInst 3120.32C

## GENERAL

The deck log is the official record of a ship's history during her commission. It presents a complete narrative of noteworthy incidents in the life of the ship and her officers and crew. Everything of significance pertaining to the ship's complement, material, operations, or state of readiness is entered in the deck log. It is a detailed source of factual data. Watch officers responsible for the maintenance of the log must appreciate the importance of their undertaking. They must ensure that all entries are complete, accurate, clear, concise, and expressed in standard naval phraseology. Taken together, the entries should constitute a true and understandable historical and legal record of the ship.

The ship's deck log must be kept with care. It must be clear enough to stand alone as the official legal record of the ship's activity and significant occurrences of any one day. The entries in the deck log for each day must give so complete an account of the events of that day, from 0000 until 2400, that reference to the previous day's log is not necessary. This is why the entry made by the midwatch must recapitulate the situation existing at midnight. This entry includes the conditions of readiness in force, the status of the engineering plant, the command organization, course and speed, other units present, and required tactical information.

The deck log, the magnetic compass record book, the engineering log, and the engineer's bell book are legal records and can be used as evidence before legal bodies. Consequently, it is important that the remarks be complete and accurate. Erasures in any of these records would bring their validity as evidence into question. The OOD must initial corrections of errors in these logs.

Logs are often consulted in the settlement of claims for pensions by persons who claim to have been injured while serving in the armed forces. A complete entry, therefore, must be made in the log concerning every injury, accident, and casualty, including accidents that could later lead to the discovery of injuries to the officers, crew, or passengers on board. This is necessary both to protect the government from false claims and to furnish a record for honest claimants.

The navigator has charge of the preparation of the deck log. Regulations require that he or she examine the log book to see that it is prepared in accordance with instructions and call the attention of watch officers to any inaccuracies or omissions in their entries. The navigator is responsible for log entries being in proper form, but the OOD is responsible for the entries made during his or her watch.

All entries must be handwritten and signed with a ballpoint pen in black or blue-black ink. The remarks must be legible, and while the junior officer of the deck or quartermaster of the watch may write the log, it must be signed by the OOD responsible for the watch.

## DECK-LOG ENTRIES

Because the deck log is handwritten, particular care must be taken in the recording of numbers. Proper nouns are to be printed, and where a signature is required, the name is to be printed under the individual's signature. The Bureau of Naval Personnel will return for remedial action logs that are illegible for any reason, including poor penmanship. No lines may be skipped, except between the beginning and end of successive watch entries. Only abbreviations that are accepted throughout the Navy by reason of long and continued usage may be entered in the log. The following are some of the most commonly used abbreviations, drawn from OpNavInst 3100.7B:

| | |
|---|---|
| UA | Unauthorized absence |
| CPA | Closest point of approach |
| OCE | Officer conducting the exercise |
| OOD | Officer of the deck |
| OTC | Officer in tactical command |
| R(L)FR | Right (left) full rudder |
| R(L) 15R | Right (left) 15 degrees rudder |
| H(R/L)R | Hard (right/left) rudder |
| R/A | Rudder amidship |
| MEET HR | Meet her |
| R(L) 050 | Right (left) to course 050°T |
| AEA ⅓ | All engines ahead ⅓ |
| AE STOP | All engines stop |
| AEA STD | All engines ahead standard |
| AEA FUL | All engines ahead full |
| AEA FLK | All engines ahead flank |
| P(S)EA ⅓ | Port (starboard) engine ahead ⅓ |
| P(S)EB ⅓ | Port (starboard) engine back ⅓ |
| 145 rpm | 145 revolutions per minute |

The following sample entries are to be used as guides for recording the remarks of a watch. They are not all-inclusive, nor are they to be construed as the only acceptable ones. Any entry that is complete, accurate, and in standard naval phraseology is acceptable.

## Midwatch

**UNDER WAY**

00–04

0000  Steaming in company with Task Group 30.5, composed of COMCARGRU 7 and COMDESRON 23, plus USS JARRETT (FFG 33) and USS RENTZ (FFG 46), en route from Pearl Harbor, Hawaii, to San Diego, California, in accordance with CTG 30.5 161514Z AUG

90. ANTIETAM (CG 54) is in station 2 in a formation 1. Formation course 220°T, speed 15 knots. Formation axis 222°T. SOPA is CTG 30.5 in USS ANTIETAM (CG 54). OTC is COMCARGRU 7 in USS LINCOLN (CVN 72). RENTZ is guide, bearing 220°T, distance 5000 yds. Condition of readiness 3 and material condition YOKE set. Ship darkened (except for running lights).

*Note:* On succeeding watches the first entry is "Under way as before."

**IN PORT**

00–04

0000    Moored starboard side to USS HEWITT (DD 966) with standard mooring lines in a nest of three ships. USS ELLIOTT (DD 967) moored outboard of HEWITT to starboard. HEWITT moored fore and aft to buoys B-5 and B-6, Norfolk, VA.
Ships present: ____, SOPA ____.

00–04

0000    Anchored in berth B-4, Trinidad, West Indies, in 12 fathoms of water, mud bottom, with 60 fathoms of chain to the starboard anchor on the following anchorage bearings: South Point Light 060, etc. Ship in condition of readiness 3, material condition YOKE set and darkened except for anchor lights. Engineering Department on 30-minute notice before getting under way. Heavy weather plan in effect. Anchor detail standing by. Wind 45 knots from 070. Weather reports indicate possibility of winds up to 60 knots before 0400. Ships present: ____, SOPA ____.

00–04

0000    Moored starboard side to pier 3, berth 35, U.S. Naval Station, Norfolk, Va., with standard mooring lines doubled. Receiving miscellaneous services from the pier. Ships present include ____, SOPA ____.

00–04

0000    Resting on keel blocks in dry dock no. 3, U.S. Naval Shipyard, Bremerton, Wash., receiving miscellaneous services from the dock. Ships present include ____, SOPA ____.

*Note:* On succeeding watches the first entry is "Moored as before," "Anchored as before," or "Dry-docked as before."

## Air Operations

ENTRIES APPLICABLE TO CARRIERS

1000 Flight quarters.

1005 Commenced launching aircraft for (carrier qualification) (refresher operations) (group tactics), etc.

1025 Completed launching aircraft, having launched 40 aircraft.

1030 Commenced recovering aircraft.

1035 Commenced maneuvering while recovering (launching) aircraft (while conducting task group [force] flight operations).

1055 Completed recovering aircraft, having recovered 40 aircraft.

1143 F-14 bureau no. 12345 of VF-31, pilot LCDR Ben B. BOOMS, USN, 000-00-0000, crashed into the sea off the port bow at latitude 30°50'N, longitude 150°20'W, and sank in 500 fathoms of water.

1144 USS ARTHUR W. REDFORD (DD 968) and helicopter commenced search for pilot.

1146 Pilot recovered by helicopter and delivered on board USS NIMITZ (CVN 68). Injuries to pilot: (description).

1215 Secured from flight quarters.

1300 F/A18, bureau no. 67890 of VFA-25, pilot ENS John P. JONES, USNR, 000-00-0000, crashed into barriers no. 2, 4, and 6, and overturned. Pilot sustained mild abrasion to left forearm and contusions to both legs. Damage to aircraft: (major) (minor) (strike).

1315 CDR A. B. SEA, USN, Commanding Officer, VFA-25, departed with 15 aircraft for Oceana, VA, TAD completed.

1330 CDR X. Y. ZEE, USN, Commanding Officer, VFA-113, landed aboard with 16 aircraft from NAS, Norfolk, VA, for TAD.

ENTRIES APPLICABLE TO ALL SHIPS

2100 Maneuvering to take plane guard station no. 1R on USS KENNEDY (CV 67). Lighting measure GREEN in effect.

2110 On station.

2115 Commenced flight operations.

2210 F-14 aircraft crashed into the sea off starboard bow. Maneuvering to recover pilot.

2214 Recovered pilot LTJG Harvey H. GOTZ, USN, 000-00-0000, VF-31. Injuries to pilot: (description).

ENTRIES APPLICABLE TO SHIPS CARRYING HELICOPTERS

1435 Flight quarters.

1455 Launched helicopter. Pilot LTJG Ray WINGS, USN; passenger BMC A. CLEAT, USN.

1505 Recovered helicopter on main deck aft.

1510 Secured from flight quarters.

## Loading and Transferring Operations

AIRCRAFT

0800 Commenced hoisting aircraft of VF-21 aboard.

1000 Completed hoisting 25 aircraft of VF-21 aboard.

*Note:* When all the aircraft of an air wing or group are hoisted aboard at the same time (i.e., during a period of a day), the entry should say "Aircraft of VF-31, VFA-113, and VS-35. . . ."

AMMUNITION

1400 Commenced loading (transferring) ammunition.

1600 Completed loading (transferring) ammunition, having received from (transferred to) USS CAMDEN (AOE 2) 400 rounds 5″/54 cal. illum. projectiles, 250 5″/54 cal. smokeless, and 250 5″/54 cal. flashless charges.

*Note:* For entries regarding expenditure of ammunition, see Gunnery, under Drills and Exercises (page 33).

## Damage

COLLISIONS

1155 USS WHIDBY ISLAND (LSD 41), in coming alongside to port, carried away 39 feet of the ship's port life line forward, with stanchions, and indented the ship's side to a depth of 4 inches over an area 10 feet long and 4 feet high in the vicinity of frames 46–51. No personnel casualties.

1401 Starboard lifeboat carried away by heavy sea. Boat and all equipment lost. No personnel casualties.

ENGINEERING CASUALTIES

1018 Lost fires in no. 1A boiler due to high water level. Maximum speed available, 18 knots.

1019 Lit fires in no. 1B boiler.

1130　No. 1B boiler on the line. All conditions normal. Maximum speed available, 27 knots.

## Drills and Exercises

GENERAL

1000　Exercised at general drills.

ABANDON SHIP

1005　Commenced abandon-ship drill.

1045　Secured from abandon-ship drill.

ALARMS

0800　Tested general, chemical, collision alarms. All conditions normal.

NBC ATTACK

1440　Set material condition ZEBRA and NBC condition WILLIAM.

1450　Set NBC condition CIRCLE WILLIAM.

1500　(Simulated) nuclear (underwater) (air) burst, bearing 045°T, distance 15,000 yards. Maneuvering to avoid base surge and fallout.

1530　Rejoined formation and took station L6 in formation.

COLLISION

1350　Held collision drill.

1354　Material condition ZEBRA set.

1410　Secured from collision drill. Set material condition YOKE.

FIRE AND RESCUE

1100　Held fire drill.

1110　Secured from fire drill.

1300　Called away the fire-and-rescue party.

1305　Fire-and-rescue party embarked in starboard boat and clear of ship.

1330　Fire-and-rescue party returned aboard. Further assistance not required.

GUNNERY

1245　Went to general quarters. Set material condition ZEBRA.

1300　Commenced missile exercise.

1304   Commenced firing. Fired one ____ missile to starboard (port).

1308   Ceased firing.

1320   Set material condition YOKE.

1325   Secured from general quarters. Ammunition expended: 89 rounds 5"/54 cal. high-explosive projectiles with 89 rounds full-service smokeless (flashless) powder cartridges with no casualties.

*Note:* For several exercises fired in close succession, the ammunition expended for all may be grouped in one entry. Normally, material condition will be set and batteries secured before securing from general quarters.


## Formations

### GENERAL

0700   Maneuvering to take station 1 in formation 49, axis 000°T. Guide is USS VALLEY FORGE (CG 50) in station A.

0800   Rotated formation axis to 180°T.

0900   Formation changed from 49 to 52. New formation guide is USS ANTIETAM (CG 54) in station B.

### OFFICER IN TACTICAL COMMAND (OTC)

0900   COMCARGRU 7 embarked in USS NIMITZ (CVN 68) assumed OTC.

1000   Commanding Officer, USS HEWITT (DD 966), was designated OTC.

*Note:* All shifts of tactical command should be logged. When the OTC is the commanding officer of the log writer's ship, the following terminology should be used: "OTC is Commanding Officer, USS VALLEY FORGE (CG 50)." In every case, the command title of the OTC (for example, COMCARGRU 7) should be used, and not his or her name and grade. Entry should state in which ship OTC is embarked.

### RENDEZVOUS

0800   USS SAMUEL B. ROBERTS (FFG 58) made rendezvous with this ship (the formation) and took designated station (took station in the screen) (took planeguard station).

2200   Joined rendezvous with TG 70.2 and took designated station no. 1 in formation 4R, with guide in USS ARTHUR W. RADFORD (DD

968) bearing 095, distance 2,400 yards, formation axis 000°.
OTC is COMCRUDESGRU 7 in USS ANTIETAM (CGN 54).

### TACTICAL EXERCISES

1000    Commenced division tactical exercises. Steering various courses at various speeds (in area HOTEL) (conforming to maneuvers signaled by COMDESRON 21) (on signals from COMDESRON 21).

### ZIGZAGGING AND SINUATING

1300    Commenced zigzagging in accordance with plan no. 1A, base course 090°T.

1400    Commenced steering sinuous course, Cam no. 1, base course 010°T.

1500    Ceased zigzagging and set course 010°T.

## Fueling

### IN PORT

1000    Commenced fueling at Naval Fuel Depot, Craney Island, draft forward 22′, aft 23′.

1130    Ceased pumping. Received 254,031 gals. of JP-5.

### AT SEA

1345    Set the special sea and replenishment detail. Commenced preparations for refueling from USS CAMDEN (AOE 2).

1426    Maneuvering to take station astern USS CAMDEN (AOE 2).

1438    On station.

1442    Commenced approach. Captain (at the conn) (conning).

1453    On station alongside port side of CAMDEN.

1456    First line over.

1510    Received first fuel hose.

1515    Commenced receiving fuel.

1559    Fueling completed. Received 233,198 gals. of DFM/F-76.

1606    All lines and hoses clear. Maneuvering to clear port side of CAMDEN.

1610    Clear of CAMDEN.

1612    Secured the replenishment detail.

## Honors, Ceremonies, and Official Visits

PERSONAL FLAGS

1200   RADM D. D. WAVE, USN, COMCARGRU 5, broke his flag in this ship.

1300   The Honorable ____, Secretary of the Navy, came aboard; broke the flag of the Secretary of the Navy.

1500   The Secretary of the Navy departed; hauled down the flag of SECNAV.

1530   COMPHIBRON 2 shifted flag from USS TARAWA (LHA 1) to USS PELELIEU (LHA 5).

MANNING THE RAIL

1000   Manned the rail as the President of the United States came aboard for an official visit. Fired 21-gun salute, broke the President's flag at the main trunk.

VISITS

1430   Their Majesties, the King and Queen of ____, made an official call on VADM D. G. FARRAGUT, USN, COMSIXTHFLT, with their official party. Rendered honors and fired a salute of 21 guns.

1530   The royal party departed. Rendered honors and fired a salute of 21 guns.

CALLS

1000   The Commanding Officer left the ship to make an official call on COMCRUDESGRU 2.

1605   RADM V. A. MOSS, USN, COMCRUDESGRU 2, came aboard to return the official call of the Commanding Officer.

## Inspections

ADMINISTRATIVE AND MATERIAL

0930   RADM S. DECATUR, USN, COMCRUDESGRU 3, accompanied by members of staff and inspecting party, came on board and commenced administrative inspection. Broke flag of COMCRUDESGRU 3.

1100   COMCRUDESGRU 3, members of staff, and inspecting party left the ship. Hauled down flag of COMCRUDESGRU 3.

1110  COMCRUDESGRU 3 broke his flag in USS BARRY (DDG 52).

**LOWER DECK**
1315  Commenced captain's inspection of lower decks, holds, and storerooms.
1400  Secured from inspection.

**PERSONNEL**
0900  Mustered the crew at quarters for captain's inspection (of personnel and upper decks).

## Navigation

**ANCHORING**
1600  Anchored in Area South HOTEL, berth 44, Hampton Roads, VA, in 4 fathoms of water, mud bottom, with 30 fathoms of chain to the port anchor on the following bearings: Fort Wook 040°T, Middle Ground Light 217°T, Sewall's Point 072°T. Ships present: ____, SOPA ____.

**CONTACTS**
1405  Sighted merchant ship bearing 280°T, distance about 6 miles on approximately parallel course.
1430  Identified merchant ship as SS SEAKAY, U.S. registry, routed independently from Aruba, NWI, to New York, NY.
1441  Passed SS SEAKAY abeam to port, distance about 2 miles.
1620  Obtained unidentified radar contact bearing 090°T, distance 28,800 yards (14 miles).
1629  Unidentified contact tracked and determined to be on course 180°T, speed 15 knots. CPA 042°T, distance 4.2 miles.
1636  Contact identified as USS BARRY (DDG 52) by USS ARLEIGH BURKE (DDG 51).
1715  Obtained sonar contact bearing 172°T, range 2,500 yards.
1717  Contact evaluated as possible submarine. Commenced attacking (tracking) (investigating).
1720  Lost contact.
1721  Contact regained bearing 020°T, range 2,000 yards. Oil slick sighted on that bearing and range. Commenced re-attack.

1724 Sonar reported hearing breaking-up noises.

1725 Contact lost.

*Note:* Contacts at sea are logged when they will pass in the vicinity of logging ship. Although the exact distance is not specified, normally contacts that pass within three nautical miles are logged.

### DRY-DOCKING

1420 Commercial tug SEAGOOSE came alongside to port. Pilot C. U. FINE came aboard.

1426 USN tug YTB-68 came alongside port bow, USN tug YTB-63 came alongside port quarter.

1431 First line to dock starboard bow.

1435 First line to dock port bow.

1440 Bow passed over sill of dock.

1442 Cast off all tugs.

1450 Caisson in place.

1455 Commenced pumping water out of dry dock.

1540 Resting on keel blocks.

1545 Pilot left the ship.

1550 Commenced receiving electrical power and fresh water from the dock.

1630 Inspection of all hull openings completed.

### OVERHAUL, CONVERSION, AND INVACTIVATION

1635 Commenced undergoing (overhaul) (conversion) (inactivation). Commenced limited log entries for duration of (overhaul) (conversion) (inactivation).

0850 Inspection of all hull openings completed.

0900 Flooding commenced in dry dock.

0918 All services disconnected from ship.

0920 Inspection of all spaces for watertight integrity completed.

0925 Ship clear of keel blocks.

0930 Handling lines secure on ship.

0935 Pilot C. U. FINE came aboard.

0950 Commenced moving ship clear of dock.

0958 Stern passed over sill.

1005 USN tug YSB 63 came alongside port bow, USN tug YTB 68 came alongside port quarter.

1009 Bow passed over sill.

*Note:* Upon termination of overhaul or conversion, deck-log entries must be recorded daily by watches.

### ENTERING HARBOR

0551 Passed Ambrose Lightship abeam to port, distance 1,000 yards.

0554 Stationed special sea detail. OOD (conning) (at the conn), captain and navigator on the bridge.

0600 Commenced maneuvering while conforming to Gedney Channel.

0650 Passed lighted buoy no. 12 abeam to starboard.

0705 USN tub no. 216 came alongside port quarter. Pilot B. A. WATCHER came aboard and took the conn.

0706 Maneuvering to go alongside the pier.

0715 Moored port side to berth 3A, U.S. Naval Ammunition Depot, Earle, NJ, with standard mooring lines. Ships present ____, SOPA is COMDESRON 21 in USS VALLEY FORGE (CG 50).

0720 Pilot left the ship.

### MOORING

1006 Moored port side to Standard Oil Dock, berth 76, Los Angeles Inner Harbor, CA, with standard mooring lines.

1015 Commenced receiving miscellaneous services from the pier.

### SIGHTING AIDS TO NAVIGATION

0102 Sighted Cape Henry Light bearing 225°T, distance about 20 miles.

0157 Passed Cape Henry Light abeam to starboard, distance 7.3 miles.

0300 Cape Henry Light passed from view bearing 315°T, distance about 20 miles.

### TIDE

0733 Commenced swinging to flood tide, stern to port.

1046 Completed swinging to flood tide, bearing 347°T.

### TIME-ZONE CHANGE

0001 Set clocks ahead 1 hour to conform with +3-zone time.

GETTING UNDER WAY

0600   Commenced preparations for getting under way. Set material condition YOKE.

0730   Stationed the special sea detail.

0750   Completed all preparations for getting under way. Draft forward 23', aft 23'.

0800   Under way for Norfolk, VA (for sea), as a unit of Task Group 20.2 in compliance with COMCARGRU 4 serial 063 (CTG 20.2 Op Order 7-73). Maneuvering to clear the anchorage. Captain (conning) (at the conn), navigator on the bridge.

0810   Standing out of Boston Harbor.

0830   OOD was given the conn. Set readiness condition 3, anchor detail on deck. (Secured the special sea detail, set the regular steaming watch.)

0845   Entered international waters.

SEA AND WEATHER

1130   Visibility decreased to 1 mile due to fog (heavy rain). Commenced sounding fog signals and stationed (extra lookouts) (lookouts in the eyes of the ship). Winds southeast 25 knots. Sea southeast 8 feet and increasing.

1212   Visibility increased to 5 miles. Ceased sounding fog signals.

*Note:* Commencement and cessation of sounding fog signals must always be entered.

## Personnel

ABSENTEES

0800   Mustered the crew (at quarters) (at foul-weather parade) (on stations) (at quarters for captain's inspection). Absentees: (none) (no new absentees) (SA Roscoe BADEGG, USN, 000-00-0000, absent without authority from muster) (FN M. A. WOHL, USN, 000-00-0000, UA since 0700 this date).

*Note:* There is no legal distinction between absence beyond leave and absence without leave. Both are logged as unauthorized absence, or UA. The initial entry indicating a person's absence suffices until he or she returns, is declared a deserter, or is otherwise detached from the ship.

0900    A systematic search of the entire ship for SA Roscoe BADEGG, USN, 000-00-0000, who missed 0800 muster, disclosed that (he was not on board) (he was found to be sleeping in BOSN's locker comp. A-301-A).

1000    NAVSTA msg 0311600Z reports that BTFN Arch CULPRET, USN, 000-00-0000, UA since 0800, 15 Apr 1999, returned to naval custody and was being held at that station pending disposition of charges.

*Note:* An entry such as the above shows that an absentee has returned to naval jurisdiction.

### RETURN OF ABSENTEES

2200    PN3 Guy ROAMER, USNR, 000-00-0000, (returned aboard) (was delivered on board by the armed services police), having been UA since 0800 this date.

2300    SH3 "C" A. HAZE, USN, 000-00-0000, UA since 0700 this date, was delivered on board under guard from NAVSTA, accused of drunk and disorderly conduct at that station. By order of the commanding officer, he was restricted to the limits of the ship pending disposition of the charges.

### REPORTS

0800    Sound-and-security watch reported. All conditions normal.

0830    Roving patrol reported all conditions normal.

### COURT OF INQUIRY

1000    The court of inquiry, CAPT A. B. SEA, USN, senior member, appointed by COMSURFPAC ltr [letter] serial 2634 of 2 Apr 1999 met in the case of the late BM3 Andrew J. SPIRIT, USN, 000-00-0000.

1030    The court of inquiry in the case of the late BM3 Andrew J. SPIRIT, USN, 000-00-0000, adjourned to meet ashore at the scene of his death.

### SPECIAL COURTS-MARTIAL

1000    The special court-martial, CDR Jonathan Q. DOE, USN, senior member, appointed by CO, USS NIMITZ (CVN 63), ltr serial 102 of 1 Mar 1999, met in the case of SA Ralph O. WEARY, USN, 000-00-0000.

1200    The special court-martial that met in the case of SA Ralph O.

WEARY, USN, 000-00-0000, recessed to meet again at 1300 this date.

*Note:* A court adjourns if it will not meet again that date, but if it is to meet again on the same date, it recesses. If known, the date and time of the next meeting are logged.

#### SUMMARY COURTS-MARTIAL

0900    The summary court-martial, LT Abel JUSTICE, USN, opened in the case of SA Ralph O. WEARY, USN, 000-00-0000.

1100    The summary court-martial in the case of SA Ralph O. WEARY, USN, 000-00-0000, adjourned to await the action of the convening authority.

#### DEATHS

0416    GM1 William P. SEA, USN, 000-00-0000, died on board as a result of _____.

#### DESERTERS

0800    PN3 Guy ROAMER, USNR, 000-00-0000, was this date declared a deserter from this ship, having been UA since 0800 1 May 1999, a period of 30 days.

#### INJURIES

1035    During drill on the 5″ loading machine, GMSN Ira M. JONAH, USN, 000-00-0000, suffered a compound fracture of the right foot when a drill shell fell on his foot. Injury not due to his own misconduct. Treatment administered by the medical officer. Disposition: placed on the sick list.

*Note:* To protect the government from false claims and to establish a record of facts for honest claimants, it is important that there be an accurate and complete entry, including all pertinent details, of *every* injury, accident, or casualty, however slight, among the officers, crew, visitors, passengers, longshoremen, harbor workers, or repairmen.

#### TEMPORARY ADDITIONAL DUTY

1400    Pursuant to COMNAVAIRPAC ltr serial 104 of 2 Feb 1999, ENS Willy A. BRITE, USN, 000-00-0000, left the ship for TAD with NAS, Barber's Point, Hawaii.

1700    ENS Willy A. BRITE, USN, 000-00-0000, having completed TAD with NAS, Barber's Point, Hawaii, returned aboard and resumed his regular duties.

## PASSENGERS

1000 Mr. Delbert Z. Brown, 000-00-0000, civilian technician, embarked for transportation to Guam, M.I. Authority: CNO 141120Z May.

*Note:* All passengers should be logged in and out with social security number.

## PATIENTS

1306 Transferred LT Lawrence A. LEVY, USN, 000-00-0000, to U.S. Naval Hospital, Yokosuka, Japan, for treatment. Diagnosis: _____.

*Note:* A ship sailing in U.S. continental waters should log a patient's transfer if his or her absence is expected to exceed thirty days; outside those waters, such a transfer should be logged regardless of how long the absence is expected to last. Diagnosis, if known, should be included.

## PERSONAL EFFECTS

1300 Personal effects of the late GM1 William P. SEA, USN, 000-00-0000, were inventoried and forwarded to _____.

## SHORE PATROL

1305 Pursuant to orders of the commanding officer, BM1 Marvin A. FORCE, USN, 000-00-0000, in charge of 17 men, left the ship to report to senior shore patrol officer, Norfolk, VA, for TAD.

0200 The shore patrol detail with BM1 Marvin A. FORCE, USN, 000-00-0000, in charge, returned to the ship, having completed TAD.

## LEAVE

1100 COMDESRON 21 hauled down his pennant and departed on 5 days' leave.

1110 The commanding officer departed on 5 days' leave.

0700 The commanding officer returned from 5 days' leave.

*Note:* Flag officers and unit commanders embarked and commanding officers are the only personnel who must be logged in and out on leave.

## Safety

DIVERS

0900    Secured injection pumps in preparation for divers going over side.

0915    Divers in the water for inspection of STBD shaft.

0945    Divers out of the water.

0950    Restored all equipment to normal operation.

MEN ALOFT

0915    Secured all transmitters and rotating antennas in preparation for personnel going aloft.

0920    Men working aloft.

0945    Personnel secured from working aloft.

0950    Restored all conditions to normal operation.

## Ship Movements

1100    USS MITSCHER (DDG 57) got under way and stood out of the harbor.

1130    USS MILIUS (DDG 69) stood into the harbor and anchored (in berth D-3) (moored alongside pier 4).

1300    USS MONTEREY (CG 61) got under way from alongside this ship and anchored in berth D-8.

1600    USS JOHN PAUL JONES (DDG 53) stood in and moored alongside (to port) (outboard) of USS MONTEREY (CG 61).

## Ship's Operational Control

0705    Changed operational control to CINCUSNAVEUR, deactivated TG 85.3, and activated TG 65.4, composed of DESRON 26 and DESRON 14, en route to Mediterranean area from Norfolk, VA.

1045    Detached by COMDESRON 26 from TG 65.4 to proceed independently to San Remo, Italy.

1435    Detached from CTU 58.3.2; changed operational control to CTU 57.4.3.

*Note:* For sample entries regarding commencement of operational control and changes thereto, see Under Way, under Midwatch (page 29), or Rendezvous, under Formations (page 34).

**Ships Present**

Ships present: USS ENTERPRISE (CVN 65) (COMCARGRU 4 embarked), USS
    CAPE ST. GEORGE (CG 71), USS CAMDEN (AOE 2), and various units
    of the U.S. Atlantic Fleet, and service craft. SOPA is COMCARGRU 4
    in ENTERPRISE (CVN 65).

Ships present: Task Group 63.1 less DESRON 4 plus USS NIMITZ (CVN 68)
    and various units of the British and French navies. SOPA is COM-
    CRUDESGRU 2 (CTG 63.1) in NIMITZ (CVN 68).

**Special Operations**

0904    Under way for special operations in accordance with CINCLANT
        patrol order 110506, 7 July 1998. Maneuvering on various
        courses at various speeds conforming to Hampton Roads
        channel. Captain (at the conn) (conning).

1125    Secured the maneuvering watch. Commenced special opera-
        tions. Commenced limiting log entries to nonoperational data
        as directed by the chief of naval operations.

1840    Ceased special operations in accordance with CINCLANT patrol
        order 110506, 7 July 1998. Commenced operating in accor-
        dance with COMSUBRON 1 transit order 2-98.

*Notes:* Upon termination of special operations, log entries should be
recorded daily by watches that adhere to the regular schedule.

The preceding entries are applicable only to ships that have
been directed by the chief of naval operations to limit the deck log to
nonoperational data. All other ships participating in a special type of
operation, which may be classified, must make all required log entries, daily by watches, and classify the log accordingly.

**Environmental Conditions**

In describing significant changes in wind, weather, and atmosphere,
terminology similar to the following should be used:

| *State of the Sea* | *Motion of the Ship* |
| --- | --- |
| Cross sea | Pitching deeply and heavily |
| Discolored water | Pitching moderately |
| Heavy sea | Pitching badly |

Heavy swell from the ____
Heavy ground swell
Heavy rolling sea
Heavy following sea
Light ground swell
Light following sea
Light swell from the ____
Luminous or phosphorescent sea
Rough sea
Short chopping sea
Smooth sea
Riptides

Pitching easily
Rolling easily
Rolling deeply
Rolling heavily
Rolling quickly
Laboring greatly

# 4

## COMMUNICATIONS

In the interest of security, transmissions by radiotelephone will be as short and concise as possible, consistent with clearness.

Allied Communications Publication (ACP) 125

Communications have been called "the voice of command." The way a ship uses communications circuits indicates professionalism in command. Indeed, without good communications every ship and every station within a ship would be isolated. As a basic function of command and control, shipboard communications are centralized in key control spaces, including the bridge, combat information center (CIC), and damage-control center. Communications systems range from the most basic, such as voice tube and buzzer, to the most modern and sophisticated satellite, and each system has specific functions and characteristics. To properly exercise command authority, the watch officer must be familiar with these systems and able to use them with facility.

### INTERNAL COMMUNICATIONS

Internal communications have to do with the ship herself and provide the means for informing and directing her company. The various systems are complicated, mastered only by the specialists responsible for their maintenance. A relatively small number of circuits and types of equipment relate to the duties of the watch officer, but he or she should have detailed knowledge of those installed in the area of the bridge and pilothouse and in the CIC.

Sound-powered telephone circuits installed in most ships include the following:

| | |
|---|---|
| JA | Captain's battle control |
| JC | Ordnance control |
| JF | Flag officer |
| 1JG | Aircraft control |
| JL | Battle lookouts |
| 2JC | Dual-purpose battery control |
| 1JS | Sonar control |
| 1JV | Maneuvering, docking, catapult control |
| JW | Ship control, navigation |
| JX | Radio and signals |
| JZ | Damage control |

The major circuits, such as the JA, JL, and 1JV, are the most commonly used. The watch officer should learn where they go, who mans them, and which station controls which circuit. The proper voice procedure to use on these circuits differs somewhat from voice-radio procedure. The OOD should know both procedures and enforce their use at all times. It may appear unimportant that informal conversation is regularly passed over the sound-powered telephones, but when an emergency arises it will be evident that only trained talkers, using standard phraseology, can get the correct word from station to station. A ship in which originality is permitted over the telephones is not only incapable of first-rate performance in an emergency but also liable to be the scene of confusion and mistakes during routine operations.

The intercommunications voice (MC) units, or "squawkboxes," installed in important stations of most ships are normally used to pass urgent information between officers and petty officers at the station or to amplify sound-powered telephone communications. Here again, circuit discipline and correct procedure must be enforced by the OOD. To avoid confusion and speed up transmissions, the standard procedure for the sound-powered phone talker is used on MC circuits.

A list of MC circuits follows:

| One-Way Systems | Purpose |
|---|---|
| 1MC | Battle and general announcements |
| 2MC | Engineers |
| 3MC | Hangar deck |
| 4MC | Damage control |
| 5MC | Flight deck |
| 6MC | Boat control |
| 7MC | Submarine control |
| 10MC | Docking control |
| 11MC | Turret |
| 16MC | Turret |
| 17MC | Antiaircraft |
| 18MC | Bridge |

| Two-Way Systems | Purpose |
|---|---|
| 19MC | Ready room |
| 20MC | Combat information |
| 21MC | Captain's command |
| 22MC | Radio room |
| 23MC | Distribution control |
| 24MC | Flag officer's command |
| 25MC | Wardroom |
| 26MC | Machinery control |
| 27MC | Sonar control |
| 28MC | Aircraft squadron |
| 29MC | Sonar information |
| 30MC | Bomb shop |
| 31MC | Escape trunk |

Certain types of ships have a general announcing system instead of the 1MC and special station-to-station systems. Regardless of the system, the principles are the same. The OOD must know what communications systems are available and who is on the other end. During an emergency, there is no time to figure it out.

Another important responsibility of the OOD is the *management* of 1MC circuits. It is a good practice to keep topside 1MC speakers off while in port, except in emergencies or for safety announcements, to minimize noise and to get the attention of the crew when something of vital importance is passed. Officer circuits should be used only when the message applies to wardroom members. The 1MC should not be used to call every member of the crew to the quarterdeck for a phone call or a visitor. Other internal circuits or the messenger should be used for this sort of task. Proper and concise use of the 1MC is the mark of a thinking, professional watch officer.

## The 1MC System

The 1MC system is the most important internal communications circuit in the ship and should be the one most closely controlled by the OOD. As mentioned in an earlier chapter, the control that the watch has over its use is one of the best indicators of how well a ship is being run. More important, however, is ensuring that messages passed over the system, particularly in critical situations, are phrased as clearly as possible. The following list of basic 1MC messages gives the standard phraseology in which they are passed.

| Event | Pipe | Word to Be Passed |
| --- | --- | --- |
| Abandon ship (prepare) | All hands | "All hands prepare to abandon ship. Execute emergency destruction. Nearest land bears ____ degrees magnetic relative position (port bow). ____ miles designated enemy (friendly)." Repeat word. |
| Abandon ship | All hands | "All hands abandon ship. Nearest land bears ____ degrees magnetic relative position (port bow). ____ miles designated enemy (friendly)." Repeat word. |
| Anchored | All hands | "Anchored, shift colors." |

| Event | Pipe | Word to Be Passed |
|-------|------|-------------------|
| Away the gig | "Long boat call" | "Away the gig, away." If the captain is not going to use his or her gig, omit the second "away." |
| Belay the word | Attention | "Belay my last." |
| Boarding | All hands | "Away the boarding party." Pass the word twice. |
| Boat call | Attention | "Away the motor whale-boat." |
| Casting off | Attention | "Stand by to cast off (ship) to port (starboard)." |
| CO arriving or departing | Number of boat gongs depends on rank | "(Title of officer)." |
| Church call | None | "Divine services are now being held in ____ (space). Maintain silence about the decks." |
| Collision (standby) | Collision alarm | "Stand by for collision, starboard (port) side, frame ____ (number). All hands close all watertight doors aft (forward) of frame ____ (number)." |
| Collision | Collision alarm | "Collision, collision, starboard (port) side, frame ____ (number)." |
| Colors (first call) | None | "First call, first call to colors." No word is passed for the execution, or for the carry-on whistle only. |
| | 1 whistle | To execute. |
| | 3 whistles | To carry on. |
| Condition III | Attention | "On deck condition III, watch (number)." |

| Event | Pipe | Word to Be Passed |
|-------|------|-------------------|
| Crew members working aloft | None | "There are men (personnel) working aloft. Do not rotate, radiate, or energize any electronic equipment while men (personnel) are working aloft." Pass the word every thirty minutes. |
| Divers | None | "There are divers working over the side. Do not operate any equipment, rotate screws, cycle rudder (planes or torpedo-tube shutters), take suction from or discharge to the sea, blow or vent any tanks, activate sonar or underwater electrical equipment, open or close any valves, or cycle trash-disposal unit before checking with the diving supervisor (name and rate) or the officer of the deck." |
| Divers (completed) | None | "Diving operations are completed." |
| Eight o'clock reports (in port) | Attention | "On deck all eight o'clock reports." |
| Eight o'clock reports (under way) | Attention | "Lay before the mast all eight o'clock reports." |
| Fire (in port) | Rapid ringing of ship's bell | "Fire, fire, fire, class ____. Fire in compartment ____ (number), (compartment name), away the in-port emergency team. Provide |

| Event | Pipe | Word to Be Passed |
|---|---|---|
| | | from repair ____ (number)." Pass the word twice. |
| Flight quarters | All hands | "Flight quarters, flight quarters. All hands man your flight quarters stations for (HIFR) (VERTREP) (land/launch). All hands not involved in flight quarters stand clear." |
| Securing from flight quarters | All hands | "Secure from flight quarters." |
| General quarters | General quarters alarm | "General quarters, general quarters. All hands man your battle stations." Pass the word twice. |
| Hoist boat | Hook on | "Stand by to hoist in (out) the whaleboat." |
| Holiday routine | All hands | "Commence holiday routine." |
| Inspection (personnel) | All hands | "Quarters for captain's personnel inspection." |
| Inspection (material) | All hands | "Stand by all lower (upper) deck spaces for inspection." |
| Inspection (berthing and messing) | All hands | "Stand by for captain's (XO's) inspection of messing and berthing spaces." |
| Knock off | Pipe down | "Knock off ship's work." |
| Late bunks | Attention | "Up all late bunks." |
| Liberty | All hands | "Liberty call, liberty call. Liberty commences for sections ____ to expire on board at ____." |
| Mail call | Attention | "Mail call." |
| Man overboard | None | "Man overboard port |

| Event | Pipe | Word to Be Passed |
|---|---|---|
| | | (starboard) side. (Type of recovery.)" Pass the word twice. |
| Mast | Attention | "All mast cases, witnesses, and division officers concerned assemble ____ (place)." |
| Material condition | Attention | "Set material condition (Yoke) (Zebra) (X-ray). Duty damage-control petty officer make reports to ____ (place)." |
| Meals | Pipe down | None. |
| Motor whaleboat | Attention | "Away the motor whaleboat." |
| Movie call | Attention | "Movie call." |
| Muster of restricted crew members | Attention | "Muster all restricted men (personnel)." |
| Officers (unidentified) | Number of boat gongs depends on rank | "(Rank of officer)." |
| Officer's call | Attention | "Officer's call." |
| Preparation for entering port | All hands | "Make all preparations for entering port. The ship expects to moor (anchor) at ____." |
| Preparation for getting under way | All hands | "Make all preparation for getting under way. The ship expects to be under way at ____." |
| Quarters | All hands | "All hands to quarters for muster, instruction, and inspection." |
| Quarters (foul weather) | All hands | "All hands to quarters for muster, instruction, and |

| Event | Pipe | Word to Be Passed |
|---|---|---|
| | | inspection, foul-weather parade." |
| Quarters (leaving port) | All hands | "Quarters for leaving port." |
| Rain squall | Attention | "Haul over all hatch hoods and gun covers." |
| Readiness reports | Attention | "All department heads make ready for sea reports to the officer of the deck on the bridge." |
| Receiving alongside | Attention | "Stand by to receive (ship) (barge) alongside to port (starboard)." |
| Relieving the watch | Attention | "Relieve the watch, relieve the watch, relieve the wheel and lookouts, on deck section ____." |
| Repel boarders | All hands | "All hands repel boarders." Pass the word twice. |
| Replenishment (refueling) | Attention | "Go to your stations, all the replenishment (refueling) detail." |
| Rescue and assistance | Attention | "Away the rescue-and-assistance detail. Muster at ____ (area). Section ____ provide (do not provide)." |
| Reveille | All hands | "Reveille, reveille. All hands heave out and trice up. The smoking lamp is lighted in all authorized spaces." |
| Secure the sea and anchor detail | Pipe down | "Secure the sea and anchor detail." |
| Secure | Pipe down | "Secure from (event)." |
| Shifting the watch | Attention | "The officer of the deck is |

| Event | Pipe | Word to Be Passed |
|---|---|---|
| | | shifting his (her) watch to the quarterdeck (bridge)." |
| Security alert | None | "Security alert, security alert. Away the security alert force. All hands stand fast." |
| Side boys | Attention | "Lay to the quarterdeck the side boys." |
| Smoking lamp (lighted) | Attention | "The smoking lamp is lighted in all authorized spaces." |
| Smoking lamp (out) | Attention | "The smoking lamp is out throughout the ship while . . ." or "The smoking lamp is out in (space or area) while . . ." |
| Special sea detail | All hands | "Go to your stations, all of the special sea detail." |
| Sweepers (at sea) | Sweepers | "Sweepers, sweepers, man your brooms, give the ship a clean sweepdown fore and aft, sweep down all lower decks, ladder wells, and passageways. Now, sweepers." |
| Sweepers (in port) | Sweepers | "Sweepers, sweepers, man your brooms, give the ship a clean sweepdown fore and aft, sweep down all lower decks, ladder wells, and passageways, take all trash to the receptacles provided on the pier." |
| Taps | None | "Taps, taps, lights out, all |

| Event | Pipe | Word to Be Passed |
|---|---|---|
| | | hands turn into your bunks. Maintain silence about the decks, the smoking lamp is out in all berthing spaces." |
| Test alarms | None | "The following is a test of the general, chemical, and collision alarms from the ____ (space)." |
| Turn to | Turn to | "Turn to, continue ship's work" or "Turn to, commence ship's work." |
| Visit and search | All hands | "Away the visit-and-search crew." Pass the word twice. |
| Working party | All hands | "Now muster a ____ (number)-hand working party (place) with (person in charge)." |

## Sound-Powered Telephone Procedures

Standard phraseology and discipline must be maintained over sound-powered telephone circuits. When unofficial conversation is the norm and discipline breaks down, information is lost or, even worse, the wrong information is passed. The discipline of sound-powered phone circuits is a reflection of the professionalism of the OOD.

When headphones are being worn by phone talkers at both stations, a message can be stated with the call-up. For example, if the CIC talker has data to pass to the bridge talker, the following is passed:

CIC talker: "Bridge, combat. Combat reports a contact bearing 040°T, 19,000 yards, on course 330°T, speed 10 knots. CPA is 270°T, 5,000 yards, at time 1045."

The receiving talker repeats the message and answers as follows:

Bridge talker:     "Bridge, aye. Contact bearing 040°T, 19,000 yards, on course 330°T, speed 10 knots. CPA is 270°T, 5,000 yards, at time 1045."

The repeat-back procedures ensure that the proper word is received.

## Standard Phraseology for Internal Communications

*Circuit Test.*   To find out if telephone stations are manned and ready, the talker at control says, "All stations, control, testing." Each talker then acknowledges in the order previously assigned. Each station responds in order but does not wait more than a few seconds for the station immediately preceding to acknowledge.

*Sending.*   When sending a message, first call the station, then identify your own station, then state the message. "Forecastle, bridge, prepare to anchor in five minutes."

*Receiving.*   When receiving a message, first identify yourself and then repeat the message. "Bridge, forecastle, prepare to anchor in five minutes, aye."

*Repeats.*   When a message is not clear to the listener at the receiving end, he or she should say, "Say again." Never use the word "repeat."

*Spelling.*   Difficult words are spelled by using the phonetic alphabet preceded by the proword (procedure word) "I spell." Pronounce the word before and after spelling it. "Forecastle—I spell— foxtrot, oscar, romeo, echo, charlie, alfa, sierra, tango, lima, echo— forecastle."

*Leaving Circuit.*   When a phone talker is relieved by another talker, the former informs the control station that he or she is shifting phones. "Bridge, after steering, shifting phones." And upon returning: "Bridge, after steering, back on the line."

*Securing.*   Before securing phones, always get permission. "Bridge, fantail, request permission to secure."

## Ship's Alarms

All ships are equipped with a general alarm, a chemical alarm, and some form of collision alarm. Each of these alarms has a distinctive sound that should be immediately recognizable to all hands. In addition to these universal alarms, some ships have special-purpose signals to provide safety or security for critical spaces and situations. Most ships have some sort of alarm system designed to provide a signal on the bridge and at the quarterdeck station, as well as at local stations, when the temperature in the magazines reaches a certain degree. Nonaviation ships that carry helicopters have an alarm that signals a helicopter crash. Ship's routine usually calls for testing the various alarms on the morning watch and before getting under way. Specialized alarms are normally tested as part of a planned maintenance system.

### Boat Gongs and Side Boys

Most ships sound gongs to indicate the prospective departure of officers' boats and the arrival or departure of visiting officers, embarked unit commanders, and the commanding officer. As boat signals, gongs are sounded *three* times ten minutes before the departure of the boat, *twice* when there are five minutes to go, and *once* with one minute to go.

When used to indicate the arrival or departure of an officer, gongs are sounded in pairs, the same number as the number of side boys the officer rates, followed by the name of the officer's command or by the word "staff." Gongs, when used this way, are not honors but merely inform those aboard of the arrival and departure of senior officers and the departure of crew's boats. In a nest, the ships may agree, or the senior commanding officer direct, that such gongs will not be sounded for captains of outboard ships making routine crossings of inboard ships. Officers rate side boys and gongs as follows:

| *Rank* | *Side Boys/Gongs* |
| --- | --- |
| Fleet admiral and vice admiral | Eight |
| Rear admiral | Six |
| Captain and commander | Four |
| Lieutenant commander through ensign | Two |

## EXTERNAL COMMUNICATIONS

As a rule, three categories of external communications relate to the watch officer: voice, visual, and record. Each of these modes meets a specific type of communications requirement, and a ship at sea is likely to be using all of them simultaneously to transmit and receive information. Technical control of all voice and record communications equipment is the responsibility of the radio watch supervisor or, on larger ships, the communications watch officer. In this regard, the term "technical control" should be clearly understood. The watch supervisor in radio does *not* control what messages are transmitted or received. What he or she does is maintain the communications path by monitoring the performance of equipment and placing traffic on a circuit.

**Voice Communications**

To an increasing extent, voice communication is the primary command-and-control tool for the watch officer on the bridge and in the CIC. Voice radiotelephone (R/T) is used to pass tactical signals, to report sensor information, and to coordinate operations between units. The use of each R/T circuit is established in the operational commander's communications plan, as is the use of the net control station, if any, and special instructions and procedures for the use of the circuit. Depending on their function, R/T circuits may be controlled by operators on the bridge, in the CIC, or at other locations. It is extremely important that there be no confusion between the CIC and the bridge over who controls, answers, or logs a given circuit, and each watch officer should confirm, as he or she begins a watch, what the circuit-guarding arrangement is.

Voice radio circuits can be established on almost any frequency but are most commonly in the high-frequency (HF) band, between two and thirty megahertz (MHz), or in the ultra-high-frequency (UHF) band, between 225 and 400 MHz. The former frequencies are usually allocated to long-range circuits for dispersed formations, while the latter are used mainly for short-range, line-of-sight communications. Because of its relative directionality and short range, transmissions over UHF have the advantage of being difficult for an enemy to detect at long range. HF transmissions, on the other hand, can be detected for thousands of miles. The following is a list of voice radio bands (V = very, L = low, M = medium):

| | |
|---|---|
| VLF | 3–30 KHZ |
| LF | 30–300 KHZ |

| MF | 300 KHz–3 MHz |
|----|----|
| HF | 3–30 MHz |
| VHF | 30–300 MHz |
| MHF | 300–3000 MHz |
| Navy HF | 2–30 MHz |
| Navy UHF | 225–400 MHz |

It is better to use higher frequencies by day and lower frequencies by night.

Correct use of the R/T should be one of the first things that a junior watch officer learns. Use of proper procedures and terminology and the ability to authenticate and quickly encode and decode information are basic skills. The competence with which a watch officer handles R/T communications is one of the most visible measures of professionalism as well as one of the best indicators of a ship's operational smartness. From time to time, every ship experiences some difficulty with voice communications. The extent to which such difficulties affect operations and the speed with which they are resolved are usually in direct proportion to the watch officer's knowledge of communications. When it appears that R/T signals are not being heard by other ships, the most common error is for the watch officer or CIC to assume that the equipment is bad and to order that it be shifted or that new gear be put on the line. As often as not, after new equipment is patched in, the problem still exists or new problems have arisen. At this point, both the OOD and the CIC watch officer are ordering new circuit patches, antennas, and equipment, and the radio watch has lost all control of the equipment setup. The problem eventually gets solved, but not without considerable frustration, misunderstanding, and loss of tempers.

To avoid this sort of confusion, watch officers in the CIC and on the bridge must allow communicators to do their job. When a circuit suddenly stops working, chances are that only a systematic investigation of all equipment, remote units, and patching systems can discover the cause. If the watch in radio is allowed to carry out its responsibility for technical control of the circuit, in all likelihood the problem will be found and corrected. If, on the other hand, the watch is constantly setting up new equipment or changing patches at the insistence of the bridge and the CIC, chances are that before long no one will have control of the situation. The watch officer who understands this and has the patience to allow communicators to do their job minimizes such trouble.

Two general categories of signals are transmitted over R/T circuits: executive and nonexecutive. Nonexecutive signals are administrative or contain information. Executive signals contain the word "execute" and require an action by the ship. They are subdivided into "delayed executive" and "immediate executive." Delayed executive signals give the OOD time to calculate the action to be carried out when the signal is executed. Immediate executive messages require an immediate response. The OOD must understand the different categories and what is required of him or her and the ship.

### Allied Communications Publication 125

One of the most important publications that the watch officer should constantly review is Allied Communications Publication 125, Communication Instructions Radiotelephone Procedure. ACP-125 is a short, unclassified, and easily readable publication that you should pick up and read cover to cover about once a month. Some of the key sections include a general discussion of communications security, the keeping of circuit logs, pronunciation of alphabet and numerals, and—most importantly—a list of "prowords." These are the key phrases and words that are universally recognized as appropriate for use on R/T circuits. Memorize all of them. There are four pages' worth in ACP-125, and if you talk on an R/T circuit, you will use them daily.

The publication also includes details on messages, operating rules, and various miscellaneous procedures for everything from reporting enemy contacts to letting everyone know that an intruder is on the circuit. ACP-125 has an absolute wealth of information, and your copy should be dog-eared from frequent review and use.

### Bridge-to-Bridge and VHF Communications

The use of VHF communications has increased dramatically. The VHF circuits are usually reserved for direct conversations between the OODs of ships to clarify intentions, weather reports, and Coast Guard safety information. With the increase in VHF communications has come a corresponding increase in net traffic. The general channel assignments, as specified by the Vessel Bridge-to-Bridge Radiotele-phone Act, are these:

| | |
|---|---|
| Channel 16 | Coast Guard emergency use |
| Channel 13 | General bridge-to-bridge traffic |

If a conversation of any length is required, the OOD should recommend switching to a channel other than 16 or 13. The Vessel Bridge-to Bridge Radiotelephone Act is applicable on waters subject to the inland rules. See U.S. Coast Guard navigation rules for complete details of this act. It is vital that the OOD carefully monitor the VHF circuits for safety information, especially when entering or leaving port. In addition, a log of applicable transmissions is required.

## Visual Communications

Visual communications are the most secure of all but are limited by both distance and visibility. Maximum use should be made of visual communications, especially when a force wants to remain undetected. All officers standing watch on deck should be able to read their own ship's flashing-light call sign and, regardless of what kind of visual watch is being kept, be constantly alert for the signals of other ships. Signal flags should be committed to memory. Learning to recognize all the flags is not difficult and is well worth the effort. Flash cards are useful in this regard and may be ordered through the Navy stock system. Most flag signals are taken from the Allied Maritime Tactical Signal and Maneuvering Book (ATP-1, vol. 2) or, when a merchant ship is being signaled, from H.O.102. The instructions for use at the beginning of these publications must be thoroughly understood in order for the officer to encode and decode signals correctly. Specific signals, even those often used, should *not* be memorized, because ATP-1 is subject to change at any time. The practice of breaking or encoding signals from memory can lead to potentially dangerous mistakes.

It is most important for the OOD to know the ships for which he or she has visual responsibility. Of particular importance is the difference between flag hoists at the dip and closed up. When in port, the OOD must be alert for the signal flags flying on units moored nearby that may indicate a special evolution such as man aloft, divers in the water, or another ship coming alongside.

**Record Communications**

Most of a ship's nontactical communications are handled by radio-teletype as record communications. The watch officer on the bridge or in the CIC is usually authorized to release various types of messages such as weather reports, bathythermograph reports, or in the case of the CIC, certain contact reports. His or her responsibility as releasing officer is to make sure that these messages are in the correct format and addressed properly. In addition, it is a good idea occasionally to check the breakdown of coded information in weather and bathythermograph messages to see whether outgoing information is correct.

## CONCLUSION

The mark of a good watchstander is his or her ability to communicate. You will instantly impress your chain of command if you master the requirements of ACP-125 and the other good information contained in this chapter. Your communication skills are central to standing an effective and safe watch.

# 5

# THE WATCH UNDER WAY

The stern and impartial sea . . . offers no opportunities but to those who know how to grasp them with a ready hand and undaunted heart.

Joseph Conrad

The position of watch officer under way carries with it unmatched responsibility and authority. When the commanding officer (CO) certifies an officer as qualified to be in charge of the underway watch, he or she is displaying a unique degree of trust in that person's judgment, ability, and intelligence. It is a trust that cannot be taken lightly, and one that must be repeatedly justified by performance. Watch-standing at sea is the most important of a junior officer's duties and is the yardstick by which his or her potential will be judged. It also offers the finest kind of reward in terms of professional achievement and personal satisfaction. Qualification as a watch officer marks the completion of the first major step toward command at sea and should be the primary initial goal of every seagoing officer.

## PREPARING FOR THE WATCH

Preparation for standing a watch under way does not begin when an officer climbs the ladder to the bridge or combat information center (CIC). Physical and psychological preparation must begin long before

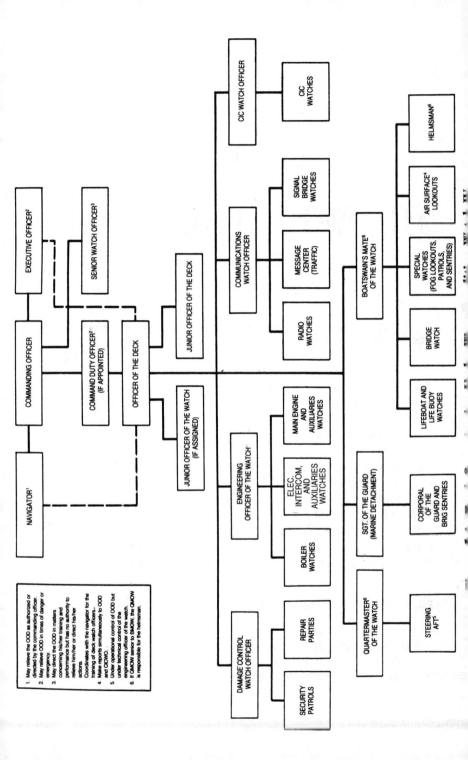

that. The performance of an officer who goes on watch tired, cold, or hungry will be impaired, no matter how capable he or she may be, and preoccupation with other matters will prevent the high level of concentration that makes the true professional. The specific way to prepare for a watch is a matter of personal preference, but there are certain things that should become habitual: being dressed properly for the situation, donning foul-weather gear if necessary; on a cold night, drinking some soup or eating hot food before taking over; and bringing one's personal equipment. This last is, again, a matter of personal preference, but a watch officer should always bring a flashlight fitted with a red lens, something to write with, a pad or notebook, and sunglasses on bright days.

## CONCENTRATION

The ability to concentrate is vital to an exacting task. This is as true for watch officers as it is for surgeons and professional athletes. A watch officer cannot under any circumstances be distracted from his or her duties. No departmental project or personal problem can be allowed to supersede concentration on the watch. If a watch officer has a personal problem that is serious enough to interfere with performance, he or she should discuss the situation with the captain or senior watch officer and, if necessary, ask to be temporarily taken off the watch bill. The CO will respect the judgment of the officer concerned.

## GETTING THE PICTURE

Standing a deck watch on a modern warship is far too demanding a task to be undertaken without advance briefing. The value of this briefing depends upon whether the officer knows what questions to ask and what to look for.

### Information from the CIC

An officer should always check in with the CIC before appearing on the bridge. The following is a partial list of the kinds of information a watch officer should expect to get from the CIC:

1. Formation disposition and the location of the officer in tactical command (OTC) and guide(s).

2. Ship's condition of readiness; which weapons are manned; the status of weapon systems.

3. What emissions-control (EmCon) plan is in effect.

4. Changes in the schedule of events, operations order, or task group commander's letter of instruction since the watch officer's last watch.

5. Which tactical voice circuits are guarded by the CIC and which by the bridge; net-control authority, if assigned; and type of call signs to be used.

6. What recognition and authentication systems are in effect.

7. What intelligence is available on enemy, allied, and other forces.

8. What intelligence-reporting requirements are assigned to the ship.

9. The assignment of surface, air, subsurface, and electronic-warfare reporting within the task group, with particular emphasis on the ship's responsibilities.

10. The status of combat air patrol, electronic-warfare aircraft, and other air assets; the ship's control duties, if any.

11. The ship's scheduled flight operations, helicopter or fixed wing.

### Information from the TAO and the CIC Watch Officer

No attempt will be made here to discuss in detail the duties of the tactical action officer (TAO), but the OOD should have a precise understanding of the command relationship between himself or herself and the TAO. The ten or fifteen minutes that the OOD takes in planning with the TAO for the upcoming watch will do a great deal toward ensuring a smooth, well-coordinated watch. When a CIC watch officer, rather than a TAO, is assigned, the same procedure should be followed even though the command relationship differs. See chapter 17 for further details.

### Information from Other Control Centers

Depending on the mission of the ship, other watch stations of importance to the OOD may be manned. In a frigate engaged in anti-submarine warfare (ASW), for example, the watch in sonar control is as important as those on the bridge and in the CIC. Therefore, before going on watch, the OOD should be familiar with the status and duties of other watch stations. In the case of a ship with an ASW mission, he or she should be aware of environmental conditions, the active and passive equipment in use and its mode operation, and the action to take if contact is gained. Similarly, in a ship whose primary mission is flight operations, the OOD must understand the capabilities and limitations of operating aircraft and be aware of the carrier's maneuvering restrictions and the type of missions to be expected on the watch. In the case of a guided-missile cruiser or destroyer with a primary antiair warfare focus, the OOD should have a general idea of missile battery status, air search and fire-control radars, combat air patrol aircraft under the ship's control, and the air threat. As noted in an earlier chapter, the watch officer should stop by the engineering control station and discuss with the engineering officer of the watch (EOOW) the status of the propulsion plant and any training, preventive maintenance, or corrective maintenance that the engineers would like to conduct, operations permitting. A tour of topside spaces will quickly prepare the oncoming OOD for heavy weather. A walk-through of other watch stations will demonstrate to the watchstanders the interest of the OOD and remind them that he or she is in charge.

## ON THE BRIDGE

When the watch officer has all the necessary information from the CIC and other watch stations, it is time to begin the turnover process on the bridge. If it is a night watch, the OOD should take the time, before and during this process, to adapt his or her eyes to the darkness. The safety of the ship at night may depend on the OOD's ability and that of the lookouts—to see in the dark. This is called dark adaptation.

All vision depends on light-sensitive nerve endings in the retina of the eye, called rods and cones, which transmit to the brain an impression of the image formed on the retina by the lens of the eye. The cones, in the center, are color sensitive. The rods, in a circle around the cones, detect variations in the light intensity and are also highly sensitive to motion. At night, when there is no color to see, the cones tend to make spots in front of the eyes if a fixed point is stared at too long; looking out of the corners of the eyes forces the motion-sensitive rods to take over. They will not tell the color of a ship ahead, but they may enable an observer to see that the ship is moving.

Daylight, in which the rods furnish color perception, is composed of all the colors in the spectrum. The cones are active only in the lower, red range of the spectrum; thus dim red lights have little adverse effect on night vision. It is possible to work on a bridge or in a pilothouse so lighted, then move out to the bridge wing and be able to see perfectly.

Exposure to white light at night greatly reduces vision. A carelessly used flashlight, an open hatch, even the flare of a match may so reduce the conning officer's perception that he or she fails to see a small craft or other object in the water.

Good night vision depends on a slow, roving gaze that systematically covers the field of vision in a simple geometric pattern. Dim objects, almost invisible if looked at directly, will be picked up. If something is sighted and then lost, the way to relocate it is to move the eyes in a circle around the spot. If the object is moving, the rods in the eyes will find it again.

The effect of bright sunlight on the eyes lasts long after the sun goes down. People exposed to strong sunlight during the day can see only half as well as others at night; they should wear dark sunglasses topside on bright days.

During those first few minutes on the bridge it is a good idea for the OOD to begin getting the feel of the watch. If it is nighttime, the OOD should stand clear of all personnel on watch while his or her eyes become adapted. Only then should the OOD start the watch by reading the captain's night orders.

## THE NIGHT-ORDER BOOK

Night orders are a statement in writing of how the captain wants the ship to be run when he or she is not on the bridge. They are divided into two parts: standing orders, which express the CO's policy and directions under *all* circumstances, and orders for dealing with the situation for each day (see Appendix A). The OOD should study and thoroughly understand the standing orders before assuming a first watch on the bridge of a ship, and should review them at least monthly and after any long period in port. The second part of the night orders contains a summary of tactical, navigational, and readiness information. Additional information and guidance are added by the captain and the navigator in the narrative sections of the orders. The night orders are signed each night by the navigator, executive officer, and captain, and the information they contain may not be changed without the permission of the captain. They are also signed by the OOD and junior officer of the deck ( JOOD) on a watch-to-watch basis. When ships are steaming in company, night intentions are often signaled by the OTC, the screen commander, or some other unit commander. Night intentions should be studied with the same care as the night orders, because they are in a broader sense the "night orders" of the CO.

## THE ORAL TURNOVER

The final and most important phase of relieving the watch is the oral turnover. At this time, the officer taking over must obtain or verify all the information needed to stand the watch, making sure that he or she understands exactly what is expected. The following is a list of the minimum amount of information to be obtained during a turnover.

### Navigational Information

1. Position of the ship, how and when determined, and fix accuracy.

2. Course and speed; engine revolutions per minute (rpm) required to keep station or maintain required speed of advance.

3. Method of plotting the ship's position (radar, OMEGA, dead reckoning, etc.) and frequency with which fixes are to be taken.

4. Time and position of expected radar or visual landfall, if any.

5. Aids to navigation in sight or expected; times and positions of expected sightings.

6. Depth of water.

7. Planned changes of course and speed.

8. Possible hazards to navigation.

9. Weather and hydrographic conditions, including winds, currents, barometer trends, and any unusual weather that may be expected.

### Tactical Information

1. The ship's station, location of the guide, and visual identification of the guide.

2. If the ship is in a line or multiple-line formation, the prescribed order, distance interval, and sequence numbers.

3. Zigzag or evasive steering plan in effect.

4. Base course, signaled speed, base speed, stationing speed, and maximum speed expected during the watch.

5. Amount and frequency of course and speed changes required to remain in station or in sector, and effects of weather on station-keeping.

6. Expected changes in formation or dispositions, attachments and detachments, and rendezvous information.

7. Maneuvering peculiarities and limitations of other ships in the formation, and approach limits for ships unable to maneuver freely.

8. Lighting and deceptive measures in force.

9. OTC's emergency instructions.

10. Status of all contacts.

## Readiness Information

1. Status of engineering plant. Speed limitation, equipment on the line, generator and boiler lineup; casualties to equipment or machinery that affect the speed or maneuverability of the ship.

2. Expected times of light-off or securing of main propulsion (boilers, gas turbines, etc.).

3. Readiness and material conditions set; expected changes to existing conditions.

4. Status of lookouts, watches, and special details, if set.

5. Status of the watch relief.

6. Unexecuted orders, signals, or evolutions.

7. Changes to scheduled evolution, watch assignments, and watchstanding personnel.

8. Officer with the conn.

9. Location of the captain and flag or unit commanders embarked.

10. Staff duty officer and staff watches assigned, if applicable.

## RELIEVING THE WATCH

Once satisfied that he or she has all the information needed to stand the watch and a grasp of the current situation, the oncoming duty officer is ready to relieve the watch. Although the relieving should certainly not be done hastily, it is discourteous to drag it out with questions about minutiae. The relief should be ready to take over about fifteen minutes before the hour. No matter how well prepared the new watch may be, it is never wise to take over during an evolution or maneuver.

Relieving a watch is, as stated in an earlier chapter, a formal process. By saying, "I relieve you, sir (or ma'am)," the new OOD is announcing to the watch that he or she has formally accepted responsibility for the watch. Use of any other terminology can leave the matter in doubt. As soon as the OOD has taken over, he or she should inform the watch by announcing clearly, "This is ____. I have the deck (and, if so, the conn)." The helmsman and lee helmsman will acknowledge this by calling out "Aye, aye, sir (or ma'am)" and repeating the course steered, magnetic heading, engine order, and rpm rung up. This procedure should always be followed when a new watch comes on duty.

## ORGANIZING THE WATCH

When the entire watch has been relieved, the OOD should check its organization to make sure that it is set up properly. There will probably be a number of people on watch undergoing watch qualification and instruction. Supervising the training of these people is an important duty for the OOD and watch leaders. The boatswain's mate of the watch (BMOW) has specific duties in regard to training the watch, as do the other senior petty officers in the section, and they should be made to take an active part in the training of the new watchstanders. It is part of the OOD's duty to see that the personnel under instruction are indeed being instructed and not merely "broken in" by nonrated crew members who happen to have been aboard for a longer time. The latter type of instruction is a sure way of establishing bad habits and a detrimentally casual attitude toward qualification.

Training is generally considered to apply to lookouts, helmsmen, lee helmsmen, and phone talkers, on the assumption that such key watchstanders as the quartermaster and the BMOW are already qualified and need no further instruction. In many ships, however, senior boatswain's mates are not on the watch bill; they assign junior-rated people or promising strikers as BMOWs under way. Although there is nothing inherently wrong with this, it often means that a nonrated boatswain striker is in charge of a watch composed of peers. Unless that person is a very strong leader, he or she may have difficulty setting and enforcing standards on the watch, and the watch officer will be deprived of the most important watch leader, trainer, and supervisor.

A watch officer in this situation will have to either train the BMOW to acceptable standards or, if that fails, find a qualified person. If the situation is serious, the best long-term solution is to take the matter up with the senior watch officer. The BMOW is the most important enlisted member of a watch team and should be able to perform to the required standards. If he or she cannot, it will be almost impossible to train the rest of the watch.

A similar situation often occurs with the quartermaster of the watch (QMOW). The duties assigned to that person are wide-ranging and require considerable knowledge as well as completion of an extensive personnel qualification standards (PQS) program. The QMOW's responsibilities in the areas of log keeping, weather observation, and navigational assistance to the OOD affect not only the operation of the watch but also such things as the accuracy of weather forecasts sent to the ship, the credibility of the deck log, and in some circumstances, the safe navigation of the ship.

A QMOW's ability to do the job properly is something that the OOD must verify by reading weather data recorded, checking the accuracy of the navigational plot, and closely examining log entries. The OOD may find, for example, that a wind whose velocity and direction have been constant for some time suddenly shifts and shows a radical change in speed when the watch is relieved. Some watchstanders are so oblivious to conditions that they will walk onto the lee wing of the bridge in a gale, record a low wind speed, and think nothing of it. When sent to a weather facility for analysis, inaccurate data can result in a ship's receiving an inaccurate forecast and, consequently, being in considerable danger. Quartermasters should be trained to observe, to use common sense, and if in doubt, to call the navigator.

Once a general idea of the qualifications of his or her watchstanders is established, the OOD can decide how and in what areas to train them for the next four hours. If the ship is steaming independently and there are no other ships or hazards in the area, emergency steering drills and procedures should always be carried out. The process of shifting steering units and steering control from station to station and making reports is not very difficult, but it must be understood thoroughly by all watchstanders, and the best way to understand it is to do it. Knowing the location and use of alarms, backup systems, and special lights is also an important training requirement, particularly on night watches. This kind of training should be pushed as hard as the tactical situation permits. It will pay big dividends, not only in terms of watch proficiency but also in the satisfaction and pride of the watchstanders. Most people enjoy knowing that they are doing something well and will appreciate the OOD's efforts to help them qualify.

Every watch station qualification is governed by a formal PQS. Checking the PQS status of each of the watchstanders and taking the opportunity to sign off PQS items is a superb way of conducting on-watch training. The watchstanders will feel a sense of accomplishment in seeing actual progress toward a goal, and the OOD will be qualifying his or her watchstanders, not just "breaking them in." Innovative ideas on training that meet with the captain's permission will prevent the development of slothful habits and help keep the team alert.

JOODs should play an important role in training the watch. Their active participation in all training will strengthen the watch team.

## THE CONN

"To conn" means to control, or direct by rudder angles and engine-order telegraph, the movements of a ship. "The conn" means the station of the conning officer. The OOD may have both the deck and the conn, but often the CO will take the conn when an intricate or dangerous maneuver is to be performed. It is also customary for the OOD to assist in such maneuvers by checking on how the members of the bridge watch are performing and by keeping a watchful eye on the entire maneuver so as to inform the CO of any danger that might escape his or her notice. Likewise, when the OOD has the conn during a delicate maneuver or in restricted waters, it is customary for the CO to be watching on the bridge. In effect, then, there is a two-person system in which one person has the conn, giving orders to the wheel and the engines, while another assists and advises.

Directing the movements of a modern warship at high speed and in proximity to other ships is a job that requires intense concentration and foresight. At night or when a number of ships are maneuvering simultaneously, it takes only a minute or two of distraction for a conning officer to become so disoriented that the ship is placed in danger. For this reason, the officer who has the conn must be able to concentrate attention on the job at hand. During maneuvers, the officer at the conn should not be concerned with getting the word passed, signing sounding-and-security logs, or any of the other duties of running the watch. When at the conn, the OOD should delegate these duties to the JOOD, and similarly, when the JOOD has the conn, the OOD should assume responsibility for carrying out the routine of the watch. Firm enforcement of the policy of not allowing the conning officer to be distracted goes a long way toward reducing the possibility of confusion in tight situations.

Although there is no official set of rules about the conn, the following principles have been accepted by experienced seagoing naval officers:

1. One and only one person can give steering and engine orders at any given time.

2. The identity of the person giving these orders must be known to the people on the bridge.

3. The OOD may delegate the conn to another officer, but he or she retains responsibility for the ship's safety.

4. The CO may take over the deck or the conn. When the CO takes over the deck, the OOD has no technical responsibility for the direction of the ship's movements, except as specifically detailed by the CO. But when the latter takes over the conn, the OOD carries out all the duties assigned to him or her by regulations and assists and advises the CO.

5. In taking the conn from the OOD, the CO should see that all personnel on the bridge watch are notified of the fact. If the CO takes over during an emergency, however, the issuing of a direct steering or engine order constitutes legal assumption of responsibility for directing the ship's movements. When taking the conn in this manner,

the CO retains that responsibility until the conn is turned over to another person.

6. Every CO establishes a procedure for letting it be known beyond doubt that he or she has assumed direct control of the ship and thereby relieved the conning officer of all responsibility for such control. The procedure for delegating control to a conning officer must be equally clear. Transfer of control is usually announced like this: "This is ____. I have the conn." All bridge personnel, but especially the helmsman and lee helmsman, must acknowledge the information with the words "Aye, aye, sir (or ma'am)." It is also customary for the helmsman and lee helmsman to respond by sounding off the course being steered, the magnetic-compass course, and the speed and rpm.

The OOD has no problem if the above principles are observed at all times. But even the best of COs is fallible and may, while concentrating on the vital matters at hand, neglect to follow recommended procedure in taking over or relinquishing the conn. Under these circumstances, it is up to the OOD to clarify the situation with a polite, "Do you have the conn, sir (or ma'am)?" or "I have the conn, sir (or ma'am)." Then he or she must see that important persons on the bridge know who has the conn.

The OOD who does not have the conn should assist the officer who does. One of the best ways of doing this is by making sure that the conning officer's orders are understood and acted upon correctly by the helmsman and other bridge personnel, and that the conning officer knows that his or her orders are being executed. The OOD may take whatever station is most conducive to maintaining a lookout.

## COMBAT INFORMATION CENTER

In modern naval operations, the CIC and the bridge function as separate parts of a tactical team. Their roles vary according to the type of operations the ship is carrying out but are never separate. Since the position of the TAO came into being, the CIC and the bridge have become even more interdependent, and no officer who stands a watch in either of these control stations should attempt to "go it alone."

It used to be the function of the CIC to collect, evaluate, display, and disseminate information pertaining to the control of the ship. In today's warships, however, the function of evaluating has been expanded to include, in some situations, actual control of the ship, its sensors, and its weapons systems. Formerly, the CO's general-quarters station was the bridge. Nowadays, he or she exercises control from the CIC, because the information available to help in decision making cannot be presented on the bridge. This arrangement in no way lessens the importance of the OOD as the officer responsible for the safety and proper operation of the ship. It does, however, require that person to possess a broad and intimate knowledge of how the CIC operates and what its capabilities and limitations are. The OOD must also know at all times what his or her command relationship with the TAO is. Confusion on this point leads, at best, to poor coordination between the bridge and the CIC, and, at worst, to disaster. It is for this reason that the prewatch briefing mentioned earlier in this chapter is so important.

Although it is equipped with a variety of sensors, evaluating devices, and data-processing equipment, the CIC does have certain limitations. The array of equipment in the modern CIC is so impressive, sometimes so overwhelming, that it is easy to forget this fact. Next to a million-dollar radar, the eyes of a lookout may seem unreliable indeed. Yet there are times when the only reliable source of information is that lookout, and the usefulness of the entire complex of systems and sensors depends on the accuracy of the information that he or she can provide. Regardless of how sophisticated a CIC may be or how well trained its watch team, it sometimes happens, especially when maneuvering at close quarters, that the information furnished to the bridge by the CIC is incomplete or inaccurate. This is where the OOD's judgment and confidence become important. The OOD must always be aware that he or she is not only a user of the information provided by the CIC but also a major contributor, evaluator, and verifier of the tactical picture. When the CIC proposes the wrong course of action, it is probably because coordination with the bridge has somehow broken down. It is the responsibility of the OOD to set the situation straight and, when there is time, to go over the event with the CIC watch officer or the TAO to find out what went wrong. What the OOD should *not* do in this kind of situation is engage in argument with the CIC watch while the situation is deteriorating.

Under most normal steaming conditions, the main channels of routine communication between the bridge and the CIC are sound-powered telephone circuits. No matter what the quality and quantity of information between the two stations, its usefulness depends on the ability of the few individuals, usually nonrated and often nondesignated, who man the circuits. The performance of phone talkers, particularly those on the bridge, can be a major source of conflict and misunderstanding. The bridge talker is often a nonrated person from a deck division who has very little idea of what goes on in the CIC and less understanding of the terms, acronyms, and figures being passed. If the bridge talker makes a mistake and is reprimanded by the OOD or, even worse, ridiculed by the CIC talker at the other end of the line, he or she may become frustrated or freeze up completely. Thus, at the very time help is most needed, the bridge talker is unable to give it.

There is an easy way to prevent this from happening. The OOD should make the bridge phone talker aware of the importance of the job and encourage familiarization with the CIC to clear up the meaning of information entrusted to him or her. On a quiet watch, when no demanding evolutions are expected, talkers can be rotated into the CIC for indoctrination on radarscopes, contact reporting, and simple procedures. At the same time, it is a good idea to man the bridge telephones and, if possible, one of the lookout stations with CIC watchstanders. It will be an education for both parties and probably a welcome change from routine duties. For special evolutions, the OOD should not hesitate to put a more senior talker on the phones, if necessary calling that person to the bridge. The same applies to bridge and engineering-control stations. The OOD should always remember that all the resources of the ship are at his or her disposal and should not hesitate to use any of them.

The most important thing to remember about bridge–CIC relations is that both watch centers are part of the ship-control team and that they share responsibility for providing the CO, the OOD, and the TAO with the best possible support of the ship's mission. Standing watch in the CIC is discussed in chapter 17.

## AIRCRAFT CARRIER FLIGHT OPERATIONS

In an aircraft carrier, the OOD meets situations not encountered in other types of ships. Flight operations themselves greatly complicate the routine of a ship. Her very size makes the efficient administration of a carrier difficult. In large carriers, the OOD is supported by a JOOD as well as a junior officer of the watch (JOOW). The latter frequently handles routine matters under way, such as passing the word, writing mast reports, and dumping trash. The JOOD handles tactical circuits and relays information between the CO and the OOD, who is, of course, in overall charge and usually has the conn.

When an aircraft carrier is operating with lifeguard destroyers, the OOD has a special responsibility to keep those destroyers informed of the progress of flight operations, unexpected changes in course and speed, and modifications to lighting measures. The lighting and shape of an aircraft carrier make it extremely difficult for another ship to visually determine her aspect, her direction of turn, and her distance. Therefore, watch officers on the lifeguard destroyers rely heavily on the carrier's OOD to tell them *immediately* of any course and speed changes. The importance of coordination between carriers and destroyers has been underscored by tragic accidents and the loss of life at sea.

It is essential for officers who stand deck watches on carriers to become familiar with those of their duties that concern aircraft. These include the following:

1. Aircraft turnups and jet blasts, and related safety precautions.
2. Operation of aircraft elevators and hangar-bay doors.
3. Operation of helicopters.
4. Cooperation between the weapons department and the air department in the matter of respotting aircraft and boats.
5. No smoking during the fueling and defueling of airplanes, helicopters, and so forth.
6. The use of rescue destroyers and helicopters in plane crashes, and the need to keep them informed.
7. Restrictions on blowing tubes (never during launching and recovery or when soot may blow over the flight deck).
8. Wind and weather conditions for flight operations.
9. Messing of air group and air department personnel before, after, and during flight operations.
10. Informing the air department when high winds are expected so that aircraft may be secured.

## HELICOPTER OPERATIONS

The use of helicopters in ASW, amphibious operations, vertical replenishment, and other logistic and tactical roles continues to increase. Most warships now either carry a helicopter or are configured so that they can operate the helicopters of other ships. An OOD should be familiar with helicopter operations in general and should have a thorough knowledge of the helicopter-operating capabilities (levels and classes of certification) of his or her own ship. If the ship carries a helicopter, the OOD should also have a basic knowledge of its limitations, special operating requirements, and operational parameters.

Wind is always a critical factor when helicopters are being operated. Each type of ship and each type of helicopter must operate within certain wind "envelopes" to spread rotors, start engines, engage rotors, and launch and recover. Relative wind directions and velocities that constitute given envelopes for both day and night operating conditions are graphically displayed in NWP-42. These tables should always be available on the bridge and, no matter how often helicopters are operated, should always be consulted before a rotor engagement, launch, or recovery is approved. Only in extreme emergency and with the CO's permission should helicopters be operated outside the envelope.

Ship's roll and pitch also affect helicopter operations. Each helicopter has a specified envelope for wind and roll and pitch in both day and night operations. It is the responsibility of the OOD to adjust course and speed not only to provide acceptable wind across the deck but also to minimize roll and pitch. As with all special evolutions, it is a good idea to keep a checklist handy to ensure that these critical conditions are provided.

### Shipboard Procedures

All OODs should be conversant with their own ship's bills and procedures for operating, fueling, and receiving helicopters. One of the best ways to begin acquiring this information on ships that have a helicopter detachment is to talk to the pilots and deck crew. They will be glad to give the OOD information, because their lives might well depend on how thoroughly he or she understands their problems and requirements.

Before any helicopter operations can be undertaken, a number of preparations must be made. The OOD is responsible for seeing that they are carried out and that the ship is ready to perform the evolution safely, smartly, and on time. The sequence of events in preparing for and conducting helicopter operations is usually as follows:

1. Pilots and crew are briefed on the mission, weather, expected ship's movement, fields to which they might be diverted, communications, and emergency procedures. It is not necessary for the OOD to know all of these things, only to have access to them through the CIC.

2. Before flight quarters is called, helicopters should be brought on deck and preflighted. The OOD and the helicopter flight crew must maintain close liaison, especially when a helicopter is being rolled out of the hangar. During this phase, ship's motion should be minimized and hard turns that may cause the ship to heel should be avoided.

3. When the preliminary checks have been completed, flight quarters should be called and a foreign object damage (FOD) walk-down done on the flight deck. The flight-operations area should be roped off and all hands periodically warned to stand clear of it. The smoking lamp should be extinguished in the area of flight operations.

4. After the detail has been manned and communications have been checked, the helicopter is given permission to start engines. At this point, the OOD should have a reasonably good idea of the flight course and should ensure that the ship will be able to maneuver for launch.

5. When the pilot is ready to engage rotors, the ship is maneuvered to within the engagement envelope and the OOD gives permission to engage. Final radio communications checks are made.

6. When the helicopter is completely ready, the pilot requests a "green deck" for launch. At this time, the ship should come to flight course, and the pilot should be informed of relative wind direction and velocity, altimeter setting, and ship's pitch and roll. The deck crew then pull out tie-down chains and wheel chocks and launch the helicopter. When the helicopter is well clear of the ship and the pilot has reported operations normal, flight quarters are usually secured and the ship returns to base course until it is time to recover.

## Conditions of Readiness

Depending on the tactical situation, the OTC usually assigns ready helicopters to such missions as search and rescue (SAR), lifeguard, and ASW and specifies a given readiness status, which can be any one of the following:

> ***Ready 5.***   Ready for launch five minutes from signal. All preflight checks complete, pilots in aircraft, and engines warmed and ready to launch. Crew at flight quarters.
> ***Ready 15.***   Aircraft spotted, rotors spread, and most preflight checks complete. Pilots in flight gear, briefed, and on call. Flight quarters not set.
> ***Ready 30.***   Aircraft ready to launch within thirty minutes. All daily preflight checks complete. Depending on limitations of ship, aircraft may or may not be spotted. Crew not at flight quarters.

Each readiness condition has advantages and disadvantages. Ready 5 provides the fastest reaction time but, because of crew fatigue resulting from the need for constant readiness to launch, cannot be maintained for long. Ready 15 does not provide as rapid a reaction time and is contingent upon the crew's ability to get to flight quarters on short notice. However, it has the advantage of requiring fewer people to be on station for a long period of time and can be maintained for days.

## Emergencies

The OOD on a ship that operates with helicopters should be familiar with basic procedures for both in-flight and on-deck emergencies, because one of the first things an aircraft in trouble will attempt to do is land on deck. He or she should be prepared to recover aircraft on very short notice and, if the situation dictates, without flight quarters being fully manned. The time the pilot has in which to land safely may be so short that the risk of recovering that person without a full flight-deck crew is justified. This is essentially the pilot's decision, and if such action is considered necessary it is probably because his or her life depends on it.

In the case of on-deck emergencies such as crashes or fires, the OOD may have to decide, after the crew is safe, whether to save the helicopter or to jettison it and thereby avoid danger to the ship. The OOD should plan in advance how to handle such a situation and know what equipment is available to assist in each kind of emergency. For example, fin stabilizers, with which some ships are equipped, contain a device that induces a large roll of the ship, a capability that could be extremely useful in getting a burning aircraft over the side. An OOD should also be very familiar with procedures for lost communications and aircraft-in-the-water accidents.

## SUBMARINE OPERATIONS

The duties of the OOD of a surfaced submarine differ from those of the OOD of a surface ship in several ways. First of all, a submarine is extremely vulnerable when she is involved in a collision. The OOD must keep this fact in mind and never allow the submarine to get into a situation where there is appreciable risk of collision. He or she must always be alert for the presence of other vessels, because the silhouette a submarine presents to another ship is deceptive. This is true both night and day, but particularly at night, because the lights of a submarine, which may not conform to the rules of the road, are grouped so closely that she gives the appearance of a fishing boat or a small ship. There is a tendency, then, for vessels approaching a surfaced submarine at night to be unconcerned. Similarly, a submarine tends to present a small "pip" on radar, which also leads to her classification by approaching ships as a small vessel.

The OOD of a submarine must be cognizant of the status of "rig for dive" at all times. An underway submarine should be ready to dive at any time. Once she has been reported "rigged for dive," permission to alter the status of that rig or to do anything that might interfere with diving must be obtained from the CO.

Because a submarine is extremely low in the water, certain safety precautions must be followed at all times at sea. Some of these are as follows:

1. No one should be allowed on the main deck without the CO's permission. Save in exceptional circumstances, all personnel going to the main deck must use life jackets and safety lines.

2. In rough seas, the OOD and lookouts should wear safety belts and have life lines secured to a part of the ship that would not be carried away by a boarding sea.

3. In rough seas, the OOD should shut the conning tower or upper-bridge hatch to prevent flooding.

4. In a following sea, the OOD should be alert to the danger of water being taken into the ship through the air-induction system. In submarines equipped with dual-induction systems, the main air-induction system should be shut and the snorkel system used to get air into the ship.

When a submarine submerges, the OOD becomes the diving officer and the conning officer takes over the functions of the OOD.

The duties and responsibilities of the OOD on a surfaced nuclear-powered submarine are not a great deal different from those on a conventional submarine. Nuclear submarines spend so little time on the surface, however, that bridge personnel may forget what those duties and responsibilities are. Following a prolonged period of submergence, the OOD should review the standing instructions and orders covering surface watchstanding and should brief the watch section as necessary.

## SEARCH AND RESCUE

The armed services and the Coast Guard jointly maintain an almost worldwide SAR organization that uses existing commands, bases, and facilities to search for and rescue people involved in air, surface, and subsurface accidents. There are three SAR areas: the Inland Region, whose designated commander is the chief of staff of the U.S. Air Force; the Maritime Region, whose commander is the commandant of the U.S. Coast Guard; and the Overseas Region, whose commander is a designated unified commander. The commander of the unit that arrives first at the scene of a disaster is known as the on-scene commander. When an accident occurs, certain radio frequencies are specified for the use of those involved in SAR operations and a carefully planned procedure is followed.

Detailed information concerning the SAR organization and its procedures can be found in most fleet instructions and operation orders. The SAR folder on the bridge and in the CIC contains the Navy Search and Rescue Manual (NWP 3-50.1) and pertinent SAR directives from current operation orders.

The OOD should be familiar with these directives and know the radio frequencies to be used, the rescue procedures, and the special signals made by ships and aircraft in distress.

## REPLENISHMENT AT SEA

Replenishment at sea (RAS) refers to the transfer of fuel, stores, mail, ammunition, and sometimes people from one ship to another while both are under way. Most replenishments are scheduled, but an "RAS of opportunity" can be ordered whenever circumstances warrant it. RAS requires special skills and maneuvering with which all officers must be familiar, because they are likely to be involved in the evolution either as OOD or as conning officer. This is especially true on destroyers and other small ships, not only because of the large number of people involved in the evolution but also because it is likely to occur often. When RAS is scheduled, the OOD should do the following things:

1. Review Underway Replenishment (NWP 4-01.4) for details of the entire procedure. Check *Knight's Modern Seamanship* for a description of the equipment used, a brief discussion of shiphandling involved, and for safety precautions to be observed.

2. Notify the heads of the departments concerned as soon as practicable.

3. Order that information about the time of the operation and the stations to be manned be passed over the 1MC circuit.

4. Supervise the use of prescribed signals while the ship is approaching and alongside the replenishing ship.

5. Assist the conning officer in relaying orders to the helmsman, operator of the engine-order telegraph, and rpm indicator.

6. Notify the EOOW as far in advance as possible so that he or she can make appropriate changes in the status of the plant, for example, lighting off extra boilers, placing generators on standby, and if refueling is scheduled, shifting the fuel load.

7. Study the characteristics and replenishment arrangements of the ship alongside of which his or her own ship will be. Set stadime-

ters to the correct masthead height for the units he or she will be working with.

8. Check to see that communications equipment includes a radio, a flashing light, electric megaphones, sound-powered telephones, flags, paddles, and wands. During the actual operation, the use of radio between delivery and receiving ships is normally confined to emergencies. Electric megaphones are used during the approach and until telephone lines are connected. Thereafter they comprise the main standby method of communicating.

## HEAVY WEATHER

One of the attributes of a good naval officer and seaman is knowledge of the weather. He or she should know what weather is expected and be prepared to meet its effects on shipboard operations.

When heavy seas and winds of high intensity are anticipated, the OOD must take the following precautions:

1. Have the word passed over all circuits "Prepare ship for heavy weather."

2. Designate divisions to rig inboard life lines on weather decks.

3. Pass, as appropriate, the word "Close all hatches on main deck forward," "Close all topside hatches forward (or aft) of frame ____," "Close all topside hatches, doors, and ports on starboard (port) side." Pass the word for personnel to remain clear of the weather decks as necessary for safety.

4. Require personnel assigned topside in heavy weather to wear life jackets and safety lines. Crew thus exposed should also wear warm jackets.

## DAMAGE-CONTROL SETTINGS

The OOD's responsibility for effective damage-control and watertight-integrity procedures is an important one. An OOD should have completed the PQS for damage control and should know the exact location and capabilities of all major and secondary damage-control systems in the ship. The OOD must see that the proper damage-control condition is set and that exceptions to that condition are reported and entered in the damage-control closure log book. When the sounding-and-security watch reports to the bridge "All secure" and presents readings, the OOD should examine them carefully before initialing them. Changes in water depth in spaces or a requirement to pump spaces frequently ought to be given close scrutiny, particularly in heavy weather when the ship may be making water because hatches or other deck openings have not been properly secured.

While opening and closing doors and hatches may seem dull, they are matters of great importance to the safety of the ship and the lives of the crew. A sudden grounding or collision can result in disaster. Even half a ship will stay afloat and permit the rescue of many crew members if her watertight integrity has been maintained. The OOD must always strive to combat carelessness and to see that the proper closure setting is maintained.

## MATERIAL CASUALTIES

The OOD must ensure, to the extent possible, that all machinery and electronic gear is operable. This means exercising foresight and testing equipment such as winches, radar, and voice circuits that may be used in the immediate future. In addition, the OOD should make certain that the right officer is notified of any material casualties that occur. He or she must know what effect a given casualty will have and make necessary reports to the OTC, as well as intraship reports. For example, the OOD should report an important electronics failure to the electronics officer as well as to the captain and admiral (if embarked), and obtain an estimate of repair time.

The OOD is interested in how a casualty affects the performance, maneuverability, or safety of the ship, *not* in how repairs are to be made, who is to do them, or how long they will take. An OOD who badgers people on the scene of a casualty not only makes no contribution but often adds to the problem and impedes its correction.

## BINOCULARS

The OOD should know how to adjust, clean, and use binoculars; know his or her own focus and interpupillary setting; and instruct lookouts and other personnel in the care and use of glasses. Careless handling, especially dropping, can soon make a pair of glasses unfit for use. The watch should be taught to use the neck strap and to keep the glasses in their case when they are not in use. Nothing is more unseamanlike and just plain wasteful of public funds than letting binoculars lie around. The top of a chart table may seem like safe stowage, but when the ship takes a roll, the user has to lean over and pick up a pair of glasses that are no longer of help. Binocular lenses should be cleaned only with lens paper.

## REFUSE DISPOSAL AND POLLUTION CONTROL

The Navy's ability to accomplish its mission requires both the conduct of daily operations in the land, sea, and air environments and good stewardship of our world's resources. The bottom line is very simple: the Navy is committed to operating in a manner compatible with the environment. National defense and environmental protection are and must continue to be compatible goals. Therefore, a very important part of the Navy's mission is to prevent pollution, protect the environment, and preserve natural, historic, and cultural resources. In order to accomplish this mission element, personnel must be aware of the environmental and natural resources laws and regulations, which have been established by federal, state, and local government. The Navy chain of command must provide leadership and a personal commitment to ensure that all Navy personnel develop and exhibit an environmental protection ethic.

You will find that the number of environmental regulations has increased significantly in recent years, and these regulations are in a continuous state of change. You must be generally familiar with an overview of federal regulations, Department of Defense (DoD) requirements, and Navy requirements that apply to Navy ships. In addition, while your ship is tied up along a pier, you as an OOD must ensure you are aware of, understand, and comply with the additional requirements imposed upon your ship by state and local governments. All the information you will need can be found in a very large and detailed instruction, OpNavInst 5090.1B, Environmental and

Natural Resources Program Manual. It contains the applicable state and local requirements for U.S. ports in which they may be moored.

One of the key items you must have complete familiarity with as an underway OOD is the regulations for overboard discharge of any matter from the ship. The basic guidelines are noted below:

***Sewage Disposal.*** As of 1 April 1981, all ships are required to be equipped with tanks capable of holding waste, transferring it ashore, or dumping it at sea beyond three nautical miles of the shore's low-water baseline.

***Garbage.*** Garbage may not be thrown overboard within the navigable waters of the United States and the contiguous zone, roughly twenty-five nautical miles to sea. In foreign waters it is a matter of courtesy to use the same standards that are used in the United States.

***Oil and Oily Water.*** Oil may not be deliberately pumped into the ocean. Bilge pumping is not permitted within fifty miles of the coastline. Caution should be exercised to prevent the spillage of oil.

***Solid Waste.*** Solid waste, trash, and refuse may not be discharged at sea within twenty-five miles of any shore.

***Hazardous Material.*** Never discharge hazardous materials at sea.

***Medical Waste.*** This is not to be disposed of at sea except in extreme circumstances, and then in weighted containers over fifty miles at sea with records maintained.

***Plastics.*** This is not disposed of at sea unless space is a constraint. The goal is to hold for at least twenty days at sea. Plastics held for longer may be disposed of over fifty miles from shore when weighted to sink and when entries are made in the deck log indicating the latitude and longitude of disposal. Food-contaminated plastics may be disposed of beyond fifty miles but not during the final three days before returning to port.

Besides the environmental dangers associated with the discharge of oil and refuse at sea, there are operational considerations. Even in midocean, trash should never be dumped over the side unless it is rigged to sink, and under no circumstances should trash be dumped during flight operations because of the danger of creating FOD. Dumping should not be permitted during ASW operations because solid material can return false echoes. It should also be obvious that the long slick left by a ship pumping oily bilges at sea would assist enemy forces in finding her. When concealment is desired, bilges should be pumped only at night, or when the sea is rough enough to break up the slick.

## REPORTS TO THE CO

Policy on reports to the CO requires exact compliance. As unimportant as some reports may appear, they all contain information that, for one reason or another, the CO needs. Exceptions or changes to what is to be reported can be made only by the CO, not the OOD. As unkind as it may seem to awaken a tired CO, it is much worse to have to call that person to the bridge unprepared when the ship is already in danger. Reports should be concise and specific and should include the OOD's proposed course of action. For example, the OOD may report a contact in this manner: "Captain, this is the OOD. I am presently on a course of 276 degrees at a speed of twelve knots. I have a contact broad on my starboard bow at nine thousand yards. She has a target angle of 330 degrees R. Her present CPA is off the port bow at one thousand yards. My intention is to alter course thirty degrees to starboard in order to open the CPA to four thousand yards off my port beam." If a certain format or sequence is prescribed by the captain for reporting information such as surface contacts, it must be adhered to exactly. No CO enjoys being awakened at night to hear a rambling discourse or a collection of disjointed information.

*In case of doubt, it is always the wisest course to call the captain.* The CO is accustomed to interrupted sleep when under way and will gain peace of mind from an OOD who pays conscientious attention to duty. Some people can acknowledge a message without being fully awake. Therefore, the OOD should make certain that important messages are understood. If possible, such messages should be delivered by the OOD in person rather than by messenger.

# 6

---

# SHIPHANDLING

The mark of a great shiphandler is never getting into a situation that requires great shiphandling.

Fleet Admiral Ernest King

Shiphandling is the most exciting and challenging aspect of a watch officer's job. The key to becoming a competent shiphandler is an understanding of the basic forces affecting the ship, knowledge of shiphandling procedures, and confidence. This chapter provides the basics, but a career of continuous study and practice is required of anyone who wants to become a fully capable conning officer.

## DEFINITIONS

**Pivot Point.** The pivot point is the point of rotation within a ship as she makes a turn. For a destroyer-type ship, it is generally about one-third the length of the ship from the bow and fairly close to the bridge (when the ship is going ahead).

**Turning Circle.** The turning circle is the path described by a ship when she turns. It varies according to the amount of rudder and speed. See figure 6-1.

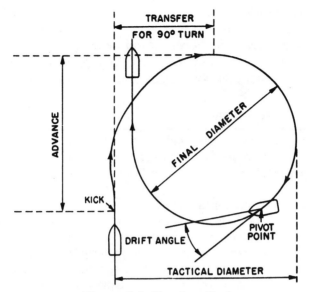

**Figure 6-1. Turning Circle**

*Advance.* For any turn, the advance is the distance gained in the direction of the original course from the time the rudder is put over until the ship is on the new course.

*Transfer.* For any turn, the transfer is the distance gained in a direction perpendicular to that of the original course from the time the rudder is put over until the ship is on the new course.

*Tactical Diameter.* For any amount of constant rudder angle, the tactical diameter is the distance made good in a direction perpendicular to that of the original course from the time the rudder is put over until the ship is on a reverse heading. It is the transfer for a turn of 180 degrees.

*Standard Rudder.* Standard rudder is the angle of rudder that, under normal conditions, gives the ship standard tactical diameter.

*Full Rudder.* Full rudder is a prescribed angle of rudder, usually a safe distance—five degrees—short of the stops, that gives the ship reduced tactical diameter.

*Hard Rudder.* This means putting the rudder over to the indicated side as far as the wheel allows.

*Acceleration and Deceleration Rates.* Acceleration and deceleration rates are those at which a ship picks up or loses headway after a change of speed.

## GENERAL PRINCIPLES

An officer who wants to become an efficient shiphandler should be aware of certain general principles and their specific application to his or her ship. Examples of these principles follow.

### Effect of the Wind Upon Turning

Most ships, particularly those with high bows, turn slowly into the wind when going ahead and rapidly when turning away from it. Conversely, they turn rapidly into the wind when backing. The effect on a particular ship can be estimated by comparing the "sail area" forward of the pivot point with that abaft the pivot point. A ship whose sail area is greater forward has the above tendencies. One with greater sail area aft has the opposite tendencies; this is particularly true of aircraft carriers. The term "sail area" refers to those surfaces of the hull and superstructure above the waterline against which the wind can exert force.

### Effect of Speed Upon Turning

With constant rudder angle, at speeds appreciably above steerageway, any increase in speed makes the turning circle larger. This is because the inertia of the ship tends to keep her going in the original direction of motion. The amount by which the turning circle increases varies from ship to ship and is most noticeable when ships of different types are operating together. Because the guide is usually a large ship and uses the same amount of rudder or standard rudder for all speeds, it is necessary to know what rudder for the ship involved will match the turning circle of the guide ship for the speed at which any turn is made.

At speeds approaching bare steerageway, a decrease in speed results in a larger turning circle. This is because the rudder acting against the inertia of the ship has less effect and tends to keep the ship moving in a straight line. For a turn at low speeds, therefore, more rudder is needed. The minimum speed at which a ship will still have steerageway should be known.

### Effect of Shallow Water

The less space there is between the ship's hull and the bottom, the less freely the screw currents flow and act upon the hull and rudder. When that space is very small, the ship may be sluggish or erratic in answering the rudder, a great deal of power is wasted, and the speed through the water is less than indicated by the propeller revolutions. Additionally, high speed in shallow water may create an effect known as squatting: the bow rides upon the bow wave and the stern sits deeper in the water.

### Time Lag in Response to Orders

There is a noticeable lag between the time an order is given to the wheel or engines and the time the effect of the response is felt. For example, to have the rudder go over at the same spot as that of the ship ahead, so that the turn is made in her wake, the order to turn must be given when the kick of the preceding ship's rudder is near the bridge of the following ship.

### Backing Power Available

In steamships, backing power may be considerably less than the power for going ahead. There are two reasons: first, because a backing turbine has fewer impeller blades, it produces less power; and second, propellers are less efficient when turning astern. "Back one-third" and "Back two-thirds" normally call for one-third and two-thirds, respectively, of the power available for backing. The turns for "Ahead one-third" and "Ahead two-thirds" are based upon one-third and two-thirds, respectively, of standard speed. There is no "back standard" speed. "Ahead one-third (two-thirds)" and "Back one-third (two-thirds)" probably do not have equal effect. Consequently, besides twisting when one engine is backing and the other is going ahead (both at one-third or two-thirds), a ship can be expected to pick up a slight amount of way in the direction of the stronger force. In a gas-turbine ship with controllable-pitch propellers, however, backing power is considerably enhanced, because it is the pitch of the propeller blade that determines the direction of the turbine force. The force generated by the turbine in this instance remains nearly constant.

## Factors That Affect Acceleration and Deceleration

The manner in which ships gain and lose headway, carry their way, and respond to changes of engine speed varies with the size of the ship, her propulsion system, her underwater lines, the condition of her bottom, the wind, and the state of the sea. A clean-bottomed, heavy ship or a ship with fine lines tends to hold her way. A foul-bottomed, heavy ship or a ship with full lines tends to pick up headway slowly in response to changes of engine speed. Gas-turbine ships are more responsive than steamships to speed changes.

## Factors That Affect Turning

An OOD should know not only how to make a normal turn but how to turn a ship in the shortest time and in the shortest possible space. A ship turns in the *shortest time* by going ahead with full power and her rudder hard over just short of the stops. The procedure for turning a ship in the *shortest possible space* depends upon the ship herself and, sometimes, upon wind conditions.

A ship with twin rudders and screws is the easiest and probably the quickest to turn as well as the least affected by wind conditions. Her rudders should simply be put over full in the direction of the desired turn and kept there. "Ahead two-thirds" on the outboard engine and "Back two-thirds" on the inboard engine should be rung up. The speed of the inboard engine can be adjusted to keep the ship from going ahead or astern as she turns on her heel.

A ship with a single rudder and twin screws is slightly more difficult to turn in a short space. If the screws are set well off from the centerline and if the turn is not adversely affected by the wind, the turn can be made by going ahead on the outboard engine and backing on the inboard engine. When the wind does adversely affect the turn, or when the screws are not sufficiently offset for a good, powerful couple, motion ahead and astern may be necessary to supplement the effect of the rudder. As a general rule, when a ship is going ahead with steerageway, her rudder should be put over in the direction of the desired turn; when a ship is going astern with steerageway, her rudder should be put in the opposite direction; when a ship has no way on or less than steerageway, her rudder should be put amidships. The amount of way on and the position of the rudder should be carefully watched. Some ships with large single rudders show a tendency somewhat similar to that of a twin-rudder ship to answer to the effect of an ahead-turning screw on the rudders even when they have a small amount of sternway. The OOD must know the characteristics of his or her own ship in this regard.

A ship with a single screw is the most difficult to turn in a short space. Most ships of this type have right-handed propellers and need to have some way on. Therefore, to turn them in a short space, headway and sternway have to be alternated. Whenever the engine is going ahead, the rudder should be thrown in the direction of the desired turn. Knowing when to shift the rudder after starting the engines backing is a matter of knowing the ship. It should usually be done shortly after the ship loses headway and then kept there until the engine is put ahead.

## HANDLING IN FORMATION

Handling a ship in company with others requires a sound knowledge of the effective tactical instructions and a thorough understanding of the relative motion of ships. Information on the first essential is found in ATP-1, vols. 1 and 2. Every officer standing deck watches at sea should be so familiar with these important directives that he or she can find at once the proper guidance for any circumstance that may arise involving the movements of the ship. The opening chapters of both these volumes are particularly important because they provide the basic concepts and definitions upon which all subsequent instructions are based.

The second essential for efficient shiphandling in formation, an understanding of relative motion, can he attained by studying and practicing problems on a maneuvering board.

An important by-product of skill in the maneuvering board is the ability to visualize problems and to solve them mentally. For a complicated evolution such as taking a distant station in a formation, a mental solution would, of course, be approximate and subject to modification by the combat information center (CIC) or a junior officer of the deck (JOOD) who actually worked out the problem. Nevertheless, a mental solution permits an instant change of course and speed, which expedites the maneuver, demonstrates a ship's smartness, and gets her "on the way." For simple problems, such as gaining ten degrees in bearing on the guide while maintaining distance, a mental solution is sufficient, because it is subject to confirmation by periodic bearings and ranges.

Developing a good "seaman's eye" should be one of a shiphandler's most important goals. Although some people have more natural ability than others in this regard, a true seaman's eye is developed only by experience, practice, and close observation of every maneuver. A shiphandler should learn to visualize and retain a picture of what is happening during a maneuver. He or she should practice correlating what is seen from the bridge wing with the bird's-eye view of the surface-search radar. Perfection of this skill not only sharpens the eye but also renders a reliable means of checking the maneuvering-board solution against what is actually seen.

When a tactical signal for maneuvering is executed, the shiphandler should be able to come to the required speed immediately and, even if there is not a complete maneuvering-board solution, put the rudder over and head in roughly the right direction. Course corrections made en route to a station do not cause major problems; being the only ship to remain on the old course and speed does.

Maneuvering signals in formation are likely to require simultaneous action by a number of ships. It is a shiphandler's responsibility, in addition to getting to the new station, to avoid interfering with or embarrassing other units and to make his or her own movements and intentions clearly understood. The shiphandler should make it a habit always to have an escape route when maneuvering with other ships and to know in advance what to do and in which direction to turn if he or she suddenly has to avoid more than one ship at a time. A common failing of inexperienced shiphandlers is to forget that there are ships astern of them. This can be disastrous. A ship that is one thousand yards on another ship's quarter and on a parallel course can become a major problem if the latter is forced to cross her bow in order to avoid a third ship.

Operating in formation with aircraft carriers places additional responsibility on the OOD. Most carriers establish a "box" around themselves—an area that other ships must avoid. At a minimum, the box prescribes the "3:2:1 rule": Other ships must never be closer than three thousand yards off the carrier's bow, two thousand yards off her beam, and one thousand yards astern. Many carriers prescribe even larger boxes, and each establishes a different-size area in her Plane Guard/Instruction to Escorts notice. Not only does a carrier's size impose maneuvering limitations on her, but the amount of rudder-induced heel is likely to be restricted if aircraft are spotted on her deck. A ship that is forward of an aircraft carrier should never turn toward her except in an emergency. If it is absolutely necessary to do so, she should indicate her intentions to the carrier. An officer (either the OOD or JOOD) should constantly have the carrier under observation. Most carriers publish a set of standard operating procedures; these should be studied by the watch officers on ships in company.

## Close Station-Keeping

Visualizing simple problems in relative motion is the key to proficient station-keeping in close formation. Although ships do not now steam in close formation as often as formerly, proficiency in this area is still an important requirement. Surface ships still must be able to steam in column, or in line of bearing, at standard distance, and in circular formation darkened at night and at high speed. Steaming in close column, which is largely a matter of speed adjustment, demands a keen appreciation of speed and how a ship carries her way.

The stadimeter is an essential instrument for ships in close formation. Every watch officer should be familiar with its use and know its capabilities and limitations. At close ranges, the stadimeter is more accurate than most radars, and it is particularly helpful in providing quick and accurate information about distance—whether it is opening, closing, or being held steady. Laser stadimeters, found on many ships today, are extremely accurate.

Distance reports should state whether distance is closing, opening, or steady. The terms "increasing" and "decreasing" should not be used because there is a chance of confusing distance reports with reports concerning bearings.

It may not be possible to take stadimeter readings on dark nights when there is not enough light, when the ship is too close for radar ranges, or when radar silence is imposed. At such times, binoculars can be used to obtain a fair estimate of distance if, during the day, when the exact distance to a ship can be measured, the extent of the binocular field that she fills has been noted. (See the quick reference guide at the end of this chapter for estimates.)

The first ship in a column, or the guide ship, should make every effort to ensure good steering and steady speed. The OOD should see that the proper revolutions are being made. The OOD on the ship astern will appreciate such efforts.

The keeping of proper distance between ships in column depends largely on the OOD's ability to detect early indications of opening or closing motion and to make proper speed adjustments to counteract that motion. In this regard, the OOD should remember that when a ship is following in the wake of another, she requires a few more revolutions than she would in still water to make good the same speed as the ship ahead; this is because she has to overcome the wake turbulence or "kick" of the preceding ship. An erratic helmsman who takes the ship in and out of another ship's wake complicates the problem of speed adjustment. The helmsman should be watched closely. Speed should be corrected with care; it must be remembered that there is a time lag before the effect of change is felt. If this lag is not allowed for, the same error may be corrected twice, requiring another correction, probably larger, in the opposite direction. Once such surging starts, it is hard to stop. An OOD would be well advised to study the time lag of the ship intently until it is known. The effect of one correction should be carefully observed before another correction is applied. Excessive use of the rudder acts as a brake. Therefore, steering should always be corrected before speed is increased.

In general, it is safer for a ship in column to be inside, rather than outside, the prescribed distance; it is easier to drop back than to close up. An OOD ought to know the allowable tolerances and keep within them, because it is also easy to hit the ship ahead if she slows without the OOD noticing. He or she should remember the fellow next astern and keep course and speed as steady as possible. The reputation of being a good ship to follow is a difficult one to earn, but it is worth trying for.

The OOD must keep in mind his or her ship's number in the column and to which side she is to sheer out in an emergency. This is the same side as that of her position when in column open order, and it follows the standard pattern—odd-numbered ships to starboard, even-numbered ships to port. When for any reason the ship gets uncomfortably close to the ship ahead, the thing to do is to ease her bow out very slightly on the side to which she would sheer out in an emergency.

Course changes for a formation in column may be made in two ways: by individual ships turning together, or by wheeling, that is, changing course in succession, each ship following the ship ahead.

When change of course is made by turning together, the rudder must be put over the proper amount promptly on the execution of the signal. The OOD must inform the helmsman of the new course and see that the latter does not swing past it or use an excessive amount of rudder in meeting the swing. Either of these errors will cause the ship to end up behind bearing in the line of bearing resulting from the maneuver. The OOD should keep the nearest ship toward which the turn is being made under constant visual observation, checking the bearing of the guide as the turn progresses with a view to detecting promptly any tendency to gain or lose bearing.

In practice, ships do not maintain perfect position, particularly when making frequent simultaneous turns, and the OOD must know how to adjust a turn to improve position. This knowledge comes mostly from experience in visualizing the situation and looking ahead. Of course, any such adjustments must consider adjacent ships on both sides.

Assuming that a ship has turned properly, the one astern will turn in the same water. The knuckle of the first ship's wake should be slightly on the second ship's bow, in the direction of the turn. Slick water inboard of the wake is caused by the stern of the ship sliding in the turn; the inboard edge of the slick marks the path of the ship's bow, the outboard edge, that of her stern.

Conning should be done from the wing of the bridge, from which the ship ahead and the one astern, if any, can be seen. Knowing exactly when to start a turn takes experience, but the OOD usually orders the rudder put over when the knuckle is abreast the bridge. If the turn is correctly timed, the bow of the ship will follow around at the inboard edge of the slick.

If the turn is made late, the ship will go outside the proper turning circle and the wake of the ship ahead may hold her there. If this happens, the OOD should not swing beyond the new course but should remain steadied and parallel to the column on the new course. When the ship next astern has completed her wheel, the OOD's ship should gradually regain station; it is almost always necessary to increase speed to regain station.

If the turn is made too early, the ship will go inside the proper circle. A slight easing of the rudder will correct this, but speed will probably have to be reduced to avoid dangerous proximity to the ship ahead. A common error in such a situation is to ease the rudder too much so that the ship crosses the wake ahead and is outside after all.

The danger of turns lies in a substantial change of course being started when a ship is too close to the ship ahead. The choice then is between making a large rudder angle to stay inside the turn, while slowing, stopping, or backing, and easing the rudder and going outside. It is safer to continue the turn inside; hesitation before easing the rudder to go outside may send the ship forging ahead while her bow is still inside the stern of the ship ahead, putting them in danger of collision.

A ship astern of one that turns too soon or too late should not attempt to follow her but should turn in the wake of the guide. If she is slightly out of position when a turn is ordered, she can maneuver to correct; if she is behind station, she can cut the corner; if too close, she can turn a bit late with full rudder.

At night or in fog, it may not be possible to see the knuckle. If the OOD keeps track of the time elapsed after the signal to execute, he or she can, on the basis of speed and distance from the guide, determine when the point of turn has been reached. This is done by utilizing the "three-minute rule," which states that in three minutes a ship travels as many hundreds of yards as the number of knots she is making. That is, a ship doing fifteen knots travels 1,500 yards in three minutes. Therefore, a ship that is one thousand yards astern of the guide at a speed of fifteen knots turns two minutes after the guide executes her turn.

## Line of Bearing

In line of bearing, station-keeping is somewhat complicated, because both distance and bearing are involved. A thorough understanding of the relative motion of ships is helpful. When the ship is in close formation, the OOD rarely has time to plot bearings and distances and obtain a solution. The problem has to be visualized and then the course and speed changed properly and promptly as soon as the OOD detects a deviation from the correct bearing and distance.

The OOD can quickly determine whether the ship is ahead or behind bearing by lining up an alidade on the prescribed bearing of the guide and then sighting through it. If the line of sight falls ahead of the guide, she is ahead; if astern, she is behind.

When ships are in line abreast, a speed that is greater or less than that of the guide causes a bearing to be advanced or retarded, with negligible variation in range. A slight change of course toward or away from the guide causes a closing or opening of range, with a slight loss of bearing. A small temporary increase of speed, normally only a few turns, can be used to counteract this small bearing change.

When the line of bearing is a column, a speed differential causes a closing or opening of distance. A change of course causes a change of bearing, with a slight opening of distance. A small temporary increase of speed can be used to counteract this small change in range.

For lines of bearing between these two extremes—line abreast and column—the effects of a course or speed differential are a little more complex. A combination of changing course and speed is usually required to maintain station.

When simultaneous turns are made in line of bearing, it is important to watch the ship toward which the turn is made for a sign that she might be turning in the wrong direction.

## Station-Keeping in Formation

Handling a ship in the main body of a circular formation is slightly easier than handling a ship in close formation, because the distance between ships is usually greater. However, because station has to be kept on a definite bearing from the guide, and at a definite distance, the problems of station-keeping are similar to those in line of bearing. The only additional determination to be made is what the range and bearing from the guide should be when a ship is moving to a new station. The CIC can be of great assistance to the OOD in these matters.

To determine the ship's range and bearing from the guide, the OOD must be familiar with the system for plotting formations by using polar coordinates. Once the formation has been plotted, the OOD can easily pick the range and bearing of the guide off the plot. A continuous plot of the formation should be kept so that ordered changes can be quickly translated into new range and bearing from the guide.

It should be borne in mind that the guide is not always at the center of a formation, and that as soon as a signal has been executed the guide is automatically on station, regardless of where she might be. This situation sometimes results in the center of the formation moving around the guide, and when it does, the other ships move a like amount in the same direction.

For any maneuver, when required range and bearing from the guide have been determined from a plot, actual range and bearing from the guide should be worked out. These figures can be used to determine the course and speed required to bring the ship to her proper station. Except for when a ship is ordered to a new station, a change of formation axis and a change in the formation itself are the only maneuvers that change either her range or her bearing, or both, in relation to the guide.

## Screening

Handling a ship in a screen is quite similar to handling a ship in the main body of a circular formation. Station-keeping procedures are the same. Determining range and bearing is, however, more complex, because the distance from the guide is greater. The OOD of a destroyer-type ship must be familiar with the maneuvering rules that govern screening ships as well as those that govern maneuvers in the various formations.

A continuous, up-to-the-minute plot of the entire formation should be kept, just as for a circular formation, so that any ordered change can be quickly translated into a new range and bearing from the guide.

To keep the plot of the screen, the OOD must know where the center of the screen is and the direction of its axis. He or she must be able to distinguish the signals that cause the screen center and to shift those that do not. And he or she must know how to determine the amount and direction of such a shift and how to allow for it in the maneuver, whether or not a reorientation of the screen is required.

An OOD must know under what conditions a screen axis changes without a specific signal, and how to determine its new direction in such cases. He or she should make every effort to start for the new station promptly. A little forehandedness will help. After each maneuver, the OOD should start anticipating the next one. He or she should check the plot and then determine the minimum change of formation course in each direction that would cause a reorientation requiring a change of station. And when it is appropriate, the OOD should determine the minimum change of course that would require an initial turn to be made in the direction opposite to that of the course change. With these figures firmly in mind, the OOD can quickly translate a signal into action and start the initial turn before the final solution has been worked out.

In working solutions, the OOD must be sure to use the course and speed for the guide that will actually be followed en route to the station. This policy is particularly applicable when the ship starts for her station before the signal that changes the guide's course or speed or both has been executed.

There are two final points to be made about screening. The first is that station-keeping should be *exact,* with the OOD ensuring that the ship is where she is supposed to be at all times. If the screen plan requires the ship to patrol a sector as opposed to maintaining a continuous, exact range and bearing from the guide, the patrolling courses and speeds should be controlled exactly. Then the OOD can afford to devote more time to other matters, perhaps delegating, under supervision, the duty of station-keeping to the JOOD.

The second point is that when a screen is being reoriented or its station changed, the OOD must keep an alert watch over the whole formation, using his or her own eyes to the maximum extent. Others can work out maneuvering-board solutions to check the OOD's quick calculations; his or her primary job under many conditions is that of chief safety officer.

### Range to the Guide

When the ship is steaming in formation, the OOD must always know the range to the guide. However, to obtain this information, he or she should not put such a burden on the surface-search radar operator in the CIC that the operator is forced to keep radar on short scale and concentrate on giving range-to-the-guide information to the deck. At night or in low visibility, when the surface-search radar must be used for detecting and tracking ships to prevent collision, this practice can be dangerous. The OOD should use a stadimeter whenever possible; it can be used at night, in good visibility, with running lights as targets. The bridge radar can also be used for checking on the CIC, freeing it from the necessity of supplying continuous ranges.

## MAN OVERBOARD

The first requirement in case of a man overboard is prompt action. An alert OOD will see that the people in his or her watch know what their duties are in such an emergency, and will be prepared, depending on weather and operating conditions, to

1. Put the rudder over to the side the person went over, to kick the stern away from him or her.

2. Immediately throw over the side a life ring with a strobe light and a smoke float or "rescue ball" to mark the spot as closely as possible.

3. Tell the JOOD, lookout, or anyone available to point at the person, if possible, and continue pointing until he or she is alongside the ship.

4. Have the word passed twice: "Man overboard, port (starboard) side."

5. Sound six or more short blasts on the ship's whistle, and make appropriate visual signals as specified in Allied Maritime Tactical Instructions and Procedures (ATP-1, vol. 1): "By day hoist OSCAR and at night (in peacetime) display two pulsating red lights or fire one white rocket (very light)."

6. Notify the CIC so that it can provide continual ranges and bearings to the person in the water.

7. Notify ships in company and the officer in tactical command.

8. Inform the commanding officer, executive officer, and flag duty officer, if appropriate.

9. Determine recovery method and pass the word. Shipboard, motor whaleboat, or helicopter recoveries are possible. Establish communication with the recovery detail.

10. Keep the recovery detail informed as to whether the recovery is to be made from the port or the starboard side of the ship.

As soon as the word "Man overboard" has been passed, the CIC should automatically mark the spot, shift the dead-reckoning tracer to the scale of two hundred yards to the inch, and begin passing ranges and bearings to the bridge.

A helicopter provides the quickest rescue, with the advantage that it can pick up a helpless person. If a helicopter is not available, a small boat may be used.

There are a number of methods of recovering a man overboard (see table 6-1 and descriptions following). The four most common are the Anderson turn, which is the fastest but requires skillful shiphandling; the Williamson turn, for night or low visibility; the racetrack turn, for fastest recovery when a ship is proceeding at high speed in clear weather; and the Y-backing, for ships with large turning circles and great backing power proceeding at slow speeds. Very large ships often use a small boat to recover a person. Small vessels also use a boat when the sea is rough and there is little chance of getting the ship close alongside the person. Under any conditions, the OOD should see to it that swimmers with life jackets and tending lines are ready to go into the water.

Regardless of which recovery method is used, the same basic principles apply. Full rudder should be used to swing the stern away from the person. If the shaft on the side toward the person can be stopped before he or she reaches the screws, it should be. If that is impossible, which is likely, the recovery should be continued without any attempt to stop the screws.

Man-overboard maneuvering for naval vessels involved in tactical evolutions can be found in ATP-1, vol. 1, chapter 5. Of specific importance are the instructions for column formation. In this situation, the ship that loses the person takes action to avoid him or her, as do the others, odd-numbered ships in the column clearing to starboard and even-numbered ships clearing to port. The ship in the best position to recover the person does so, and keeps the other vessels informed of her actions.

The person should be recovered in the shortest possible time. Large ships usually use the Williamson method. Small ships, in good weather, use the racetrack method. At night or in low visibility, the Williamson turn, though not the fastest recovery method, must be used to bring the ship back along her track. No matter what the method, the best final position is beam to the wind slightly to wind-

**Table 6-1. Methods of Recovering a Man Overboard**

| METHOD AND PRIMARY CONDITIONS FOR USE | DIAGRAM OF SHIP ON COURSE 090 (NUMBERS REFER TO THE EXPLANATION) | EXPLANATION | ANALYSIS | |
|---|---|---|---|---|
| | | | ADVANTAGES | DISADVANTAGES |
| **Anderson Turn** Used by ships that have considerable power and relatively tight turning characteristics. | <br><br>⊗ = MAN | 1. Put the rudder over full to the side from which the person fell. Stop the inboard engine.<br>2. When clear of the person, go ahead full on the outboard engine only. Continue using full rudder.<br>3. When about two-thirds of the way around, back the inboard engine two-thirds or full. Order all engines stopped when the person is within about 15° of the bow, then ease the rudder and back the engines as required to attain the proper final position.<br>4. Many variations of this method are used, differing primarily in respect to the use of one or both engines and the time when they are stopped and backed to return to the person. The variation used should reflect individual ship's characteristics, sea conditions, personal preferences, etc. | Speed | Requires proficiency in shiphandling because the approach to the person is not straightaway. Often impossible for a single-propeller ship. |
| **Williamson Turn** Used in low visibility because it makes good the original track. Used when it is believed that a person fell overboard some time previously and is not in sight. | | 1. Put the rudder over full to the side from which the person fell. Stop the inboard engine.<br>2. When clear of the person go ahead full on all engines. Continue using full rudder.<br>3. When heading is 60° beyond the original course, shift the rudder without having steadied on a course. Sixty degrees is proper for many ships. However, the exact amount must be determined through trial and error.<br>4. Come to the reciprocal of the original course, using full rudder.<br>5. Use the engines and rudder to attain the proper final position (ship upwind to the person and dead in the | Simplicity. Makes good the original tract. | Slowness. Takes the ship relatively far from the person, when sight of him or her may be lost. |

water with the person alongside, well forward of the propellers).

| | | | |
|---|---|---|---|
| **Racetrack Turn** (two 180° turns) Used in good visibility when a straight final-approach leg is desired. | A variation of the one-turn method that provides a desirable straight final approach to the person.<br>1. Put the rudder over full in the direction corresponding to the side from which the person fell. Stop the inboard engine.<br>2. When clear of the person, go ahead full on all engines. Continue using full rudder to turn to the reciprocal of the original course.<br>3. Steady for a distance that will give the desired run for a final straight approach.<br>4. Use full rudder to turn to the person.<br>5. Use the engines and rudder to attain the proper final position (ship upwind of the person and dead in the water with the person alongside, well forward of the propellers). | Straight final-approach leg facilitates a calculable approach. Ship will return to the person if he or she is lost from sight. Reasonably last. Effective when wind was from abeam on original course. | Slower than one-turn methods. |
| **Y-Backing** Used by submarines because of their low height of eye. | 1. Put the rudder over full to the side from which the person fell. Stop the inboard engine.<br>2. When clear of the person, back the engines with full power, using opposite rudder.<br>3. Go ahead. Use the engines and rudder to attain the proper final position (ship upwind of the person and dead in the water with the person alongside, well forward of the propellers). | The ship remains comparatively close to the person. | Most ships back into the wind or seas, causing poor control. |
| **Delayed Turn** Used when word is received that a person fell overboard, is in sight, and is clear astern of the ship. | 1. Put the rudder over full to the side from which the person fell. Go ahead full on all engines.<br>2. Ahead towards the person.<br>3. Use the engines and rudder to attain the proper final position (ship upwind of the person and dead in the water with the person alongside, well forward of the propellers). | Fastest method when person is in sight and already clear astern of the ship. Provides a straight run in the critical final phase. | Does not ensure return to the person. Requires good visibility. Takes the ship farther from the person than other methods.<br><br>*Continues on next page* |

**Table 6-1.—Continued**

| Method and Primary Conditions for Use | Diagram of Ship on Course 090 (Numbers Refer to the Explanation) | Explanation | Analysis | |
|---|---|---|---|---|
| | | | Advantages | Disadvantages |
| | | | Effective when wind was from ahead or astern of ship on original course. | |
| **Boat Recovery** Used by ships that do not have maneuverability to make a good approach to the person. Used when the ship is dead in the water and the person is close aboard but not alongside. Can be used in conjunction with any of the methods shown above. | | 1. Put the rudder over full to the side from which the person fell. Stop the inboard engine. 2. When the person is clear, back all engines full almost to stop the ship. Use the rudder to the side of the ready lifeboat to provide a slick in which the boat can be lowered. Stop the engines while the ship still has very slight headway to permit better control of the boat and to keep it out of the propeller wash. | Simple. The ship remains close to the person. Does not require that a particular final position be attained. | The person must be in sight. Sea and weather conditions must be satisfactory for small-boat operations. |

ward of the person, with all way off. When in this position, the ship provides a lee for the person, and because she will make more leeway she will drift toward rather than away from the person. It is important that the person be kept *forward* of the main condenser injection intakes, particularly if there is a possibility that he or she still has a parachute attached; a parachute can clog the intakes, which are ordinarily aft of the midships section on either side. In her final position, the ship should have the person just off her leeward bow.

## REPLENISHMENT AT SEA

The Navy's ability to project sea power over long ocean distances depends on its ability to sustain itself at sea for long periods without land-based support. It is the mission of the Combat Logistics Force (CLF) to provide this support with fuel, stores, provisions, and ammunition. In addition to the naval vessels that constitute the CLF, many ships of the Military Sealift Command (MSC) have been designated to provide underway logistic support.

Replenishment at sea (RAS) is the most commonly encountered evolution, and the manner in which it is executed is one of the basic yardsticks by which a ship's performance is measured. It presents one of the most challenging, exciting, and satisfying opportunities for shiphandling that a watch officer will be given. It can teach more about seamanship and shiphandling than almost any other evolution. Standard doctrine for RAS is outlined in Underway Replenishment (NWP 4-01.4), which also contains a tabulation of the locations and functions of the replenishment stations on all CLF ships. ATP-16 provides the same kind of information for NATO's replenishment ships.

To begin RAS, a replenishment ship comes to a steady course and speed, which are usually dictated by wind and seas or, if the weather is calm, by the course the formation wants made good. The receiving ship takes station astern of the delivering ship and waits for her to signal her readiness to replenish.

Weather conditions permitting, the normal speed of the guide ship is between thirteen and fifteen knots. Speeds less than eight knots are not advisable because they reduce rudder effect. At speeds greater than fifteen knots, venturi effect (the pressure differential created around the hull of a moving ship) calls for greater lateral separation. See R. S. Crenshaw's *Naval Shiphandling* for a detailed description of how to bring a ship alongside a delivery ship.

The delivery ship indicates preparations for receiving a ship alongside by flying Romeo at the dip on her rigged side. The receiving ship replies that she is ready to come alongside by flying Romeo at the dip on her rigged side. When the delivery ship is ready for the approach, she hoists Romeo close up. The receiving ship hoists Romeo close up and increases speed by three to ten knots over signaled underway-replenishment (UnRep) speed. She slows down so as to be moving at replenishment speed when in position. When the ships are in proper relative position, transfer rigs are passed and hooked up; when the first line is secured, both ships haul down Romeo. They both fly Bravo if fuel or ammunition is being transferred.

Fifteen minutes before the receiving ship expects to complete replenishment, her OOD orders Prep hoisted at the dip to notify the next ship scheduled to replenish. On completion of the replenishment, all nets, slings, lines, and hoses are returned to the delivery ship.

Just before disengaging, when the fuel transfer is complete, the receiving ship hoists Prep close up, and when the last line is clear she hauls it down. When the side has been cleared, the conning officer increases speed by five to ten knots, depending on ship type, and clears ahead, gradually changing course outboard. Propeller wash caused by radical changes in speed and course is likely to have a bad effect on the steering of the delivery ship, and a dangerous situation might develop if a ship is on her other side.

The most important tasks of the OOD during an UnRep are the coordination of the multitude of preparations and the management of the bridge team while the ship's focus (and the captain's) is on the evolution itself. The OOD must have the crew on station on time but should avoid wasting the crew's time with needless waiting. Two hundred people waiting thirty minutes on station are a hundred hours that could be better spent. Coordination with the weapons officer and the executive officer and watching the progress of other ships conducting UnRep at the same time will help the OOD to call the right time. During the process the OOD must make sure that critical functions such as navigation and communication are being correctly carried out. Of utmost importance is a plan for the stage following UnRep. The OOD should be alert for hints of problems in the areas of steering and propulsion. Anticipating possibilities is just as important as technical knowledge.

## PILOTS

A pilot is merely an advisor to the commanding officer. The presence of a pilot on board shall not relieve the commanding officer or any subordinates from their responsibility for the proper performance of the duties with which they may be charged concerning the navigation and handling of the ship.

Navy Regulations, Article 0856

Only in the following special circumstances does the presence of a pilot, even if he or she has the conn, relieve the commanding officer of any responsibility for the safety of the ship: when a ship is entering a dry dock; when a ship is traversing the Panama Canal with a licensed canal pilot on board; and when a ship is required by the harbormaster to move within a harbor while not under her own propulsion, using only tugs (dead stick). When a pilot is taken on board, the OOD should be sure that the bridge watch understands who has the conn and whose orders to the engine and the helm should be obeyed. Most pilots are accustomed to handling merchant ships, and frequently their commands to the helm and engines differ from standard naval commands. When this is the case, the commanding officer should direct the OOD to relay the pilot's orders to the helm, using proper naval terminology.

If possible, the pilot should be advised of the differences in power and speed between his or her orders and the OOD's. When ordering ahead dead slow, for example, the OOD rings up a one-third bell and advises the pilot how many knots the bell was for. As long as the captain, the pilot, and the OOD know how much power is being asked for, differences in terminology can be overcome. The same holds true for orders to the helm. Although pilots usually give orders in degrees of rudder, they often call for "hard rudder," which on most naval vessels is used only in emergencies. The proper procedure in this case is to call on the helmsman for "full rudder," because this is the naval term for what the pilot means.

Most pilots are superb seamen and shiphandlers and the best of them are only too pleased to share their knowledge. Often the commanding officer leaves the conn with the OOD and asks the pilot to act as an adviser to the OOD for the purpose of training. An OOD who is fortunate enough to be in this situation should take the opportunity to learn all he or she can.

Occasionally, especially in out-of-the-way places, a ship finds herself with a pilot who does not understand her characteristics or who simply does not come up to professional standards. In this case, the captain will normally take the conn and either modify the pilot's instructions or politely ignore them. The OOD must pay particular attention to what the helmsman and lee helmsman are doing, because they can easily be confused as to which orders they should follow.

## QUICK REFERENCE FOR THE WATCH OFFICER

Every watch officer needs to do a little mental arithmetic to get through a watch. While the maneuvering board, naval tactical data system, and whole CIC watch team are available to back the OOD up with detailed maneuvering solutions, it is useful to have a quick way to obtain initial courses, speeds, and distances, and to check solutions from other means. A few of the more common tricks include the following:

*Three-Minute Rule.* A ship will travel a distance equal to her speed in knots times one hundred yards every three minutes. Example: A ship going fifteen knots will cover 1,500 yards every three minutes.

*Radian Rule.* For every degree difference in bearing divided by sixty and multiplied by the range equals the horizontal separation. Example: A contact, dead in the water (DIW) or on a reciprocal course, is three degrees off the bow of your ship at a range of two miles. You want to determine your CPA (horizontal separation) quickly. Multiply 3/60 times the range of two miles (four thousand yards) to obtain the CPA of two hundred yards.

*Sliding-into-Station Rule.* Multiply the speed differential in knots times fifty yards for a steam plant and times twenty-five yards for a gas turbine to slide into station. Example: You want to end up parallel to an oiler going sixteen knots. Your approach speed is twenty-three knots, or seven knots overspeed. For a steamship, you would want to cut engines and slide into station seven times fifty yards or about 350 yards short of her position. For a gas turbine, with its quicker response, multiply by twenty-five, or 175 yards.

***Stopping the Ship.*** To stop within one length at five knots, back two-thirds; in two lengths at ten knots, back full. In all cases, if the objective is to get the way off the ship, go to back emergency/ flank immediately.

***Rule of Binoculars.*** A frigate (FFG/FF) will fill the field of standard (7 × 50) binoculars at about three hundred yards, a cruiser/ destroyer (DD 963/DDG 51/CG 47) at about 350, and a carrier at about 450 yards.

***Rule for Underway Replenishment.*** To make an approach at 120 feet (standard) or 150 feet (wide, in the case of a difficult course or inclement weather), bearing offset from the base course to the tangent of the side of the replenishment ship should be as follows at the given distances:

| Range to Replenishment Ship (yards) | 120 feet | 150 feet |
|---|---|---|
| 600 | 4 degrees | 5 degrees |
| 500 | 5 degrees | 6 degrees |
| 400 | 6 degrees | 7.5 degrees |
| 300 | 8 degrees | 10 degrees |
| 200 | 12 degrees | 15 degrees |

In other words, when six hundred yards from the replenishment ship with a course of 150 degrees as Romeo corpen (replenishment course), the starboard side of the replenishment ship should bear 146 degrees to effect a 120-foot approach, and 145 degrees to effect a 150-foot approach.

***Distance to the Horizon.*** The distance to the horizon in nautical miles is 1.14 times the square root of the height of eye in feet. A few representative calculations include:

| Height of Eye (feet) | Horizon (nautical miles) |
|---|---|
| 50 | 8.1 |
| 75 | 9.9 |
| 85 | 10.5 |
| 100 | 11.4 |
| 110 | 12.0 |

**Rule of Anchoring.** A simple chart to cover the stopping times upon approaching an anchorage would be as follows:

| Yards to Berth | Steam | Gas Turbine |
|---|---|---|
| 1,000 | 5 knots | 10 knots |
| 800 | All stop | |
| 500 | | 5 knots |
| 250 | Back 1/3 | All stop |
| 100 | | Back 1/3 |
| When backing | Drop | Drop |

**Scope Guide.** The scope of chain required out for winds at a level of less than force seven is as follows:

| Water Depth (fathoms) | Chain |
|---|---|
| 7 | 30 |
| 7 to 12 | 45 |
| 12 to 20 | 60 |

## SOME QUICK RULES OF SHIPHANDLING

1. All conning orders must be given in a loud, clear, authoritative voice.

2. The conning officer should always be looking forward, not immersed in the administration of the watch or tied to a communications circuit.

3. Develop a practiced seaman's eye and strive to conn with rudder commands, not by giving courses. Remember, when the conning officer gives a rudder order, *he or she* controls the rudder; when the conning officer gives a course to steady on, the *helmsman* controls the rudder.

4. When approaching a pier, anchorage, or another ship, the conning officer should have both a plan to complete the evolution and an alternate plan.

5. Always be aware of the forces operating on the ship. One knot of current is the equivalent of thirty knots of wind.

6. Know how to use the anchor. It can save the ship in many difficult situations.

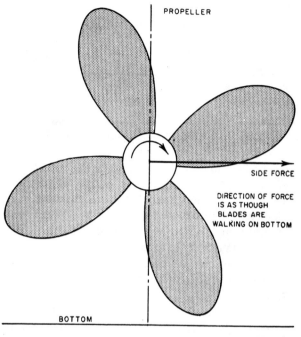

SIDE FORCE

DIRECTION OF FORCE
IS AS THOUGH
BLADES ARE
WALKING ON BOTTOM

BOTTOM

**112.49**

**Figure 6-2. Side Force**

7. The ship's bow will turn into the wind if making way; if not making way, it may end up broadside to the wind. If backing, the ship, especially is she is single-screwed, will back into the wind.

8. Here are a few shiphandling points for UnRep:

—A bow overtaking a stern will push the bow out.

—While alongside, ships tend to move laterally toward each other.

—When two sterns cross, they attract.

9. Engines have relative responsiveness; gas turbines are by far the fastest to respond to orders, because the throttles in the pilot-house are directly connected to the engines. Diesels are fairly responsive. Steam plants are slow in responding.

10. When giving rudder/engine commands, generally follow the rule of thirty: The sum of rudder and engine speed should not exceed thirty unless you are willing to have the ship heel over hard, that is, fifteen degrees rudder plus fifteen knots. At twenty-five knots, use only five degrees, and so forth.

11. Propellers will move the stern laterally as though they were touching the ground, that is, clockwise screw motion will turn the stern to starboard when viewed from astern. See figure 6-2.

12. Never take a chance with a ship for the sake of showmanship.

13. Ships do not back with precision.

14. Always bear in mind the direction to fair water when under way.

15. The conning officer should always physically sight the rudder angle indicator to make sure the helmsman puts the rudder over in the right direction. Likewise, the side of the turn should always be physically checked prior to the turn.

16. In a maneuver with another ship, the conning officer on the other vessel should be absolutely certain of any impending turn.

17. When you first sight a vessel on the horizon, immediately begin to take visual bearings to determine if there is bearing drift. If it appears to be slight, start a maneuvering board and compare solutions with the CIC.

18. Wind can help or hurt the problem. Think through the consequences of the wind's effect.

19. The most sensitive part of many modern ships is the bow, where the sonar dome is located.

20. When a ship is going ahead close to a bank or a seawall, the bow will be forced out and the stern sucked in. When the ship backs down, this tendency is reversed.

21. Never depend on a line, particularly for maneuvering a larger ship near a pier.

22. Before undertaking a demanding situation as a conning officer, review the applicable sections of standard shiphandling references. *Knight's Modern Seamanship* and Crenshaw's *Naval Shiphandling,* are the two best.

23. Make up a file or a series of index cards with tactical data, ship's characteristics, engine orders, and the like for ready reference

until you are fully familiar with the ship. Seek such information from the more senior officers.

24. When tugs are made up, take care not to overpower them with the ship's engines and rudder. Be careful of tugs' lines, and be aware of the time lag often required for a tug to position itself.

25. Enjoy having the conn and handle your ship with confidence and pleasure.

# 7

# SAFE NAVIGATION

The commanding officer is responsible for the safe navigation of his or her ship or aircraft, except as prescribed otherwise in these regulations for ships at a naval shipyard or station, in dry dock, or in the Panama Canal.

Navy Regulations, Article 0857

The winds and waves are always on the side of the ablest navigator.

Edward Gibbon

The officer of the deck shall be aware of the tactical situation and geographic factors which may affect safe navigation and take action to avoid the danger of grounding or collision in accordance with tactical doctrine, the U.S. Coast Guard Navigation Rules of the Road, and the orders of the Commanding Officer or other proper authority.

OpNavInst 3120.32C

Young officers are inclined to look upon accidents at sea as events that are as inescapable as being struck by lightning. On the contrary, collisions and groundings can usually be avoided by the intelligent application of the fundamental principles of good seamanship combined with good judgment and common sense.

## COLLISIONS

Analyses of collisions frequently show that one or more of the ten following mistakes were made:

1. Failure to realize in time that there was a risk of collision.
2. Failure to notify the commanding officer of a potentially dangerous situation.
3. Failure to check for steady bearing in a closing situation until too late.
4. Reliance on the combat information center (CIC) and consequent failure to make a sound evaluation of the situation on the bridge.
5. Poor judgment in evaluating the effects of wind and tide.
6. Failure to understand the tactical characteristics of the ship.
7. Injudicious use of the ship's power.
8. Failure of bridge personnel to keep a sharp visual lookout.
9. Failure of the CIC and the bridge to ensure that the conning officer understood tactical signals.
10. Making a radical change in course without informing ships in the vicinity.

The most significant overall cause of collisions, however, is the failure of the bridge and the CIC to check each other's actions through a systematic approach to comparing maneuvering-board solutions, fixes, and tactical signals. If the CIC and the bridge work together and check each other, very few problems emerge.

Most of these mistakes are elementary and, though it is hard to believe that able, intelligent officers would make them, discouragingly common. It does not require genius to stand a proficient deck watch, but it does require vigilance, alertness, a highly developed sense of responsibility, and good judgment.

Most of these mistakes are discussed farther along in this book; the others need little elaboration. The timely use of navigational lights in uncertain or dangerous maneuvering, even under simulated or actual battle conditions, is proper. It should be evident in these days of radar that lights will yield only incidental information to an enemy who might be nearby. Running-light switch panels should be

## Table 7-1. Distance of Visibility of Objects at Various Elevations above Sea Level

| HEIGHT IN FEET | DISTANCE IN GEOGRAPHIC OR NAUTICAL MILES | HEIGHT IN FEET | DISTANCE IN GEOGRAPHIC OR NAUTICAL MILES | HEIGHT IN FEET | DISTANCE IN GEOGRAPHIC OR NAUTICAL MILES |
|---|---|---|---|---|---|
| 1 | 1.1 | 31 | 6.4 | 100 | 11.4 |
| 2 | 1.6 | 32 | 6.5 | 105 | 11.7 |
| 3 | 2.0 | 33 | 6.6 | 110 | 12.0 |
| 4 | 2.3 | 34 | 6.7 | 115 | 12.3 |
| 5 | 2.6 | 35 | 6.8 | 120 | 12.5 |
| 6 | 2.8 | 36 | 6.9 | 125 | 12.8 |
| 7 | 3.0 | 37 | 7.0 | 130 | 13.0 |
| 8 | 3.2 | 38 | 7.1 | 135 | 13.3 |
| 9 | 3.4 | 39 | 7.1 | 140 | 13.5 |
| 10 | 3.6 | 40 | 7.2 | 145 | 13.8 |
| 11 | 3.8 | 41 | 7.3 | 150 | 14.0 |
| 12 | 4.0 | 42 | 7.4 | 160 | 14.5 |
| 13 | 4.1 | 43 | 7.5 | 170 | 14.9 |
| 14 | 4.3 | 44 | 7.6 | 180 | 15.3 |
| 15 | 4.4 | 45 | 7.7 | 190 | 15.8 |
| 16 | 4.6 | 46 | 7.8 | 200 | 16.2 |
| 17 | 4.7 | 47 | 7.8 | 210 | 16.6 |
| 18 | 4.9 | 48 | 7.9 | 220 | 17.0 |
| 19 | 5.0 | 49 | 8.0 | 230 | 17.3 |
| 20 | 5.1 | 50 | 8.1 | 240 | 17.7 |
| 21 | 5.2 | 55 | 8.5 | 250 | 18.1 |
| 22 | 5.4 | 60 | 8.9 | 260 | 18.4 |
| 23 | 5.5 | 65 | 9.2 | 270 | 18.8 |
| 24 | 5.6 | 70 | 9.6 | 280 | 19.1 |
| 25 | 5.7 | 75 | 9.9 | 290 | 19.5 |
| 26 | 5.8 | 80 | 10.2 | 300 | 19.8 |
| 27 | 5.9 | 85 | 10.5 | 310 | 20.1 |
| 28 | 6.1 | 90 | 10.9 | 320 | 20.5 |
| 29 | 6.2 | 95 | 11.2 | 330 | 20.8 |
| 30 | 6.3 | | | | |

kept set up, and bridge personnel should be drilled in turning them on quickly.

Frequent compass checks of the bearings of all closing ships are essential. They are the best and most important means of preventing

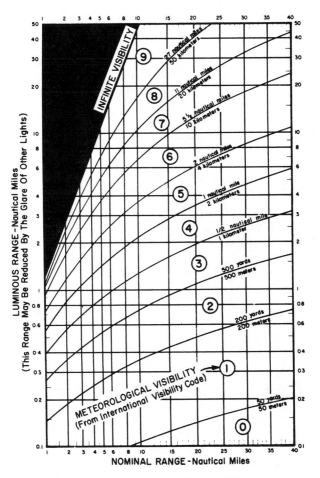

**Figure 7-1. Luminous Range Diagram**

collisions at sea. In low visibility, bearings should be checked by radar. A steady bearing with decreasing range means that collision is imminent. Even a slowly changing bearing is warning of a dangerous situation. *Action must be taken.* This means notifying the captain if time permits, changing course, or stopping and backing.

## GROUNDINGS

Like collisions, groundings are generally attributable to human error. Most of the common errors listed below involve duties that are the responsibility of the navigator but of which the OOD should be cognizant:

1. Laying down the ship's intended track too close to known shoal water, or over water too shallow for the ship's draft.

2. Failure to plot danger and turn bearings on the chart ahead of time.

3. Reliance on radar navigation alone.

4. Failure of the OOD to notify the captain and the navigator as soon as he or she doubts safety of position.

5. Improper application of known gyro error.

6. Failure to use visible aids to navigation.

7. Failure to have available the latest *Notice to Mariners* concerning temporary dislocation of aids to navigation.

8. Failure to use a dead-reckoning plot effectively.

9. Failure to fix position by distance run between successive bearings when only one landmark was identified.

10. Failure to stop and assess the situation or take emergency action when doubt of safe position first arose.

11. Failure to use fathometer and line of soundings.

12. Failure to account for set and drift and to apply the proper course correction.

13. Misidentification of lights and other fixed aids to navigation.

14. Failure to adjust course to remain on the dead-reckoning track.

15. Failure to take fixes frequently enough.

16. Too much reliance on nonfixed aids to navigation, such as buoys.

Again, most of the errors that result in groundings are violations of the basic principles of navigation, and, as with collisions, the inescapable conclusion is that disaster results from carelessness and lack of good judgment rather than ignorance. All too often the OOD gives in to the temptation to take a chance, to slop through the watch instead of expending energy in doing the job correctly. It does

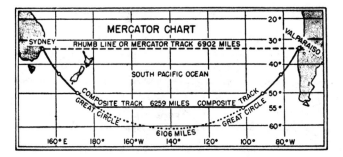

**Figure 7-2. Rhumb Line and Great Circle Course on a Mercator Chart**

not take a master mariner to slow, stop, change course, or notify the captain and navigator whenever the ship's position is in doubt.

Checking the gyro should be the concern of the OOD. Gyrocompasses can suddenly develop large errors, and the only way to detect them quickly is to be aware at all times of the relationship between the gyro and the magnetic compass. The quartermaster of the watch logs the readings of both in a compass record book. He or she should know the importance of this routine chore. When a gyro error has been detected and measured, it must be applied to the course to be steered *in the right direction.* A useful mnemonic device is "Compass least, error east, and compass best, error west." When converting from gyro to true, add easterly and subtract westerly, that is, G + E = T.

## RADAR NAVIGATION

Radar has become internationally accepted as the primary means of fixing a ship's position. Properly used, it permits ships to navigate safely at greater distances from land and under worse weather conditions than traditional visual methods. The danger is that it is so easy to navigate by radar that a false sense of security, a precursor to disaster, is likely to be created.

The OOD's responsibility for safe navigation is in no way lessened by the fact that the CIC or the quartermaster is navigating by radar.

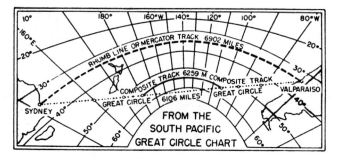

**Figure 7-3. Rhumb Line and Great Circle Course on a Great Circle Chart**

The clear radar pictures that some topographies provide can be deceptive; radar sometimes yields fixes that look accurate but are in fact miles wide of the ship's position. This is especially so in areas where the shoreline is low and sandy and the terrain behind it rises gradually. Furthermore, the clarity of a radar picture can change as a ship's position changes, and a feature that stands out clearly from one angle may begin to "break up" or disappear altogether when seen from another angle. If this happens when a ship is approaching a turn bearing and no dead-reckoning plot or other navigational tools have been applied, she can easily lose her bearings and get into trouble.

When radar is being used in close or restricted waters, it should be cross-checked with whatever other aid to navigation is available. The bridge and the CIC should always lay out the same track, take fixes at the same time, and constantly compare fixes. In this way, differences in the ship's position can be discovered and action taken before it is too late. The importance of the relationship between the CIC and the bridge can never be overstressed, especially in regard to navigation.

## DEAD-RECKONING PLOT

In the days before electronics, when good fixes were rare, hard to get, and highly valued, the dead-reckoning (DR) plot was one of a navigator's most important aids. It still is.

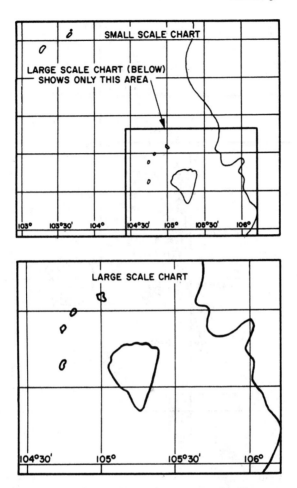

**Figure 7-4. Small- and Large-Scale Charts**

When a ship's actual position is in doubt, a DR plot (modified, if necessary, by known factors, such as current) is the best estimate of that position. A good navigator has either the actual or the DR position of the ship instantly available at all times. The mechanics of navigating—the accumulation of fixes that show where the ship has been—is of secondary importance. A navigator's primary duty is to

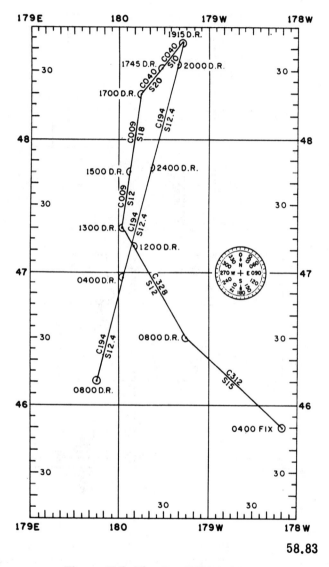

58.83

**Figure 7-5. Plotting DR Position**

know where the ship is going, not where she has been. For this purpose, a DR plot is invaluable and must always be maintained on the chart in use.

The "Six Rules of DR" state when a DR position must be plotted:

1. Every hour on the hour.
2. Every course change.
3. Every speed change.
4. Every fix or running fix.
5. Every line of position.
6. From each fix or running fix (plot a new course line). See figure 7-5.

## THE NAVIGATOR AND THE OOD

In addition to those duties prescribed by regulation for the head of a department, he or she will be responsible, under the Commanding Officer, for the safe navigation and piloting of the ship. The navigator will receive all orders relating to his or her navigational duties directly from the Commanding Officer and will make all reports in connection therewith directly to the Commanding Officer. . . . The duties of the navigator will include advising the Commanding Officer and the Officer of the Deck as to the ship's movements, and if the ship is running into danger, as to the safe course to be steered.

OpNavInst 3120.32C

The navigator and the OOD share responsibility for knowing the navigational situation of a ship. When the navigator is on the bridge, he or she is usually doing the actual navigation and recommending to the OOD changes in course and speed to make good a track or to keep the ship out of danger. Nevertheless, the OOD has the responsibility, in the words of the regulation, to "take appropriate action" to ensure the safety of the ship. When the navigator and the OOD do not agree on the course of action to be taken, the navigator may, if authorized in writing to do so, relieve the OOD. The navigator must, however, immediately inform the commanding officer (CO) that he or she has done so. This very rare situation is not likely to develop if both the navigator and the OOD understand and are paying attention to the navigation of the ship. It is likely to arise if the OOD is taking little interest in the navigation, because the navigator or an assistant is

# USS VALLEY FORGE (CG-50) NIGHT ORDERS

FROM:_____ TO: _____ TIME ZONE: _____

OTC/XB _____ XV _____
XW _____ XC _____
XX _____ XY _____
XS _____ XT _____
XN _____ XD _____
XL _____ XH _____
XP _____ XK _____
XR _____ XU _____
XJ _____ XQ _____
FOTC _____ AFOTC _____

## TACTICAL DATA

FORMATION_____ GUIDE _____
BASE COURSE_____ SPEED _____

STATION ASSIGNMENT_____
_____

## PLANT STATUS

| | | | | | | | | | | |
|---|---|---|---|---|---|---|---|---|---|---|
| 1A | 1B | | 1 | 2 | 3 | | | | 2A | 2B |
| 2A | 2B | | 4 | 5 | 6 | | 1 | 2 | 3 | 3A | 3B |
| ENGINES | | | FIRE PUMPS | | | GENERATORS | | | 400HZ CONV. | |

## WEATHER DATA

SUNRISE _____ SUNSET _____ MOONRISE _____ MOONSET _____

FORECAST: _____
_____

MANEUVERING INSTRUCTIONS: _____
_____
_____
_____
_____
_____

**Figure 7-6. Captain's Night Orders**

## USS VALLEY FORGE (CG-50) NIGHT ORDERS

TACTICAL SITUATION:

_____

_____

_____

_____

THREAT SECTOR _____

EMCON _____

| WEAPONS | C2WC | 1 | 2 | 3 | USW | 1 | 2 | 3 |
|---------|------|---|---|---|-----|---|---|---|
| POSTURE | AWC  | 1 | 2 | 3 | SUW | 1 | 2 | 3 |

DRILLS/EVENTS: _____

_____

_____

MODIFICATION TO PRE-PLANNED RESPONSES:

_____

_____

ACTIVE DOCTRINE STATEMENTS:

_____

_____

COMMENTS: _____

_____

_____

_____

John Paul Jones, CO, CG50

**Figure 7-6.—*Continued***

| SYMBOL | DESCRIPTIVE LABEL | MEANING |
|---|---|---|
|  ⊙ | FIX | An accurate position determined without reference to any previous position. Established by visual or celestial observations. |
|  △ | FIX | A relatively accurate position, determined by electronic means. This symbol is also used for a fix when simultaneously fixing by two means, e.g., visual and radar; sometimes used for radio/navigation fixes, without reference to any former position. |
|  ◠ | DR | Dead reckon position. Advanced from a previous known position or fix. Course and speed are reckoned without allowance for wind or current. |
|  ▣ | EP | Estimated position. Is the most probable position of a vessel, determined from data of questionable accuracy, such as applying estimated current and wind corrections to a DR position. |

**Figure 7-7. Navigation Plotting Symbols**

on the bridge and doing the navigating. The navigator's position as the authoritative adviser on the safe navigation of the ship does not relieve the OOD of any responsibility.

Additionally, because of the navigator's unique responsibility for safe navigation at all times, the OOD should keep that person informed of anything that may be pertinent. The OOD should never hesitate to consult the navigator, day or night, on questions about safe navigation.

When a ship is in formation, the OOD routinely makes the course and speed changes dictated by the tactical situation and not directly related to the safe navigation of the ship. The OOD should nevertheless inform the navigator of any such changes other than minor alterations necessary to maintain station. He or she should also ensure that the dead-reckoning plot is revised to reflect course and speed changes (except for station-keeping) held for more than five minutes. This should be done even when a ship changes station. A ship's change of station from one side to the other of a large formation can have a significant effect on her geographical position.

## FOG AND LOW VISIBILITY

Radar has made possible the most complicated maneuvering and piloting under all conditions of visibility. However, this does not reduce in any way the responsibilities of a CO. Extensive use of radar has led many inexperienced officers to think they can neglect the older and more reliable means of safeguarding a ship. Radar is an *aid* against disaster, not a *guarantee*. In reduced visibility, either the OOD or the junior officer of the deck should be outside the pilothouse, using binoculars and listening for fog signals. "Radarscope fixation" must be avoided. Aviators are taught to scan their instruments and check the air around them constantly. They are warned never to become fixed on one instrument for too long. The OOD should develop the same habits. Rather than become anchored at a radar repeater or at the centerline pelorus, he or she should be constantly on the move, checking both bridge wings and the area astern of the ship and periodically scanning the radar repeaters.

An OOD must understand the capabilities and limitations of the radars. He or she should know how to operate all the remote-control gear, who is responsible for the maintenance of radar, and how to reach them in a hurry. The OOD should have the radars warmed up and checked before dark, when fog descends, and when it begins to rain or snow.

It is important to use surface-search radar in poor visibility. At night and when visibility is poor, radar repeaters on the bridge and in the CIC should be on different ranges. Surface-search radars should be kept energized when a ship is under way (but not necessarily emitting when operating under emissions-control [EmCon] condition), and they should be checked and calibrated at intervals. Keeping all radar repeaters, both in the CIC and on the bridge, on the same range is dangerous, because it can lead to concentration on the immediate area at the expense of detecting contacts in the distance, or vice versa. It should be noted that the courts have held the failure of a government vessel to make use of radar while under way in low visibility to have contributed directly to a collision. This philosophy appears in rule 2 of the International Regulations for Preventing Collisions at Sea, which states that "nothing in these rules shall exonerate any vessel, or the owner, master or crew thereof, from the consequences of any neglect to comply with these rules or of the neglect of any precaution which may be required by the ordinary practice of seamen, or by the special circumstances of the case."

## LOOKOUTS

Every vessel shall at all times maintain a proper lookout by sight and hearing as well as by all available means appropriate in the prevailing circumstances and conditions so as to make a full appraisal of the situation and the risk of collision.

International Regulations for Preventing Collisions at Sea, rule 5

International Regulations for Preventing Collisions at Sea, commonly known as the rules of the road, specifies clearly that a lookout must be both looking and listening. This is an important point because many lookouts are not aware that, even under normal steaming conditions, they have a responsibility to maintain a watch by sight and sound. In low visibility, the duty of the lookout to report what he or she hears is especially important; the lookout should be provided with a telephone talker so that he or she can concentrate on listening for fog signals. A lookout who is wearing phones when charged with listening for signals is *not* standing a proper watch.

Lookouts should not be trained by casual instruction from their peers or by a so-called break-in watch. They should be included in a formal qualification program that includes training in reporting procedures, recognition and identification, and the use of sound-powered telephones. A lookout should be encouraged to report everything seen, even floating material, and his or her reports should always be acknowledged. If they are not acknowledged, the lookout may begin to think that his or her efforts are wasted and subsequently not report anything. Lookouts should be rotated as frequently as possible, at least hourly. When the weather is bad, they should be the first members of the watch to be issued foul-weather gear, and they should be relieved as often as necessary. In extremely cold or windy weather, a lookout's efficiency drops to almost zero after half an hour of duty.

## PSYCHOLOGICAL FACTORS

During World War II, Fleet Admiral Chester W. Nimitz, in a letter to the Pacific Fleet, stressed the impact that psychological factors can have on safe navigation:

> There are certain psychological factors which have fully as much to do with safety at sea as any of the more strictly technical ones. A large proportion of the disasters in tactics and maneuvers comes from concentrating too much on one objective or urgency, at the cost of not being sufficiently alert for others. Thus, absorption with enemy craft already under fire has led to being torpedoed by others not looked for or not given attention; while preoccupation with navigation, with carrying out the particular job in hand, or with avoiding some particular vessel or hazard, has resulted in collision with ships to whose presence we were temporarily oblivious. There is no rule that can cover this except the ancient one that eternal vigilance is the price of safety, no matter what the immediate distractions.
>
> No officer, whatever his rank and experience, should flatter himself that he is immune to the inexplicable lapses in judgment, calculation, and memory, or to the slips of the tongue in giving orders, which throughout seagoing history have so often brought disaster to men of the highest reputation and ability. Where a mistake in maneuvering or navigating can spell calamity, an officer shows rashness and conceit, rather than admirable self-confidence, in not checking his plan with someone else before starting it, *if time permits.* This is not yielding to another's judgment; it is merely making sure that one's own has not "blown a fuse" somewhere, as the best mental and mechanical equipment in the world has sometimes done.

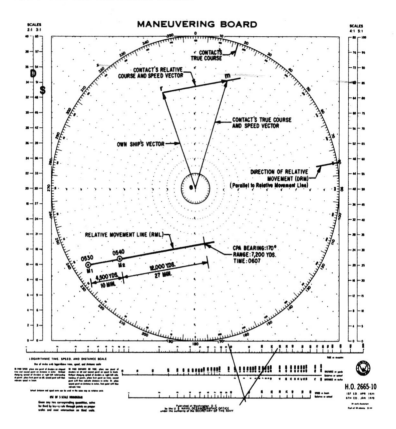

**Figure 7-8. Solving for CPA Course and Speed (Source: QM2, Navy Rate Training Manual, 1986, pp. 5–8)**

## MANEUVERING BOARD

One skill the capable watch officer must polish is processing contact information via the maneuvering board, or "mo board." Despite the increasing use of combat system and computer-generated maneuvering solutions, the use of the maneuvering board and dividers will not disappear, nor should it be allowed to. Whenever a contact is perceived to pose a risk of collision, the competent watch officer will

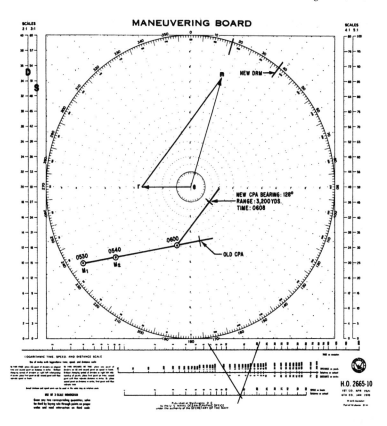

**Figure 7-9. Solving for a New CPA (Source: QM2, Navy Rate Training Manual, pp. 5–11)**

see that a maneuvering-board solution is prepared both in the pilot-house and in the CIC, should the ship be manned for that.

In fact, many COs order that a maneuvering-board solution be worked on any contact with a closest point of approach (CPA) of less than some set distance, perhaps five thousand yards. The reasons for doing so are plain: When the watch officer has to plot position and calculate true course and speed, CPA, and all the other information available on the maneuvering board, he or she is paying full attention to contact situations. In an age of machine-generated solutions on cathode-ray tubes, a maneuvering-board solution gives a comforting sense of indispensable human input.

The intent in this brief section is not to provide a detailed description of how to do the "mo board." Those skills are well taught in precommissioning programs and at many of the schools the typical watch officer attends after earning a commission. Rather, the objective is to provide a few salient examples in maneuvering-board format of the most common problems faced by the watchstander: the true course/speed and CPA of a nonmaneuvering contact, true wind, stationing, and maneuvering to adjust CPA, among others. For the watch officer who already has a basic understanding of the maneuvering board, these examples serve as a quick reference.

Whenever working a maneuvering board, it is important to be precise and consistent with measurements taken from both the radar and the dividers on the maneuvering board itself. Here are a few general pointers:

1. Use the largest scale possible for speed and distance, and try to use the same scale for both. Use the same scales throughout each problem.

2. Be careful, and double-check yourself.

3. Work in true bearings, not relative.

4. Label all points, and use arrowheads to indicate direction.

5. Actual speed vectors always originate at the center of the board.

6. At least three "cuts" are required on each contact before an accurate solution can be determined.

## SUMMARY OF FIX ACCURACIES AND INTERVALS

| Area | Distance from Land | Accuracy | Rec Interval |
|---|---|---|---|
| Restricted waters | <2 NM | 50 yds | 2 min |
| Piloting waters | 2–10 NM | 100 yds | 3–15 min |
| Coastal waters | 10–30 NM | 500 yds | 15 min |
| Enroute navigation | >30 NM | 1500 yds | 30 min |

## NAVIGATION IN THE ELECTRONIC AND INFORMATION AGE

There are many new electronic navigation systems entering the fleet. Most are built around the Global Positioning System (GPS) which takes highly accurate input from a constellation of satellites and provides precise positioning data to ships. An example of the new systems building from GPS is the Electronic Chart Display Information System (ECDIS), which provides an electronic chart and takes a direct feed from GPS to show the ship's position, course, and speed on an electronically displayed "chart." There are also inexpensive, small versions of these electronic chart systems available through commercial outlets, some for a few thousand dollars. Many ships are installing such systems, and using them as a "back check" to the traditional paper, pencil, and charts that have now been used for centuries on ships at sea.

GPS is wonderful. It provides accuracy from two to seven meters in most cases, although there are still some areas of the world where accuracy is reduced. They are annotated in the publications accompanying the GPS systems. It is easy to use, extremely reliable, and readily accessible. Backups, in the form of hand-held GPS receivers, are also common on all U.S. Navy ships as well. All in all, GPS and the associated electronic navigation systems have much to recommend them.

However, as a result of the electronic aids, it is increasingly easy to overlook some of the real essentials of navigation and piloting, such as the geometry behind the visual fix, the correct use of dead reckoning, and close coordination between the bridge and CIC. The basics—use of the radian rule, calculation and understanding of gyro error, using celestial navigation, teamwork, and communications—cannot be replaced by a new GPS system and a set of electronic charts sent on diskettes.

As a watch officer, you must use all the tools at your disposal. You will find that in most situations, you will be able to navigate your ship safely and easily with GPS and electronic charts. There will be times, however, when you will be glad for the excellence of your piloting team and their visual fixes; you will be happy to have a written record of your track through a difficult channel; and you will understand that to stand a safe watch you must navigate using a wide variety of systems.

# 8

---

# STANDARD COMMANDS

Each person on watch shall use phraseology customary to the service when issuing orders.

OpNavInst 3120.32C

Nowhere in the Navy are terminology and phraseology as important as in commands given by the conning officer to the helmsman or the engines. Because misunderstanding or ambiguity can so quickly lead to disaster, there must be no possibility of a command being misunderstood, and there need be no confusion if official terminology and phraseology are used. Shortcuts and individual variations are to be discouraged; all the enlisted people who man ship-control instruments should become accustomed to receiving their commands in the same form.

## MANNER OF GIVING COMMANDS

Commands should be given in a clear voice, loud enough to be heard, and the tone should be incisive.

The word "helm" should not be used in any command relating to the operation of the rudder. Commands to the helmsman are given in a logical sequence. The first word is "right" or "left," which indicates the direction in which the helmsman is to put the wheel over. The second word indicates how far it is to be put over, for example, "Right *standard* rudder." The purpose of giving a command in this manner is to ensure quick and accurate compliance by the helmsman, who starts turning the wheel instantly upon hearing "right" or "left." By the time the amount of rudder has been specified, he or she can bring the rudder-angle indicator to rest on the exact number of degrees. One exception is when ordering hard rudder. In that case, the sequence is "*hard* right (left) rudder," indicating that the maximum rudder should be applied as rapidly as possible in the indicated direction.

Similarly, in a command given via the engine-order telegraph, familiarly called the lee helm, the first term, "port (starboard) engine" or "all engines" indicates to the operator which handles or knobs to move. The next word, "ahead" or "back," tells in which direction to move them. The last part of the command, "one-third," "full," etc., gives the amount of the speed change and tells the operator where to stop his or her instrument. Standard commands to the engines are these:

1. "All engines ahead one-third (two-thirds, standard, full, flank)" or "All engines back one-third (two-thirds, full)."

2. "Starboard (port) engine, ahead one-third (two-thirds, standard, full)" or "Starboard (port) engine, back one-third (two-thirds, full)."

In an emergency, normal acceleration and deceleration tables are sometimes abandoned and orders are given for the ship to go ahead or back with all available power as quickly as possible. In such instances, the proper command is "All engines ahead (back), emergency." The operator should then ring up "Ahead flank" (or "Back full") three or more times in rapid succession.

The exact number of revolutions to be made on each engine should be indicated to the engine room by the revolution indicator. If the number of revolutions desired is not the exact number for the speed ordered, the former must be specified: "*Indicate* one one seven revolutions." The word "revolutions" should always be included in this order to prevent confusion with orders concerning course or bearings. When increasing or decreasing revolutions by small increments, the exact number of revolutions desired should also be stated, for instance, "Indicate one one seven revolutions," rather than "Up two" or "Take off three."

When practical, the number of revolutions desired should be ordered rather than the speed desired. This would not be practical if, for instance, the OOD were on the wing of the bridge, unable to see or remember the revolutions required, and felt that he or she should not move. In such a situation, the OOD should say, "Indicate turns for ____ knots," and require a report of the turns rung up, as well as a repetition of the command. The turns-per-knot table should be memorized as soon as possible. The method of ordering speed varies from ship to ship, even within a class. Check the commanding officer's standing orders upon reporting aboard and before conning.

One-third speed and two-thirds speed are one-third and two-thirds of the prescribed standard speed. The revolutions for these speeds are the number of revolutions per minute (rpm) required to achieve those fractions of standard speed. Full speed and flank speed are greater than standard speed. They are usually based on fractional increments of standard speed. The rpm for these speeds are also those actually required to achieve them. When small adjustments in speed are desired, the only command usually necessary is the one ordering the change in revolutions. However, when revolutions are ordered that will result in a speed within a different increment, that increment should also be rung up on the engine-order telegraph.

It is important that all commands be repeated loud and clear, just as they were given by the officer at the conn, by the helmsman or lee helmsman. This practice serves as a check on the officer who originated the command and provides an opportunity for correction of any slip of the tongue, such as "left" when "right" was meant.

It is equally important to require the person at the helm or lee helm to report when he or she has complied with the command. The conning officer must acknowledge this final report with a "Very well."

## STEERING COMMANDS TO THE HELM

When a specific amount of rudder is desired:

    Command:  "Right full rudder (or right standard rudder)."
    Reply:       "Right full (standard) rudder, aye, sir (or ma'am)."

Report: "My rudder is right full (standard), sir (or ma'am)."

When the rudder order is given in degrees:
 Command: "Left ten degrees rudder."
 Reply: "Left ten degrees rudder, aye, sir (or ma'am)."
 Report: "My rudder is left ten degrees, sir (or ma'am)."

When the helmsman is to steady on a specific course:
 Command: "Steady on course ____."
 Reply: "Steady on course ____, aye, sir (or ma'am)."
 Report: "Steady on course ____, sir (or ma'am). Checking ____ magnetic."

When maximum possible rudder is required:
 Command: "Hard right rudder."
 Reply: "Hard right rudder, aye, sir (or ma'am)."
 Report: "Rudder is hard right, sir (or ma'am)."

*Note:* The danger in using hard rudder lies in the possibility of jamming the rudder into the stops. For this reason, it is rarely used except in emergencies. If hard rudder is chosen when there is no emergency, the conning officer may reduce the possibility of jamming the rudder by first ordering full rudder and then increasing the rudder to hard, allowing the helmsman more control of the rudder's movement.

When the amount of rudder is to be increased:
 Command: "Increase your rudder to ____ (right full, right ten degrees, etc.)."
 Reply: "Increase my rudder to ____, sir (or ma'am)."
 Report: "My rudder is ____ (right full, right ten degrees, etc.)."

When the amount of rudder is to be decreased:
 Command: "Ease your rudder to ____ (standard, left ten degrees, etc.)."
 Reply: "Ease my rudder to ____, sir (or ma'am)."
 Report: "My rudder is ____ (standard, left ten degrees, etc.)."

When the rudder is increased or decreased while the ship is turning to an ordered course:

Command: "Right standard rudder, steady on course 270."

Reply: "Right standard rudder, steady on course 270, aye, sir (or ma'am)."

Command: "Increase your rudder to right full, steady on course 270."

*Note:* When the rudder is increased or decreased, the conning officer must restate the desired course.

Reply: "Increase my rudder to right full, steady on course 270, aye, sir (or ma'am)."

Report: "My rudder is right full, coming to course 270, sir (or ma'am)."

When course change is less than ten degrees:

Command: "Come right, steer course ____."

Reply: "Come right, steer course ____, aye, sir (or ma'am)."

Report: "Steady course, checking course ____ magnetic, sir (or ma'am)."

When the rudder angle is to be reduced to zero:

Command: "Rudder amidships."

Reply: "Rudder amidships, aye, sir (or ma'am)."

Report: "My rudder is amidships, sir (or ma'am)."

When the course to be steered is that which the ship is on at the instant the command is given:

Command: "Steady as you go."

Reply: "Steady as you go, course ____, sir (or ma'am)."

Report: "Steady on course ____, sir (or ma'am). Checking course."

*Note:* Injudicious use of this order could cause momentary loss of control over the ship's swing if the helmsman is required to use a large rudder angle to carry out the order. To prevent this, the order should be preceded by "Rudder amidships." This, of course, requires anticipation on the conning officer's part to ensure a correct heading. In this situation, the conning officer should always maintain positive control of the rudder.

When the swing of the ship is to be stopped without steadying on any specific course:

Command: "Meet her."

Reply: "Meet her, aye, sir (or ma'am)."

*Note:* Immediately after the reply is given, the conning officer must order a course to be steered.

Command: "Steady on course ____."

Reply: "Steady on course ____, aye, sir (or ma'am)."

Report: "Steady on course ____, sir (or ma'am). Checking course ____."

When equal and *opposite* rudder is desired relative to that previously ordered:

Command: "Shift your rudder."

Reply: "Shift my rudder, aye, sir (or ma'am)."

Report: "Rudder is ____ (an angle equal but opposite to that previously ordered)."

When the heading of the ship is to be determined at a given moment:

Command: "Mark your head."

Report: "Head is (exact heading at that moment), sir (or ma'am)."

*Note:* If the helmsman appears to be steering properly but the ship is not on her correct heading, the conning officer should use this command to compare the helmsman's compass repeater with other repeaters on the bridge.

When the helmsman appears to be steering badly or is continually allowing the ship to drift from the ordered course:

Command: "Mind your helm."

Reply: "Mind my helm, aye, sir (or ma'am)."

*Note:* No report necessary.

When the ship is in a situation where minor deviation from an ordered course may be permitted to one side but none may be permitted to the other side (for example, when alongside another ship for refueling):

    Command:  "Steer nothing to the left (right) of course ____."

    Reply:      "Steer nothing to the left (right) of course ____, aye, sir (or ma'am)."

*Note:* No report necessary.

Whenever ordering a course change, the conning officer should perform the following activities:

1. Check the side to which he or she intends to turn to make sure that it is safe to turn in that direction.

2. The ship's speed determines how quickly her head will swing. At very low speeds, a large angle of rudder may be required to bring about a course change; at very high speeds, a large rudder angle may cause her to swing so rapidly that she cannot be safely controlled. All conning officers should be familiar with the tables of turning speeds and turning diameters for their ship. This information is contained in the ship's tactical data book. Generally, the sum of rudder order plus speed in knots should not exceed thirty or else there will be a probability of fairly heavy rolls.

3. After giving a rudder order, the conning officer should monitor its execution by checking the rudder angle indicator to ensure there was no misinterpretation of the command.

4. In a turn without an ordered course, the helmsman should call out the ship's head for each ten degrees that the ship swings. If the conning officer does not want the helmsman to do this, he or she should give the helmsman the order "Belay your headings." The helm should reply, "Belay my headings, aye, sir (or ma'am)."

## ENGINE-ORDER COMMANDS TO THE LEE HELM

Engine orders are always given in the following order:

1. *Engine.* Which engine is to be used. If both engines are to be used, the command is "All engines." On single-screw ships the command is always "Engine."

2. *Direction.* Ahead, back, or stop.

3. *Amount.* Ahead one-third, two-thirds, full, flank. Back one-third, two-thirds, full.

4. *Shaft revolutions desired.* Number of revolutions in three digits for the desired speed in knots. Shaft revolutions are not used for backing orders.

## Examples

When a twin-screw ship is to go ahead on both engines to come to a speed of six knots:

| | |
|---|---|
| Command: | "All engines ahead one-third. Indicate zero eight eight revolutions for six knots." |
| Reply: | "All engines ahead one-third. Indicate zero eight eight revolutions for six knots, aye, sir (or ma'am)." |
| Report: | "Engine room answers all ahead one-third. Indicating zero eight eight revolutions for six knots, sir (or ma'am)." |

When different orders are given to port and starboard engines, revolutions should not be specified:

| | |
|---|---|
| Command: | "Port engine ahead one-third, starboard engine back one-third." |
| Reply: | "Port engine ahead one-third, starboard engine back one-third, aye, sir (or ma'am)." |
| Report: | "Engine room answers port ahead one-third, starboard back one-third, sir (or ma'am)." |

When the order is to only one engine, the report must include the status of both engines:

| | |
|---|---|
| Command: | "Starboard engine ahead one-third, port engine back one-third." |
| Reply: | "Starboard engine ahead one-third, port engine back one-third, aye, sir (or ma'am)." |
| Report: | "Engine room answers starboard engine ahead one-third, port engine back one-third, sir (or ma'am)." |
| Command: | "Starboard engine stop." |
| Reply: | "Starboard engine stop, aye, sir (or ma'am)." |

Report:      "Engine room answers starboard engine stop. Port engine back one-third, sir (or ma'am)."

When there are to be small changes of speed, for example, when the ship is alongside another for refueling or to keep station on the formation guide:

Command:  "Indicate one zero zero revolutions."

Reply:       "Indicate one zero zero revolutions, aye, sir (or ma'am)."

Report:     "Engine room answers one zero zero revolutions for three revolutions over eleven knots, sir (or ma'am)."

On many gas-turbine ships with controllable reversible-pitch propellers, at speeds below twelve knots, the ship's speed is controlled by varying the pitch of the propeller blade, measured as a percentage. This requires additional orders at lower speeds, as in:

Command:  "All engines ahead one-third. Indicate ____ rpm's, ____ percent pitch for ____ knots."

Reply:     "As normal."

Report:    "As normal."

*Note:* This will vary from ship to ship, even within a class. Check the captain's standing orders.

When maneuvering in restricted waters, getting under way, docking, or mooring, ships usually use what are known as maneuvering bells. Under these circumstances, only engine, direction, and amount are given. Revolutions are not specified. Depending on the type of ship, each engine amount is equivalent to a standard number of knots, for example, one-third equals five knots, two-thirds equals ten knots, etc. When maneuvering bells (or "maneuvering combination") are desired, the conning officer must order the helmsman as follows:

Command:  "Indicate maneuvering combination (bells)." (By convention, this is usually an engine order for nine nine nine revolutions.)

Reply:     "Indicate (nine nine nine) revolutions for maneuvering combination (bells), sir (or ma'am)."

Report:    "Engine room answers (nine nine nine) revolutions for maneuvering combination (bells), sir (or ma'am)."

Some commanding officers develop variation in the maneuvering bells to indicate one-half of the power increment, often by indicating seven seven seven or eight eight eight. This tells the throttleman to cut standard acceleration or deceleration and power levels in half for more explicit shiphandling around the pier. The watch officer should consult the commanding officer's standing orders to see if this practice is acceptable on the ship.

## COMMANDS TO LINE-HANDLERS

Many a good approach to landing is offset by the improper use of mooring lines. Using them properly requires knowledge of the standard commands to line-handlers. The following examples and definitions are in common use in the fleet and form the basis of all orders to lines. Orders should state the number of the line, when appropriate, and telephone talkers should be used for transmitting them.

Mooring lines are numbered from bow to stern in the order in which they are run out from the ship: 1, bow line; 2, after bow spring; 3, forward bow spring; 4, after quarter spring; 5, forward quarter spring; 6, stern line. The breast line amidships is not numbered.

| Command | Meaning |
| --- | --- |
| "Stand by your lines" | Man the lines, ready to put them over, cast them off, or take them in. |
| "Let go" or "Let go all lines" | Slack off to permit people tending lines on the pier or on another ship to cast off. |
| "Send the lines over" or "Put over all lines" | Pass the lines to the pier, place the eye of each over the appropriate bollard, but take no strain. |
| "Take a strain on (line 3)" | Put the line under tension. |
| "Slack (line 3)" | Take tension off the line and let it hang slack. |
| "Ease (line 3)" | Let out enough of the line to lessen tension. |
| "Take (line 3) to the capstan" or to "power" | Lead the end of the line to the capstan, take the slack out of it, but put no strain on it. |

| | |
|---|---|
| "Heave around on (line 3)" | Apply tension on the line with the capstan. |
| "Avast heaving" | Stop the capstan. |
| "Hold what you've got on (line 3)" | Hold the line as it is. |
| "Hold (line 3)" | Do not allow any more line to go out. ("Hold" commands should be used with extreme caution because they require the lines to be held even to parting.) |
| "Check" | Hold heavy tension on line but let it slip as necessary to prevent it from parting. |
| "Surge" | Hold moderate tension on the line but let it slip enough to permit the ship to move. |
| "Double up" | Pass additional bights on all mooring lines so that there are three parts of each line to the pier. |
| "Single up" | Take in all bights and extra lines, leaving only a single part of each of the normal mooring lines. |
| "Take in all lines" | Have the ends of all lines cast off from the pier and brought on board. |
| "Cast off all lines" | Used when secured with *another* ship's lines in a nest. Cast off the ends of the lines and allow the other ship to retrieve her lines. |
| "Shift" | Used when moving a line along a pier. Followed by specification of the line and where it is to go: "Shift no. 3 from the bollard to the cleat." |

When a ship's auxiliary deck machinery is to be used to haul in a line, the command given is "Take one (no. 1 ) to the winch (capstan or power)." This may be followed by "Heave around on one (no. 1)" and then "Avast heaving on one (no. 1)."

The proper naval term for the line-handling drum on the anchor windlass is "warping head." Usage, however, has given authority to the synonyms "winch," "capstan," and "power."

## COMMANDS TO TUGS

Tugs are normally handled by two-way VHF radio. However, the following whistle and hand signals are still in use. They may be transmitted to tugs by flashing lights, but only when whistle or hand signals cannot be used.

### Whistle Signals

A blast lasts two to three seconds. A prolonged blast lasts four to five seconds. A short blast lasts about one second. Care must be exercised to ensure that whistle signals are directed to and received by the tug for which they are intended. Whistles of different tones have been used successfully to handle more than one tug.

| Signal | Meaning |
|---|---|
| One blast | From stop to half-speed ahead |
| One blast | From half-speed ahead to stop |
| Four short blasts | From half-speed ahead to full-speed ahead |
| One blast | From full-speed ahead to half-speed ahead |
| Two blasts | From stop to half-speed astern |
| Four short blasts | From half-speed astern to full-speed astern |
| One blast | From half-speed or full-speed astern to stop |
| One prolonged blast, two short blasts | Cast off, stand clear |

Whistle signals are usually augmented by hand signals.

### Hand Signals

| Signal | Meaning |
|---|---|
| Arm pointed in direction desired | Half speed (ahead or astern) |
| Fist describing arc | Full speed (ahead or astern) |
| Undulating movement of open hand, with palm down | Dead slow (ahead or astern) |
| Open hand held aloft, with palm facing the tug | Stop |

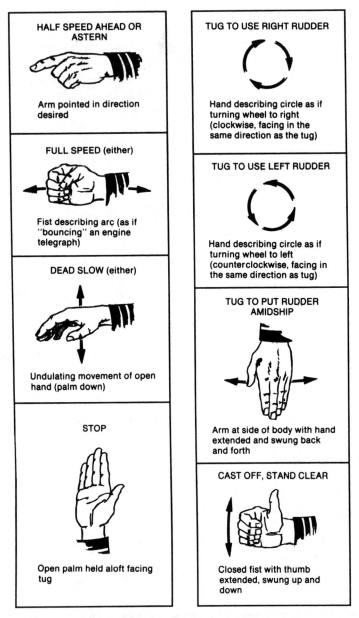

**Figure 8-1. Tugboat Hand Signals**

| | |
|---|---|
| Closed fist with thumb extended, swung up and down | Cast off, stand clear |
| Hand describing circle as if turning wheel to the right (clockwise), facing in the same direction as the tug | Tug to use right rudder |
| Hand describing circle as if turning wheel to the left (counterclockwise), facing in the same direction as the tug | Tug to use left rudder |
| Arm at side of body with hand extended, swung back and forth | Tug to use rudder amidship |

A tug must acknowledge all whistle and hand signals with one short toot (one second or less) from her whistle. The exceptions are the backing signal, which must be acknowledged with two short toots, and the cast-off signal, which must be acknowledged by one prolonged and two short toots.

## AUXILIARY POWER UNITS

Auxiliary power units (APUs) on some newer classes of naval vessels have given an increased maneuvering capability in close quarters. APUs are electrically driven, trainable motors positioned near the bow of the ship.

| *Command* | *Meaning* |
|---|---|
| Train port APU ninety degrees | Position port APU to push the ship toward 090 degrees relative |
| Energize port (starboard) APU | Port (starboard) APU on |
| Stop port (starboard) APU | Port (starboard) APU off |

## BOW THRUSTERS

Bow thrusters on amphibious ships are used to marry the ship's bow with a causeway for amphibious landings. Additionally, they improve maneuverability near the pier or in close quarters. The bow thruster is an electrically driven, controllable-pitch propeller (CPP) located near the bow inside a transverse hull tube.

| *Command* | *Meaning* |
|---|---|
| Bow thruster starboard one-half | Bow thruster will move the ship to starboard. CPP will slew to 50 percent. |
| Bow thruster stop | Bow thruster CPP will slew to 0 percent pitch. |

# 9

## WEATHER

If you don't like the weather, stick around. It'll change.

Popular saying

The coldest winter I ever spent was a summer in San Francisco.

Attributed to Mark Twain

The weather—we are surrounded by it, discuss it endlessly, and spend millions of dollars attempting to predict it. Understanding the weather is essential if a professional watch officer is to effectively stand his or her watch. Yet weather receives little attention in traditional commissioning programs and Navy schools, and we generally don't know enough about it when knowledge is what we most need.

## CLOUDS

The first and most obvious feature of the weather at sea is the clouds. There is much to be learned from each cloud layer, and each represents different aspects of the interaction of wind and waves. A capable watch officer has at least a nodding acquaintance with the major cloud formations and can give a general indication of what each portends. The following are some of the key cloud formations:

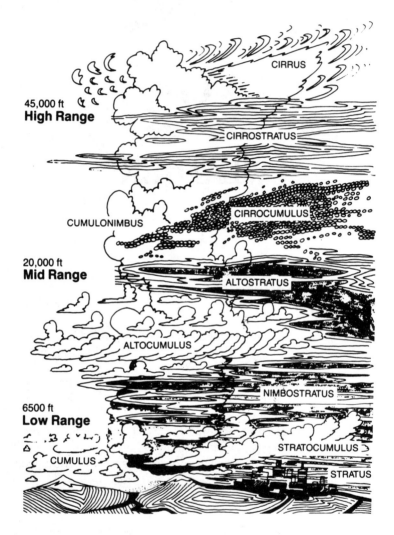

**Figure 9-1. The Ten-Cloud Genera**

*Cirrus.* These delicate white clouds commonly make feather-like plumes across the sky. They have little shading, occur at very high altitude, and are generally composed of ice crystals. They can indicate the direction of a storm.

*Cirrocumulus.* Also called mackerel sky, these clouds look like thousands of cottonballs pasted together. They generally indicate the approach of a storm.

*Cirrostratus.* These faint veils of cloud can cause halos to appear around the sun and the moon. They are often a precursor of rain.

*Altocumulus.* These clouds look like flat globes arranged in lines or waves. They differ from cirrocumulus clouds in casting shadows.

*Altostratus* Thick cirrostratus clouds without any halo, these appear as part of a thin veil or sheet and can completely obscure the sun and the moon. Either heavy snow or light rain can fall from altostratus clouds.

*Nimbostratus.* These covered, shapeless clouds are slightly illuminated from behind. When precipitation occurs, it is normally continuous, although it does not always reach the ocean.

*Stratocumulus.* These layers or patches of clouds are composed of rolls, generally soft gray. They occasionally have dark spots.

*Stratus.* These low, even clouds assemble just above the earth. Their presence can give the sky a hazy appearance. Drizzle is the precipitation normally associated with stratus clouds.

*Cumulus.* These dense clouds rise from a horizontal base into gently rounded projections. They can create strong and unpredictable updrafts.

*Cumulonimbus.* These heavy cloud masses resemble towers or mountains, and their upper levels have a full appearance. They are associated with heavy rain, snow showers, violent hail, and thunderstorms.

## FOG

Fog can be the mariner's worst enemy, particularly when a ship enters or leaves port. Fog is formed when warmer air moves over colder water. Great fog banks can develop just offshore, particularly in the North Atlantic and the Aleutians. Fog generally forms at night

**(A)**

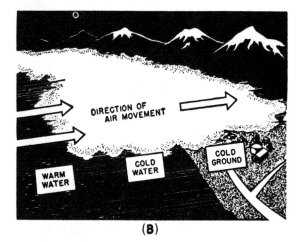

**(B)**

**Figure 9-2. Coastal Fog. This shows how it is formed and how dissipated: (A) by day when the ground is warm, and (B) by night when the ground is cold.**

and lingers until morning, when heat from the sun evaporates the droplets or an offshore wind drives them away.

One way to predict the formation of fog is to determine the difference between the wet- and dry-bulb temperatures. Fog generally forms when the wet-bulb depression is four degrees or less. Keeping a continuous record of the depression will serve the watch officer well by helping to predict dangerous conditions.

## FRONTS

The seam where one air mass or weather system meets another is a front. The colder mass, which is heavier, forces the warmer mass aloft, usually forming clouds and inclement weather. When fronts converge, the front on the surface is occluded.

Cold fronts are usually fifteen to fifty miles wide; warm fronts can be as wide as three hundred miles. The area where a warm and cold front meet is normally low pressure.

When a cold front is approaching, the horizon will darken in the direction of the front. A fast cold front, with cumulonimbus clouds, can cause violent and sudden thunderstorms or showers. When the cold front passes, the temperature drops, pressure rises, and the sky clears rapidly.

The appearance of a warm front, usually preceded by cirrus clouds, brings a variety of cloud formations, including (in rough order) cirrostratus, altostratus, nimbostratus, and stratus. Visibility is poor, generally because of fog, rain, or drizzle. Thunderstorms can develop ahead of the front.

A stationary front, as the name implies, is a region where two air masses abut each other without much movement. As a general rule, the weather and clouds along a stationary front are similar in character to those found along a warm front.

An occluded front occurs when a cold front overtakes a warm front, forcing warm air up and leaving a front on the surface that may be either cool or warm. An occluded front generally displays characteristics similar to those of a warm front.

## ATMOSPHERIC PRESSURE AND ISOBARS

Every watch officer must understand atmospheric pressure, as it is one of the best indicators of weather activity. With the ship's barometer, variations in atmospheric pressure can be measured accurately. Pressure readings are given in inches of mercury, and at the earth's surface the baseline reading is 29.92 inches. As a general rule, a high barometer (over thirty inches) portends fair weather, while a low or falling barometer presages deteriorating weather. The bridge quartermaster, who is trained in weather observation, will report the barometric pressure to the watch officer every hour, also indicating whether the barometer is rising or falling and giving the amount in hundredths of an inch: "Sir (or ma'am), the barometer has fallen two-hundredths in the past hour." Because an air mass moves from a high-pressure region to a lower-pressure one, a knowledge of barometric pressure in different regions provides clues about the direction and movement of frontal systems and the air masses that form the weather (wind, precipitation, etc.). More important than a single "snapshot" reading is an understanding of the *relative* changes in the barometer from hour to hour and of any deviation in the expected reading for a given geographical area during the season of the measurement. The watch officer should notify the commanding officer and navigator, and probably the first lieutenant and operations officer, of changes in the barometer that seem excessive or out of the ordinary.

As a general rule, a steady barometer means good weather. A falling barometer (either below normal for the region or time of year, or simply declining in the immediate region) normally presages wind and rain, especially when coupled with increasing temperature and moisture. A sudden fall (more than four-hundredths of an inch in an hour) can mean heavy winds. A rising barometer, especially with decreasing moisture and temperature, generally portends milder, drier weather. A rapid rise can mean unsettled conditions with a variety of weather shifts.

A map of pressure areas and the movement of air masses depicts frontal systems and lines of equal pressure called isobars. Isobars do not join or cross, and by studying them, you can obtain a fairly good idea of weather in a given region. The difference in pressure between isobars gives an indication of wind strength (the greater the difference between high and low pressure over a given distance, the stronger the wind). If isobars are close to each other, the wind generated by the pressure differential will generally be stronger. Conversely, when there is more room between the isobars, winds will be lighter. On a map or chart, an elongated area of low pressure is re-

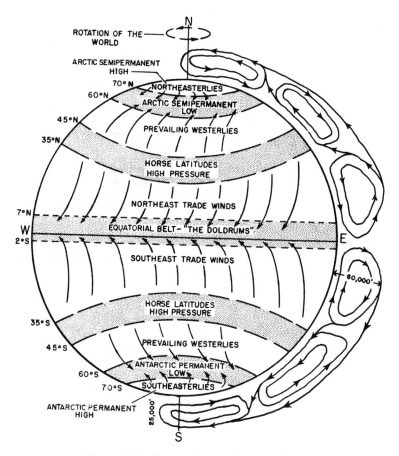

**Figure 9-3. General Circulation of Air**

ferred to as a trough or trough line. Troughs are associated with strong weather and occasionally violent wind shifts.

In areas of high pressure the wind blows outward, while in areas of low pressure it blows inward. In the northern hemisphere, the combination of the earth's rotation and the structure of the isobars causes the air to circulate in a clockwise direction around high pressure centers and in a counterclockwise direction around low pressure centers. The opposite is true in the southern hemisphere.

## Table 9-1. Apparent Wind Speed

| Knots | Indication |
|---|---|
| Less than 1 | Calm, smoke rises vertically |
| 1–3 | Smoke drifts slowly |
| 4–6 | Wind felt on face |
| 7–10 | Wind extends light flag |
| 11–16 | Wind raises dust, cinders, etc. |
| 17–21 | Wind waves and snaps flags briskly |
| 22–27 | Wind whistles through rigging |
| 28–33 | Walking into the wind becomes difficult |
| 34–40 | Wind generally impedes walking |

## WEATHER PROVERBS

Often the best person to predict the weather is the experienced watchstander or member of the bridge team. The chief or first-class quartermaster on most ships will have a "feel" for the weather. Here are a few of the phrases and proverbs they often utter:

Red sky at night, sailors delight (good weather coming).

Red sky at morning, sailors take warning (weather deteriorating, generally in the afternoon).

Greenish tint to the sky (a deep low-pressure area to the north or west).

Yellow sunset (coming strong winds).

Sunrise low in the sky (light winds and fair weather).

Sunrise high in the sky (winds and cloudiness).

Mares' tails and mackerel scales make tall ships carry low sails (cirrus clouds [mares' tails] and cirrocumulus clouds [mackerel scales] often indicate pressure lows and possible warm fronts).

## NAVY WEATHER FORECASTING

For the watch officer on a naval vessel, many excellent weather information services are available. The point of contact is generally the ship's navigator (occasionally the operations officer), with the specific point of contact often being the quartermaster of the watch (QMOW) on the bridge.

The best overall information on the Navy's oceanographic support system is Commander, Naval Meteorology, and Oceanography

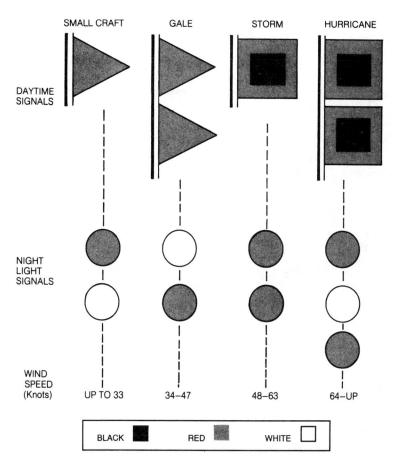

**Figure 9-4. Small Craft, Gale, Storm, and Hurricane Warnings. Screened areas are red.**

Command, Instruction 3240.1K, the U.S. Navy Oceanographic and Meteorological Support System Manual. This comprehensive publication details all the support services available, including tropical cyclone warnings, daily forecasts, warnings of destructive extratropical weather systems, high-sea warnings, ice conditions, storm tide or surge warnings, area analyses and prognostic charts, severe local

**Table 9-2. Beaufort Scale and Estimating True Wind by Sea Conditions**

| Knots | Beaufort Number | Wave Height (Feet) | Description | Sea Conditions |
|---|---|---|---|---|
| 0 | 0 | 0 | Calm | Sea smooth and mirrorlike. |
| 1–3 | 1 | ¼ | Light air | Scalelike ripples without foam crests. |
| 4–6 | 2 | ½ | Light breeze | Small, short wavelets; crests glassy and do not break. |
| 7–10 | 3 | 1 | Gentle breeze | Large wavelets; some crests begin to break; occasional white foam crests. |
| 11–16 | 4 | 3 | Moderate breeze | Small waves, becoming longer; fairly frequent white foam crests. |
| 17–21 | 5 | 6 | Fresh breeze | Moderate waves, taking a more pronounced long form; many white foam crests; there may be some spray. |
| 22–27 | 6 | 12 | Strong breeze | Large waves form; white foam crests more extensive everywhere; there may be some spray. |
| 28–33 | 7 | *15 | Near gale | Sea heaps up, and white foam from breaking waves blown in streaks in the direction of the wind. |
| 34–40 | 8 | †20 | Gale | Moderately high waves of greater length; edges of crests break; foam blown in well-marked streaks in the direction of the wind. |
| 41–47 | 9 | ‡30 | Strong gale | High waves; dense streaks of foam in the direction of the wind; crests of waves begin to roll over; spray may reduce visibility. |
| 48–55 | 10 | ‡40 | Storm | Very high waves with long overhanging crests; foam in great patches blown in dense white streaks in the direction of the wind; visibility reduced. |
| 56–63 | 11 | ‡50 | Violent storm | Exceptionally high waves; sea completely covered with long white patches of foam lying in the direction of the wind; visibility reduced. |
| 64 and over | 12 | ‡60 | Hurricane | Air is filled with foam and spray; sea completely white with driving spray; visibility very much reduced. |

* Duration of sixteen hours, not fully arisen.
† Duration of twenty hours, not fully arisen.
‡ Duration of twenty-four hours, not fully arisen.

weather, satellite environmental data, and acoustic range predictions. These are available to the watch officer by a variety of means, including fleet broadcast and fleet facsimile broadcast. Additionally, specialized support services for specific operations, including optimum track ship routing (OTSR), route weather forecasts (WEAX), oceanic fronts and eddy positions (FREDDY), and fleet operating area forecasts, are available upon request. Specific support is available for the Great Lakes. Here are a few of the more common reports received on a ship:

**Wind Warnings.**   Issued as necessary by message at twelve- or twenty-four-hour intervals.

**High-Sea Warnings.**   Issued every twelve hours wherever waves in an ocean area equal or exceed 12 feet in height.

**OTSR.**   OTSR helps ships on voyages in excess of fifteen hundred nautical miles save fuel and time by providing best-weather routing.

On larger ships, a meteorology detachment is assigned for forward deployments.

A second publication of general interest to the naval watch officer is Commander, Naval Forces, Atlantic/Pacific Instruction 3140.2, Tropical Cyclone Evasion. This is a simple, comprehensive review of how to avoid typhoons and hurricanes.

## STORMY WEATHER

Shiphandling in a storm is a required skill for any watch officer. How to predict storm paths and how to escape them are equally important. A sound knowledge of weather greatly reduces the chance that a watch officer will place the ship in danger.

A cyclone is a violent windstorm that results from the presence of areas of dramatically low pressure. A tropical cyclone is also called a typhoon in the western Pacific or a hurricane in the Atlantic and eastern Pacific. Cyclones have well-defined areas and paths that are difficult to predict. These storms are extremely dangerous to both shipping and, when they make landfall, populated areas. A few clarifying definitions follow:

**Tropical Disturbance.**   This is a system of wind, generally one hundred to three hundred miles in diameter, that originates in

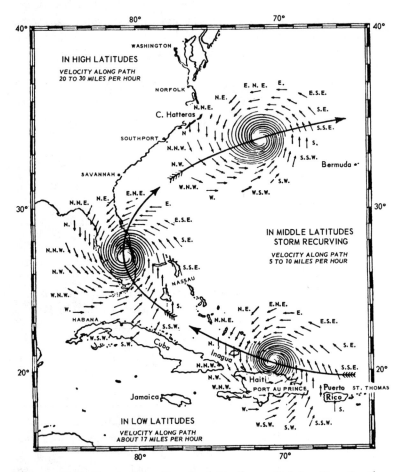

**Figure 9-5. Track of a Tropical Cyclone Originating in the West Indies**

the tropics and has maintained a distinct character for at least twenty-four hours.

*Tropical Depression.* This consists of one or more closed isobars beginning to rotate in a pattern, with wind speeds no higher than thirty-three knots.

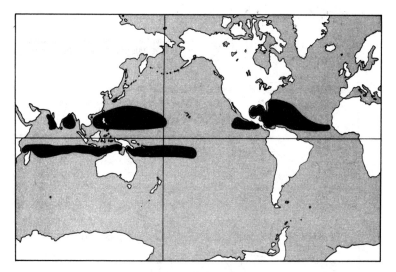

**Figure 9-6. Source Regions of Tropical Cyclones**

*Tropical Storm.* This has closed isobars and wind speeds from thirty-four to sixty-three knots.

*Typhoon or Hurricane.* This is a mature storm with winds over sixty-four knots and a distinct eye.

Rainfall in a tropical storm is heady, particularly in the center, and winds are forceful. Wind circulates counterclockwise in northern latitudes and clockwise in southern latitudes. The eye of a storm is usually five to thirty miles in diameter, and there winds are calm although the seas remain heavy. Interestingly, the South Atlantic is generally free of tropical storms because of the proximity of the African and South American land masses.

Despite the sophisticated weather-tracking and prognostication devices available to the watch officer, a tropical cyclone can form with extreme rapidity and overtake an unsuspecting ship with ease. The watch officer should learn and heed the signs discussed above, particularly during hurricane or typhoon season.

The basic device that indicates the formation of a storm is the barometer. Barometric pressure falls steadily when the air is hot,

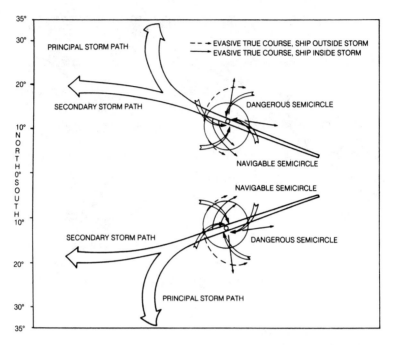

**Figure 9-7. Storm Evasion**

moist, and heavy. Wind begins to pick up. In advance of heavy winds, the sea rises in a long, low swell, and light plumes of cirrus clouds appear in an arc over the horizon. Some observers have reported a humming sound caused by increasing wind speed. Rain squalls appear and gradually increase to heavy showers and then to torrential downpours. The barometer continues to fall as the sea churns with ever-larger waves.

Determining the bearing of a storm is a simple matter. In the northern hemisphere where the storm whirls counterclockwise, the center will be about 110–120 degrees to the right of a watch officer facing the wind. The wind hauls in one direction or the other, depending on the semicircle in which the ship finds herself. The next step in the problem, determining distance to the storm center, is more difficult. The following scale presents a rough idea:

| Average Fall of Barometer | Distance from Center |
|---|---|
| 2/100s to 6/100s | 250 to 150 miles |
| 6/100s to 8/100s | 150 to 100 miles |
| 8/100s to 12/100s | 100 to 80 miles |
| 12/100s to 15/100s | 80 to 50 miles |

A storm can move up to fifty miles per hour, although speeds of five to twenty miles per hour are far more common.

After determining range and bearing to the center, the watch officer has to ascertain the track of the storm. The basic track can be determined by taking three to five bearings on the center, roughly two hours apart. If the wind hauls to the right, the ship is in the dangerous semicircle; if it hauls to the left, the ship is in the navigable semicircle. If the wind continues from the same direction and the barometer continues to fall, the storm is headed directly for the ship. The eye of the storm is a fairly good radar target, and the storm can be tracked on radar.

As a general rule, the best method for maneuvering in a storm in the northern hemisphere is as follows:

1. If the ship is in the right (dangerous) semicircle, put the wind on the starboard bow and make as much headway as possible without subjecting the ship to danger. If it is necessary to heave to, face into the sea.

2. If the ship is in the left (navigable) semicircle, put the wind on the starboard quarter and hold on that heading. If it is necessary to heave to, proceed stern into the sea.

3. If the ship is ahead of the storm center, bring the wind two points on the starboard quarter, and maintain that heading to make for the left (navigable) semicircle.

4. If the ship is behind the storm center, avoid the center by the most practical route, keeping in mind that the storm will eventually curve northeastward.

Attempting to outrun the storm by "crossing the T" is problematic because of the heavy swells that build rapidly ahead of the storm. Additionally, unpredictability makes it dangerous to approach the storm closely from ahead. The storm may follow the path toward the warmest waters, although this will have little influence over its path if the storm is moving fast.

# 10

## THE RULES OF
## THE ROAD

Without the rule of law, civilization soon turns to barbarism.

Tacitus

The intent of this brief chapter is not to present a detailed analysis of the international and inland navigation rules and regulations but rather to provide the watch officer with a handy reference summarizing these rules so that they may be accurately and professionally followed.

This chapter discusses the International Regulations for Prevention of Collisions at Sea, 1972 (72 COLREGS). It also discusses the Inland Navigation Rules, which were enacted by law on 24 December 1980 and became effective for all inland waters except the Great Lakes on 24 December 1981. The inland rules became effective on the Great Lakes on 1 March 1983. Some differences do remain between the international and inland rules, although they are fairly similar.

On 19 November 1989, nine amendments to the 72 COLREGS became effective. These nine amendments are technical in nature and are reflected in this discussion. The Coast Guard has adopted several amendments to the inland and international rules and annexes, which are also reflected.

The best source for studying the rules of the road is the U.S. Department of Transportation, United States Coast Guard Publication "Navigation Rules, International-Inland," which is Commandant Instruction M16672.2C. This handy and well-illustrated publication is available on your ship (check with the navigator, CIC officer, or senior watch officer) and from any Coast Guard station, and contains the actual text of the rules. If you want additional interpretation, there are several books published by the Naval Institute Press, including *Farwell's Rules of the Nautical Road,* seventh edition, and *Handbook of the Nautical Rules of the Road,* second edition. *Farwell's* is considered the classic of the profession on this subject, and is currently being edited by retired Royal Navy captain Richard Smith, a master navigator and well-known author.

While the books mentioned above are quite good, there is simply no substitute for studying and reading the rules of the road directly from the Coast Guard text. It doesn't take very long to read through the rules, and you should set aside some time to do this every couple of months while you are assigned to sea duty and standing watch.

What follows is a summary of the rules, with emphasis on sections that are more difficult to remember on short notice. This is for quick reference only; every watch officer should have a complete understanding of the rules based on reading, study, testing, and seminar discussion with other members of the wardroom.

***Rule 1: Application.*** This sets out areas in which the rules apply. International rules apply to all vessels upon the high seas and all waters navigable by seagoing vessels. Inland rules apply to all vessels on the inland waters of the United States. Rule 1, both international and inland, also contains a permit for submarines to display an intermittent flashing amber (yellow beacon) with a sequence as follows: one flash per second for three seconds followed by a three-second off-period.

***Rule 2: Responsibility.*** Nothing in the rules exonerates any vessel from the consequences of neglect to comply with the rules, to take the ordinary precautions, or to heed the special circumstances of a case. Due regard must be paid to all dangers of navigation and collision and to any special circumstances making a departure from the rules necessary to avoid immediate danger.

***Rule 3: General Definitions.*** Key definitions include the following.

Vessel: Any craft, including nondisplacement craft and seaplanes, used or capable of being used as a means of transportation on water.

Power-driven vessel: Any vessel propelled by machinery.

Sailing vessel: Any vessel under sail, provided that propelling machinery is not being used.

Vessel engaged in fishing: A craft fishing with nets, lines, trawls, or any other apparatus that restricts maneuverability. This does not include vessels with fishing apparatus that does not restrict maneuverability, such as trolling lines.

Seaplane: Any aircraft designed to maneuver on the water.

Vessel not under command: A craft unable to maneuver as required by the rules and which cannot keep out of the way of another vessel.

Vessel restricted in its ability to maneuver: A craft whose maneuverability is restricted because of work such as underway replenishment, air operations, mine clearance, towing, working navigation marks, or laying submarine cable/pipeline.

Vessel constrained by draft: A power-driven vessel severely restricted in its ability to maneuver because of the relation between draft and depth of water (international rules only).

Underway vessel: A vessel not at anchor, made fast to the shore, or aground.

***Rule 4: Application.*** The steering and sailing rules apply in any condition of visibility.

***Rule 5: Lookout.*** Every vessel must at all times maintain a proper lookout by sight and hearing as well as by all available means appropriate in the prevailing circumstances and conditions so as to make a full appraisal of the situation and the risk of collision.

***Rule 6: Safe Speed.*** All vessels must travel at a safe speed to enable them to "take proper and effective action to avoid collision and be stopped within a distance appropriate to the prevailing circumstances and conditions." The factors that should be taken into account in determining safe speed include visibility; traffic density; the maneuverability of the vessel; background light at night; the state of the wind, sea, and current; the proximity of navigational hazards;

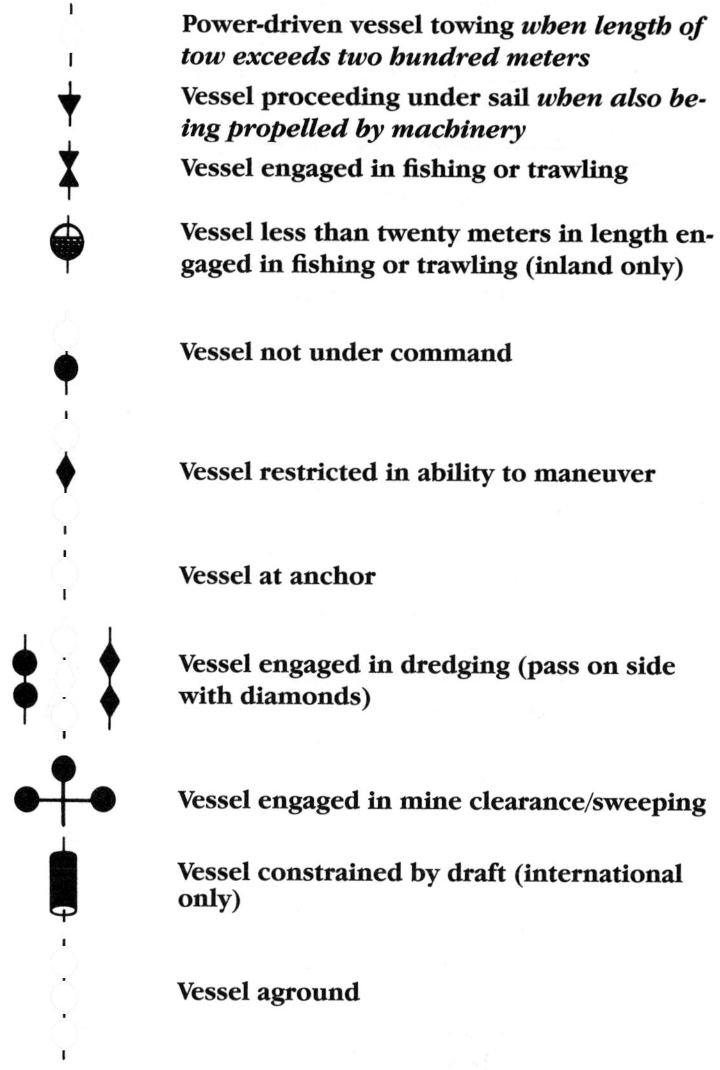

Power-driven vessel towing *when length of tow exceeds two hundred meters*

Vessel proceeding under sail *when also being propelled by machinery*

Vessel engaged in fishing or trawling

Vessel less than twenty meters in length engaged in fishing or trawling (inland only)

Vessel not under command

Vessel restricted in ability to maneuver

Vessel at anchor

Vessel engaged in dredging (pass on side with diamonds)

Vessel engaged in mine clearance/sweeping

Vessel constrained by draft (international only)

Vessel aground

**Figure 10-1. Day Shapes. These are international and inland, unless otherwise indicated.**

and draft in relation to the depth of water. If there is radar aboard, factors relating to radar must be taken into account.

**Rule 7: Risk of Collision.** All vessels must use "all means available . . . to determine if risk of collision exists." If there is any doubt, risk is deemed to exist. Radar must be properly used. A factor to consider is whether the compass bearing of an approaching vessel changes appreciably. Risk sometimes exists even when an appreciable bearing change is evident, particularly when one vessel is approaching a very large vessel or tow or a vessel at close range.

**Rule 8: Action to Avoid Collision.** Any such action should be positive and made in ample time; an alteration of course and/or speed should be readily apparent to another vessel observing visually or by radar. A succession of small alterations of course and/or speed should be avoided. The effectiveness of such action must be carefully checked until the other vessel is finally past and clear. To avoid collision or allow more time to assess the situation, a vessel should slacken speed or take all way off by stopping or reversing engines.

**Rule 9: Narrow Channels.** Keep to starboard. Smaller ships must not impede the passage of larger ones constrained to the channel. Fishing and crossing vessels must not impede a channel. Overtaking vessels still give way. Avoid anchoring in a narrow channel.

**Rule 10: Traffic Separation Schemes.** These specific rules should be reviewed prior to entering such waters. You must remain in assigned lanes, join or leave at a slight angle, and cross at a right angle. Avoid separation zones altogether.

**Rule 11: Application.** This entire section (Conduct of Vessels in Sight of One Another) applies to vessels in sight of one another.

**Rule 12: Sailing Vessels.** This gives specifics of sailing rules of the road having to do with wind.

**Rule 13: Overtaking.** Any vessel overtaking another must keep out of the way of the vessel being overtaken. Being overtaken is defined as coming up with another vessel from a direction more than 22.5 degrees abaft her beam. At night, the overtaking vessel would be able to see only the stern light of the vessel being overtaken and not the sidelights. If in doubt, you are overtaking and should behave accordingly. Any subsequent alteration of the relationship between the two ships does not change the responsibility of the original overtaker

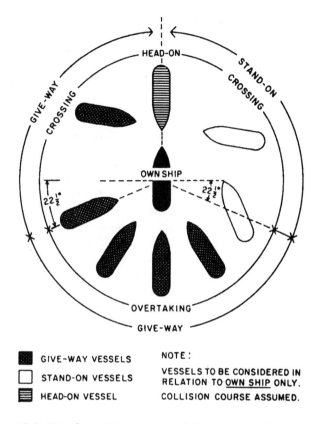

**Figure 10-2. Head-on, Crossing, and Overtaking Situations**

to keep out of the way until finally past and clear of the vessel being overtaken. See figure 10-2.

***Rule 14 Head-On Situation.*** This is defined as two vessels meeting on reciprocal or nearly reciprocal courses involving the risk of collision. Both should alter to starboard so that each will pass the other on the port side. The situation occurs when one vessel sees another ahead or nearly ahead, and by night sees masthead lights in a line, or nearly so, and both sidelights. If any doubt exists, assume a head-on situation exists.

***Rule 15: Crossing Situation.*** When crossing with risk of collision, the vessel that has the other on its starboard side must keep out of the way and, if circumstances permit, avoid crossing ahead of the other vessel. This normally means that the vessel having the other on its port hand is "privileged" ("stand on"). This is a simple mnemonic: Port hand privileged. Generally, the correct course for the give-way vessel is to turn to starboard, thus passing astern of the stand-on vessel. (The stand-on vessel is the one maintaining course and speed.)

***Rule 16: Action by Give-Way Vessel.*** When you are the give-way vessel, take early and substantial action to keep well clear. This should be obvious to the other vessel both visually and on its radar.

***Rule 17: Action by Stand-On Vessel.*** When it becomes apparent that the give-way vessel isn't getting out of the way, the stand-on vessel *may* take action to avoid collision by its maneuver alone. The stand-on vessel *must* take action when the situation reaches a stage where the give-way vessel's action alone cannot avoid collision. To avoid collision in a crossing situation, a craft shouldn't alter course to port for a vessel on its port side. Nothing in this rule relieves the give-way vessel of the obligation to keep out of the way.

***Rule 18: Responsibilities Between Vessels.*** The simplest means of understanding the relative responsibilities of vessels is a list going from the most privileged vessel (gives way to no other) to the least privileged (gives way to all others).

| *International* | *Inland* |
| --- | --- |
| Vessels aground/anchored | Vessels aground/anchored |
| Vessels not under command | Vessels not under command |
| Vessels restricted in ability to mancuver | Vessels restricted in ability to maneuver |
| Air operations | Air operations |
| Alongside operations | Alongside operations |
| Underwater operations | Underwater operations |
| Minesweeping | Minesweeping |
| Towing (restricted) | Towing (restricted) |
| Vessels constrained by draft | Does not apply inland |
| Vessels fishing/trawling | Vessels fishing/trawling |
| Sailing vessels under sail | Sailing vessels under sail |

Power-driven vessels        Power-driven vessels
   Seaplane                    Seaplane

**Rule 19: Conduct of Vessels in Restricted Visibility.**   This applies when vessels are not in sight of one another when in or near an area of restricted visibility. A vessel should proceed at a safe speed adapted for conditions of restricted visibility, with engines ready for immediate maneuver; use radar to determine the risk of collision and take appropriate action; avoid altering course to port for a vessel forward of the beam, except when overtaking; and avoid altering course toward a vessel abeam or abaft the beam. Whenever a fog signal is heard forward of the beam, the vessel should reduce speed to bare steerageway and if necessary take all way off.

**Rule 20: Application.**   This covers lights and shapes and discusses the application period for them. Lights are on sunset to sunrise only, except in restricted visibility. Shapes should be displayed during the day.

**Rule 21: Definition.**   This defines lights as follows.

Masthead light: white, 225 degrees (that is, covered by the light), 22.5 degrees abaft the beam each side.

Sidelights: red/green, 112.5 degrees, 22.5 degrees abaft the beam each side.

Stern light: white, 135 degrees, 67.5 degrees forward each side.

Towing light: yellow, 135 degrees, 67.5 degrees forward each side.

All round: white, 360 degrees.

Flashing: yellow, 120 flashes per minute.

Special flashing (inland only): yellow, 50 to 70 flashes per minute.

**Rule 22: Visibility of Lights.**   This gives ranges of lights as follows.

*Vessel greater than fifty meters*

| | |
|---|---|
| Masthead | 6 miles |
| Sidelight | 3 miles |
| Stern light | 3 miles |
| Towing | 3 miles |
| White, red, green, or yellow (as required) | 3 miles |
| Special flash (as required, inland only) | 2 miles |

*Vessel greater than twelve meters but less than fifty meters*

| | |
|---|---|
| Masthead | 5 miles |
| Vessel less than twenty meters | 3 miles |
| Sidelight | 2 miles |
| Stern light | 2 miles |
| Towing light | 2 miles |
| White, red, green, or yellow (as required) | 2 miles |
| Special flash (as required, inland only) | 2 miles |

*Vessel less than twelve meters*

| | |
|---|---|
| Masthead | 2 miles |
| Sidelight | 1 mile |
| Stern light | 2 miles |
| Towing light | 2 miles |
| White, red, green, or yellow light | 2 miles |

*Inconspicuous, partly submerged, or objects being towed*

| | |
|---|---|
| White all-round light | 3 miles |

**Rule 23: Power-Driven Vessels Under Way.**    While the best method of studying the rules of lights is to use a well-illustrated guide such as *Farwell's Rules of the Road,* some basic guidelines are set out here and in the rules that follow.

Power-driven vessel: A larger power-driven vessel (greater than fifty meters) must have sidelights, a stern light, and a second masthead light abaft of and higher than the forward one.

Air-cushion vessel: This craft should show the all-round flashing yellow light where it can best be seen.

Small vessel: Generally, a small vessel will show a single all-round white light and sidelights if possible.

**Rule 24: Towing and Pushing Vessels.**    A towing vessel should have two white lights with a diamond day shape and a yellow towing light astern. In inland waters, two yellow stern lights are added.

**Rule 25: Sailing Vessels Under Way and Vessels Under Oars.**    The mnemonic for sailing lights is "Red over green, sailing queen." The red over green, however, is optional. The day shape (when a sailboat is under power) is a small cone pointing down at the engine.

**Rule 26: Fishing Vessels.** "Green over white, trawling at night; red over white, fishing at night"—so the mnemonic goes. The day shape is two black cones with their points together, or a basket for vessels under twenty meters (sixty feet).

**Rule 27: Vessels Not Under Command or Restricted in Their Ability to Maneuver.** Not under command: "Red over red, the captain is dead" is the operative mnemonic, with two black balls as the corresponding day shape.

Restricted in ability to maneuver: Red over white over red for lights, with a corresponding day shape of ball-diamond-ball. If a dredge is working, the side to pass on has two green lights, the fouled side two red. There are two diamonds on the good side and two balls on the fouled side ("diamonds are better than pearls"). A vessel towing or conducting aviation or alongside operations exhibits the same lights and day shapes. Minesweeping operations require three green lights, one masthead light, and one light on each side of the operation area, with black balls for day shapes.

**Rule 28: Vessels Constrained by Draft.** These require three red lights in a vertical display by night, or a single black cylinder/can by day (shown only in international waters).

**Rule 29: Pilot Vessels.** "White over red, pilot ahead" is the mnemonic. If at anchor, the vessel displays a single black ball.

**Rule 30: Anchored Vessels and Vessels Aground.** Anchored vessels display a single white light forward and high in the ship, unless they are greater than fifty meters, in which case they display a second white light aft and lower than the after white light. The day shape for a vessel at anchor is a single black ball. Aground vessels display "Red over red, navigator's dead," with three black balls ("one for the captain, one for the executive officer, and one for the navigator") for the day shape.

**Rule 31: Seaplanes.** Do the best you can; exhibit lights and day shapes as similar in characteristics and position as possible.

**Rule 32: Definitions.** This rule defines a few terms for sound and light signals.

Whistle: Any sound-signaling appliance that meets certain technical specifications.

Short blast: One second.
Prolonged blast: Four to six seconds.

**Rule 33: Equipment for Sound Signals.** A vessel longer than twelve meters requires a whistle and bell; one longer than one hundred meters also requires a gong. A craft less than twelve meters requires some means of signaling.

**Rule 34: Maneuvering and Warning Signals.** This rule marks the greatest point of divergence between the international and inland rules. In international rules, the signals demonstrate immediate action; in inland rules, the signals demonstrate intent and must be agreed on by the parties involved. Briefly, the international rules are as follows:

One short: "I am altering my course to starboard."
Two short: "I am altering my course to port."
Three short: "I am operating astern propulsion."

The international overtaking sequence is as follows:

Two prolonged, one short: "I intend to overtake you on your starboard side."
Two prolonged, two short: "I intend to overtake you on your port side."
One prolonged, one short, one prolonged, one short: "Agreement."
Five or more short: "Danger."
One prolonged: "Blind bend."

The inland rules for vessels within sight of one another and meeting or crossing within half a mile of each other are briefly as follows:

One short: "I intend to leave you on my port side."
Two short: "I intend to leave you on my starboard side."
Three short: "I am operating astern propulsion."
Same signal in return: "Agreement."
One short: "I intend to overtake you on your starboard side."
Two short: "I intend to overtake you on your port side."
Same signal in return: "Agreement."

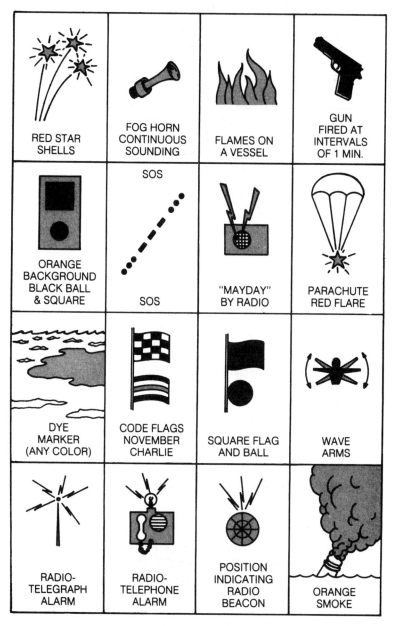

**Figure 10-3. Distress Signals (72 COLREGS)**

Five short: "Danger."
One prolonged: "Blind bend."

### Rule 35: Sound Signals in Restricted Visibility.

| Vessel | Signal |
|---|---|
| Power driven, making way | One prolonged, two minutes |
| Power driven, under way, not making way | Two prolonged, two minutes |
| Not under command, restricted sailing, fishing, towing | One prolonged, two short, two minutes |
| Towing | One prolonged, three short |
| Anchored | Bell forward, gong aft Optional prolonged-short-prolonged |
| Aground | Anchorage plus three strokes on the bell before and after the rapid ringing of the bell |
| Piloting | Four short |

**Rule 36: Signals to Attract Attention.**   Vessels should make a sound or light signal to attract attention and not embarrass any vessel in the process.

**Rule 37: Distress Signals.**   See figure 10-3.

**Rule 38: Exemptions.**   This sets out a few exemptions to light requirements for older vessels.

**Annex 1: Positioning and Technical Details of Lights and Shapes.**

**Annex II: Additional Signals for Fishing Vessels Fishing in Close Proximity.**

**Annex III: Technical Details of Sound-Signal Appliances.**

**Annex IV: Distress Signals.**   See figure 10-3.

**Annex V: Pilot Rules.**   These are inland rules only.

**COLREGS Demarcation Lines.**   These lay out the exact lines between international and inland rules based on geographic points in the United States.

**Vessel Bridge-to-Bridge Radiotelephone.**   This gives details of operating bridge-to-bridge radiotelephones. As a general rule, in U.S. waters, a radiotelephone set on channel 13 is required for most vessels, particularly power-driven ones over three hundred tons, passenger vessels over one hundred tons, and towing vessels over twenty-six tons. Dredges and floating plants likewise have radiotelephones.

Other administrative information (penalty provisions, duties related to casualty assistance, injunctions) is also included in the COL-REG publication.

# 11

## ENGINEERING

At the heart of any ship is an engineering plant that moves the hull through the water, makes fresh water from the sea, provides electrical power and hotel services, and in general permits the ship to perform her mission and support her crew. Over the past fifteen years, an increasing number of frontline U.S. Navy and Coast Guard warships have been commissioned with gas-turbine and diesel-propulsion plants. Additionally, a large number of U.S. ships have steam-propulsion plants. A small number are nuclear powered.

While it is impractical and unnecessary to elaborate in this small volume on the details of running each type of engineering plant, it is useful for the deck watch officer to have solid knowledge of the plants as well as broad knowledge of engineering casualty control, damage control, and general propulsion/auxiliary issues. The discussion that follows is aimed at the nonengineering officer of the watch. Volumes that offer more detail for the watch officer include *Introduction to Naval Engineering* and *Engineering for the Officer of the Deck* (Naval Institute Press). One particularly good reference work on engineering is a new book from the Naval Institute Press entitled *Ready to Answer All Bells: A Blueprint for Successful Naval Engineering*, by Lieutenant Commander David Bruhn. Published in 1997, this fine work is highly recommended. The intent here is to provide quick reference on basic engineering issues as they pertain to the topside watch.

## RELATIONSHIP OF THE OOD AND THE
## ENGINEERING OFFICER OF THE WATCH

The engineering officer of the watch (EOOW) is one of the principal assistants to the OOD. He or she reports directly to the watch officer, generally via an MC circuit ("bitch box"), growler, or telephone. The EOOW is also responsible to the engineering officer for the safe operation of the plant and the execution of the engineer's and captain's standing orders for propulsion and auxiliary systems. In the course of a normal watch the OOD and EOOW converse several times, generally about routine shifts in equipment status in the plant, minor problems or concerns, and routine reports. The requirements vary from ship to ship and plant to plant. The documents that shape the routine reports flowing between the EOOW and OOD are the standing orders of the commanding officer (CO), the engineer's standing orders, the night orders of the CO and the engineer, and the Standard Ship's Organization and Regulations Manual (SORM).

In an emergency, the EOOW normally makes his or her first report of a casualty or problem to the watch officer, and it is the responsibility of the OOD to pass the information to the CO and take whatever action is necessary from the bridge. The EOOW is generally responsible for informing the chief engineer of the problem; the engineer then informs the captain in far greater detail as to the nature of and solution to the problem. To give an example. . . .

The EOOW of a cruiser is informed that there is a hot lineshaft bearing on the No. 2 shaft. The EOOW informs the OOD of the casualty and begins engineering operational sequencing system (EOSS) procedures. The OOD calls the CO and informs him or her of the casualty and the impact on the ship's maneuverability. The OOD takes maneuvering action to slow the ship if necessary, informs the officer in tactical command (OTC) and other ships in company if necessary, and avoids shipping if necessary. The EOOW then calls the engineer, who generally proceeds either to the central control station (central, or CCS) or to the vicinity of the casualty to assess the situation. The engineer subsequently calls the CO to explain the cause of the problem (faulty temperature sensor, replacing sensor, estimated time of repair twenty minutes, etc.) and its impact on the ship's ability to maneuver. The EOOW then calls the OOD to give a more detailed explanation of the casualty and to mention any constraints on the plant.

Communications between the EOOW and the watch officer must be concise and clearly understood. They should be repeated over the circuit so that both watch stations are in full agreement as to the information that was passed. An example: The EOOW informs the OOD, "Bridge, Central, I have a hot lineshaft bearing, bearing 2D, request you slow to standard." The OOD replies, "Central, Bridge, hot lineshaft bearing 2D, slowing to standard, aye." And the EOOW confirms: "Central, aye."

By constantly practicing the repeat-back method, even during routine conversations, the OOD and the EOOW see to it that during an emergency the information will be accurate and quickly passed.

The watch officer must also learn to let the EOOW handle a crisis as it occurs and to avoid demanding an excessive amount of information during the critical early seconds of a casualty. At that time, the EOOW is focused on keeping the plant stable, and the last thing he or she needs is a constant drumbeat of questions and comments from the pilothouse. The watch officer who falls into this may be trying to keep the captain informed, but he or she needs to realize that when the situation has stabilized, the EOOW will be calling the CO with a full explanation. Far better than badgering is to let the EOOW get initial responses and begin casualty control.

The watch officer's real concerns in the event of a casualty are simple: to gather enough information to give the captain a quick report, recognizing that more detail will shortly be coming from the engineer; to understand any maneuvering implications of the casualty, for example, a locked shaft or the loss of an engine on a shaft; and to foresee anything that could suddenly affect the routine of the ship, for example, a fuel leak. Beyond this, the EOOW must be permitted to correct the casualty and restore the plant to full readiness.

If the watch officer has a problem with an EOOW that he or she believes is not forthcoming with information or is uncooperative, the situation should be discussed with the senior watch officer or engineering officer upon conclusion of the watch. The wrong thing is to enter into prolonged confrontation with the EOOW during the watch.

## BASIC ENGINEERING KNOWLEDGE

There is a body of basic knowledge that each watch officer should have about the plant over which he or she is ultimately responsible. In the Navy, this is the knowledge a junior engineering officer of the watch (JEOOW) should have as part of the personnel qualification system (PQS), and it is fundamental to the proper execution of the watch. Watch officers are generally tested by a qualification board prior to assuming the watch. While not extensive or all-inclusive (because, after all, an EOOW is always on duty as a reference source for the OOD), this knowledge must be mastered by the watch officer. Until it is fully committed to memory, the watch officer may want to jot down particulars on index cards, which can be carried in a pocket for referral and study.

While this information varies, as a baseline each watch officer should know the following:

*Propulsion.* The basic method of propulsion, amount of shaft horsepower generated, number of engines/boilers, basic drive train, basic thermodynamic cycle, steering system, main lubricating-oil system, shafting and bearing supports for the main shafts, fuel-oil filling and distribution system, and aviation-fuel filling and distribution system.

*Electrical.* The number of generators, specifications for generators, the basic configuration of the electrical distribution system, the layout of load centers, the power source for critical loads (steering, vital combat systems, propulsion systems, etc.), special frequency systems (400-Hz generators, distribution), the emergency power supply (emergency diesels, uninterruptable power supply, etc.), the casualty power-distribution system, and the degaussing system.

*Auxiliaries.* The number of evaporators, the rating, the amount of feed and fresh, air conditioners, dry air, chill water, air compressors (high pressure and low pressure), and main and secondary drainage systems.

*Damage Control.* Major systems (HALON, installed carbon dioxide, AFFF/FP180, HICAP, etc.), the capabilities of each, the use of portable firefighting systems, the fire-main layout, the number of fire pumps, normal pressure, installed educators, ventilation, and the countermeasure washdown system.

***Engineering Control.*** The layout of central, the location of control mechanisms for most major engineering systems, and a basic understanding of controls for key equipment.

In addition to or in place of index cards, many ships publish an engineering department handbook that includes the information indicated above. Similarly, many ships have a damage-control handbook with a great deal of useful information.

## THE GAS-TURBINE PLANT

The advantages of a gas-turbine plant include its light weight and compact structure, extremely quick startup times, relative quietness, minimal manpower requirements, easily replaceable engines, reliability, efficiency at high rates of speed, and cleanliness. Some of the disadvantages include the requirement for a lot of fuel storage, inefficiency when there are small or partial loads, huge consumption of air, which can be dangerous in a nuclear/biological/chemical (NBC) environment, and mechanical problems with the controllable reversible-pitch propeller system and clutches (especially in the DD 963 class).

From the perspective of the watch officer, the major advantages of the gas-turbine plant are rapidity of response and operations that are almost casualty-free. Because the throttle control for propulsion gas-turbine engines is normally on the bridge, response to engineering commands is virtually instantaneous. The ship moves ahead and astern within seconds of the throttle movement on the bridge. The engineering plant is unusually reliable. The OOD will encounter a few basic casualties, but the likelihood of major shaft-stopping problems is minimal. With two engines available on each of twin shafts in most plants, it takes only moments to start one engine if there is a problem with the other.

## THE CONVENTIONAL STEAM PLANT

The advantages of a steam plant include efficiency at cruising speed, reliability, reasonable efficiency at partial loading, and the usefulness of steam for auxiliary systems (heating, distilling, etc.). Disadvantages include the size of the plant, its startup time, the requirement for large fuel tanks, low endurance at high speeds, inefficiency at lower speeds, and above all, the manpower requirement.

Steam, dependable and effective as a means of propulsion, will be used in the foreseeable future on many older ships and some new warships. In the nuclear variant (discussed below), steam propulsion will be used for the largest surface combatants (aircraft carriers) and submarines. Some of the casualties associated with steam plants require a watch officer to slow the ship considerably. The watch officer provides permission for the EOOW to conduct blowdowns, light off and secure boilers and generators, pump bilges, and place vital machinery or equipment out of commission for preventive maintenance.

## THE NUCLEAR STEAM PLANT

The advantages of a nuclear steam plant include, above all, endurance, the lack of requirement for air during combustion (rendering it safe during NBC warfare), and reliability. Disadvantages include the cost of construction, maintenance, and training of the work force to maintain the plant; weight; startup time; radiological and environmental problems and risks; and the length of overhauls.

The nuclear steam plant is reliable and run by specialists. The relationship between the watch officer and the EOOW is similar to that associated with other plants.

## THE DIESEL PLANT

The advantages of a diesel plant include exceptional efficiency at all loads, low cost, smaller reduction gears, reliability, low manning levels, and simplicity of adaptation. Disadvantages include the amount of maintenance and the frequency of overhauls, the consumption of an inordinate amount of lubricating oil, noise (especially disadvantageous for ships involved in antisubmarine warfare or convoy duty), and problems resulting from the need to drive a single shaft with three or more diesels.

## THE ENGINEERING OPERATIONAL
## SEQUENCING SYSTEM (EOSS)

The watch officer needs a basic appreciation of the concept of EOSS. The complexity of the modern plant requires standardized guidelines for normal operations and casualties. Watchstanders in the engineering plant are provided with specific checklists and step-by-step procedures to deal with every conceivable situation.

The two parts of EOSS that the watch officer may hear about from the engineer are engineering operational procedure (EOP), which covers normal activities such as starting a main engine, switching duplex strainers, and bringing a forced-draft blower on the line, and, of more importance to the watch officer, engineering operational casualty control (EOCC). EOCC refers to actions watchstanders take in the event of a casualty in the plant. Engineering watchstanders memorize the immediate actions required and, in the event of a casualty, immediately inform the watch officer on the bridge of any actions required there. Once the casualty is under control, specific recovery steps outlined in the EOCC are followed.

## UNDERSTANDING THE ENGINEERING OFFICER OF THE WATCH

A quick review of this excerpt from OpNavInst 3120.32C is always useful for the officer of the deck. It provides an excellent overview of what your counterpart down in engineering is doing. Because most OODs go on to become EOOWs, it is also helpful from a professional perspective.

> BASIC FUNCTION. The Engineering Officer of the Watch (EOOW) is the officer or petty officer on watch designated by the Engineer Officer to be in charge of an Engineering Department watch section. He/she is responsible for safe and proper performance of engineering department watches following the orders of the Engineer Officer, the Commanding Officer, and higher authority.
>
> b. DUTIES, RESPONSIBILITIES, AND AUTHORITY. The Engineering Officer of the Watch shall:
>
> (1) Supervise personnel on watch in the Engineering Department (except damage control), ensuring that machinery is operated according to instructions, required logs are maintained, machinery and controls are properly manned, and all applicable inspections and safety precautions are carried out.
>
> (2) Ensure that interior communications circuits are properly manned and that circuit discipline is maintained and correct procedures and terminology are followed.

(3) Ensure that all orders from the OOD concerning the speed and direction of rotation of the main engines are executed promptly and properly.

(4) Immediately execute all emergency orders concerning the speed and direction of rotation of the screws.

(5) Immediately inform the OOD and the Engineer Officer of any casualty which would prevent the execution of engine speed orders or would affect the operational capability of the ship.

(6) Ensure that directives and procedures issued by higher authority which concern the operation of machinery in the Engineering Department are followed.

(7) Keep informed of the power requirements for operations. Ensure that the propulsion and auxiliary machinery combinations will effectively meet operational requirements. Advise the OOD and the Engineer Officer when any modification of the propulsion plant or major auxiliaries is required.

(8) Supervise and coordinate on-the-job training for engineering personnel on watch.

(9) Assume such other responsibilities as the Engineer Officer may direct.

(10) In addition, on nuclear-powered ships, the EOOW will also be governed by the requirements of the Engineering Department Manual for Nuclear Propulsion Plants (when applicable).

# 12

# THE WATCH OFFICER IN PORT

The Command Duty Officer in port is that officer or authorized Petty Officer designated by the Commanding Officer to carry out the routine of the unit in port and to supervise the Officer of the Deck in the safety and general duties of the unit. In the temporary absence of the Executive Officer, the duties of the Executive Officer will be carried out by the Command Duty Officer.

OpNavInst 3120.32C

## THE COMMAND DUTY OFFICER

The primary responsibility of the in-port duty section is the safety and security of the ship. The command duty officer (CDO), designated by the commanding officer, must lead watchstanders in discharging this responsibility. He or she customarily stands duty for a twenty-four-hour period and sets the tone for the duty section's performance. The CDO reports to the executive officer or, in that person's absence, the commanding officer. Routine reports made to the commanding officer by the OOD should also be made to the CDO. If the executive officer is temporarily absent, the heads of departments or their designated representatives report to the CDO concerning matters affecting the operation and administration of their departments. The CDO should conduct frequent inspections to ensure the safety and security of the ship. Additionally, he or she has the responsibility of drilling duty emergency parties.

Clearly, this is a critical position that requires a great deal of preparation. Navy regulations state that the CDO is an officer eligible for command. In fact, the CDO may be required to get the ship under way on a moment's notice; although he or she rarely takes this action, the possibility shows how well prepared a CDO must be to accept the responsibilities of the watch. A good CDO does not execute responsibilities from the confines of the wardroom but rather makes frequent rounds of the ship and keeps informed as to her status. Commanding officers and executive officers have specific guidelines for the CDO; the following suggestions can help him or her maintain high standards for the duty section:

1. The CDO should conduct frequent and random inspections throughout the ship, keeping an eye out for hazards, cleanliness, crew appearance, work in progress, material condition, and shipwide security.

2. The CDO should always inform the quarterdeck of his or her whereabouts and how he or she may be contacted.

3. The CDO should attempt to be on the quarterdeck for the arrival and departure of the commanding officer and executive officer so that they can pass along any necessary information.

4. The CDO should pay close attention to drills by emergency response teams and critique them. He or she should be creative, vary the scenario to cover common contingencies, and remember to have the rescue-and-assistance team train.

5. The CDO should inform the commanding and executive officers if a drill will be conducted while they are on board. This courtesy goes a long way to alleviating their anxiety when a drill is called away.

6. The CDO should be on deck to observe special evolutions such as colors and sunrise. These evolutions are a sign of a ship's pride and professionalism, and the CDO's personal interest always helps to make them run smoothly and efficiently.

7. The CDO should watch for sudden and unexpected changes in weather (particularly a change in barometric pressure readings of .04 or more in any one hour). This is critical if boat operations are being conducted.

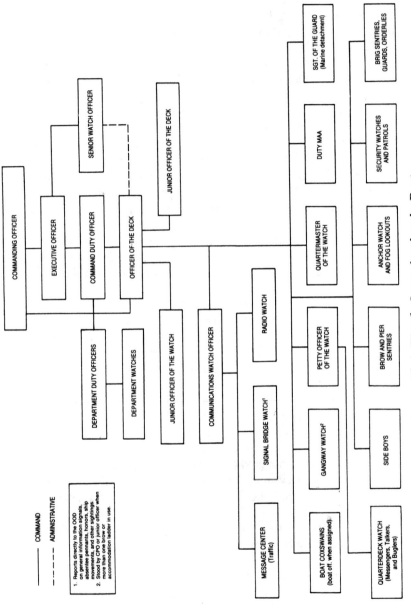

**Figure 12-1. Watch Organization in Port**

8. The CDO should know the status of the ship's boats at all times.

9. The CDO should frequently spot-check hazardous storage areas to ensure proper storage of volatile material.

10. The CDO should always know the status of the engineering plant and frequently check it.

11. The CDO should require the quarterdeck to inform him or her immediately of any changes in fire-main pressure or any unusual readings observed by sounding-and-security or roving patrols.

12. The CDO should mentally prepare to respond to emergencies and should have emergency telephone numbers, such as those of the base fire department, ambulance, security, and chaplain, within reach.

13. The CDO should ensure that preparations are made for upcoming events. For example, if the ship expects to get under way the following day, he or she should make sure that arrangements have been made to clear away paint floats, doughnuts, etc. The CDO should think at least one day ahead of the duty day.

14. If in doubt, the CDO should call the commanding officer or executive officer for assistance.

The CDO sets the standards for the duty section. Slovenly appearance, lack of interest in drills and exercises, or a lethargic attitude toward duty will be reflected by the watch team. On the other hand, an exuberant, visible, and concerned CDO will lead the way to a taut and safe watch.

## THE OFFICER OF THE DECK

The officer of the deck in port is that officer or petty officer on watch designated by the Commanding Officer to be in charge of the unit. He/she is primarily responsible for the safety and proper operation of the unit.

OpNavInst 3120.32C

When a ship is in port, the OOD's responsibilities are considerably less complex than when she is at sea. This does not mean, however, that the job is any less demanding. Though not faced with tactical problems, maneuvering, or signals, the OOD in port is occupied with a seemingly endless series of things to supervise, inspect, and control. He or she is expected to make timely and sound decisions on matters that are, in their own way, nearly as important as anything that happens at sea. If the OOD is to stand watch properly, he or she must be at least as well prepared as at sea and must be ready to respond quickly to a variety of situations.

A chief petty officer or petty officer who is assigned as OOD in port has the same status as a commissioned or warrant officer so assigned, and his or her orders have the same force. This person is designated in writing by the commanding officer and in most ships is required to complete the section of the surface-warfare officer's personnel qualification standards test that relates to the OOD in port.

## PREPARING FOR THE WATCH

Considerable preparation in the form of reviewing ship's routine, receiving instructions from local commanders and from the senior officer present afloat (SOPA), and learning policy concerning special situations is necessary before taking over a deck watch in port. The basic information that the OOD needs is usually kept in a notebook on the quarterdeck. Some of the most important things that OODs in port must consider are listed below; experience or special circumstances will suggest others.

If the ship is pierside, the OOD should know:

1. Evolutions that may occur during the watch.
2. The status of visitors.
3. Quarterdeck search procedures in effect.
4. The local security climate.
5. The last time security watches reported.
6. The status of the ship's propulsion machinery.
7. Current material condition of readiness.
8. Who the SOPA is and what other commanders and flagships are present.
9. What flags and pennants are flying.
10. The status of crew aloft, crew over the side, or divers in the water.
11. What guard ships (military, medical, etc.) are present, what radio circuits are guarded, and whether visual guards are posted.

12. What services the ship is receiving from the pier.

13. The status of all boats in the water, in skids, out of commission, away on trips, scheduled for trips, and so forth, and the status of fuel in boats.

14. The status of ship's vehicles—location, drivers, trips planned, fuel, and so forth.

15. The weather, and changes anticipated.

16. The amount of rise and fall of the tide, the state of the tide, and the time of the next change in the tide.

17. The status of aircraft.

18. Who the CDO is and how he or she may be reached.

19. The status of ship's restricted crew, prisoners, or medical cases.

20. What orders are currently in effect or unexecuted.

21. The location of the commanding and executive officers.

If the ship is at anchor, the OOD should also know:

1. The anchorage bearings.

2. The nature of the holding ground, the depth of water, and the scope of chain on deck.

3. The position of the ship on the chart.

4. Anchor(s) in use.

5. Anchor(s) ready for letting go.

6. Steaming notice required.

7. Other ships present and their location.

8. When the ship is moored to a buoy or buoys, the amount of chain or wire used.

## SMART APPEARANCE

In port, more than at any other time, the initial impression a visitor receives is based almost solely on the appearance and smartness of the quarterdeck and the watch. This impression is all-encompassing: It is created by crew, officers, and captain. Thus the appearance of a ship, her boats, and her crew is a major responsibility of the OOD. He or she must not only know the proper standards of cleanliness and smartness but also enforce them. It takes little practice to note such things as loose bits of line, slack halyards, and sloppy execution of the colors ceremony. But it takes energy, initiative, and patience to correct them. Junior officers vary in their powers of observation and in their attitude about action. The better an officer's reputation for standing a taut watch and for being intolerant of anything that downgrades the ship, the more readily the crew will respond. An officer with such a reputation is not likely to have watchstanders on the quarterdeck in frayed or soiled uniforms, or to allow crew on liberty that are not properly groomed. He or she will, in short, find high standards easy to maintain. On the other hand, an officer who is slovenly and does not have the pride to stand a proper watch will be continually beset. Superiors will be constantly calling him or her on the appearance of the ship, and the crew will not be responsive. Every officer should resolve early on to run a taut and efficient watch. People respect an officer who knows his or her job and performs it fairly and pleasantly, but in accordance with directives and the traditionally high standards of the Navy.

## WATCH ORGANIZATION

The Commanding Officer will establish the watches necessary for the safety, security, and proper operation of the command.

OpNavInst 3120.32C

Prior to taking over a watch, the OOD must find out what watches are being manned, who is manning them, and to whom each watchstander reports. Because few watch teams are centered in one place, as they are when the ship is under way, this information is important for getting the watch started smoothly. The oncoming OOD should be informed of any changes to the watch bill that have been authorized, of watches posted for special evolutions, and of watch conditions that differ from those promulgated in the plan of the day.

### The Petty Officer of the Watch

The petty officer of the watch is the primary enlisted assistant to the officer of the deck in port. When assigned, the Boatswain's Mate of the Watch and/or the Quartermaster of the Watch will carry out the duties of the petty officer of the watch.

OpNavInst 3120.32C

The petty officer of the watch (POOW) is the OOD's right-hand person and should be given responsibility for overall supervision of the watch team. The POOW is usually the person closest to the OOD in qualification and experience, and is specifically responsible for assisting him or her in training and inspecting the watch. If properly trained and briefed by the OOD, the POOW can serve as a second pair of eyes and double-check the ship's routine. In addition to the duties required by naval and ship's policy, such as log keeping and supervising boats, he or she should be, under the OOD, the leader of the watch team. The POOW is normally armed with a .45-caliber pistol.

## The Messenger of the Watch

Normally nonrated, the messenger of the watch is detailed by the OOD and the POOW to perform various routine duties, such as waking watch reliefs, escorting visitors, and periodically sprucing up the quarterdeck. Messengers should not be considered qualified until they have been aboard a ship long enough to know the location of all major working spaces, offices, staterooms, and other frequently visited areas. A sure way to give the impression of a sloppy ship is to provide a visitor with a messenger escort who does not know his or her way around. When a watch is expected to be unusually active, two messengers should be assigned.

## The Sounding-and-Security Patrol

The sounding-and-security patrol is required to make his or her rounds in a random fashion and to report to the OOD hourly. The small size of the average in-port duty section makes this duty particularly important. With most of the crew ashore on liberty, this watchstander is likely to be the only person in a position to discover flooding, fire, or a breach of the ship's security. Therefore, his or her performance should be closely monitored by the OOD and, whenever possible, double-checked by the POOW. It is a good practice for the OOD periodically to quiz the sounding-and-security watch to ensure that he or she is actually checking the spaces assigned. Failure of this watchstander to make a report to the quarterdeck must be immediately investigated.

## The Master-at-Arms

The duty master-at-arms is normally a petty officer first or second class who stands no other watches during the duty day. He or she is responsible for conducting periodic musters of restricted crew, supervising the performance of extra duty, and conducting a number of routine inspections of various spaces to check for cleanliness. When a working party is called away, the duty master-at-arms should be placed in charge of mustering and supervising it.

One of this person's most important duties is to enforce standards of order and discipline. When a disciplinary problem is discovered or suspected, the duty master-at-arms should be called away at once, given instructions by the OOD, and charged with investigating the situation. In cases of drunken or disorderly conduct the duty master-at-arms may be empowered to obtain assistance from other senior petty officers in the duty section.

## Cold-Iron Watch

In ships whose main machinery is inactive or that have no auxiliary watch on duty below, a "cold-iron watch" is stationed. This consists of members of the engineer watch who, at regular intervals, inspect all machinery spaces for violations of watertight integrity and for fire hazards.

## EXTERNAL SECURITY

In port, the security of the ship is one of the most important duties of the OOD. Threats to her security may be natural, caused by fire and heavy weather, or they may arise from an almost infinite range of deliberate human actions. Tight security is a necessity at all times, and no matter how quiet and uneventful a watch may seem, the OOD should never allow it to be relaxed. Of growing concern is the terrorist threat to U.S. naval vessels. No ship is ever immune to this threat, which can be carried out in a variety of unconventional ways. Fanatic America-haters are willing to die for their cause. The quarterdeck watch team must always assume that the danger of terrorism is present and must not allow lax security procedures.

If a breach in security is discovered, the OOD has a trained self-defense force. The type of ship and her mission determine who constitutes this force. Members are specifically designated and trained in security procedures, which the OOD should know and fully understand. The OOD should call away the security force if the ship or crew is in any way threatened. The team follows established procedures to ensure the security of the ship. The OOD should never hesitate to initiate a security alert; if there is any doubt, he or she should call it away. The OOD should also periodically drill this team at the discretion of the CDO.

## Control of Visitors

Commanding Officers are responsible for the control of visitors to their commands and shall comply with the relevant provisions of the Department of the Navy Security Manual for Classified Information and other pertinent directives.

Navy Regulations

Almost every naval vessel in commission must be prepared for the control, identification, and supervision of visitors. Depending on the security requirements in force, the OOD may be required to issue passes for visitors, check whether there is written authorization for them to come aboard, and provide them with escorts. No matter how busy the quarterdeck gets, the OOD must always maintain control over visitors. They should not be allowed to wander from the quarterdeck or to proceed without escort simply because they claim to know the way.

In general, dealers and tradespeople or their agents are admitted only as authorized by the commanding officer for the following purposes:

1. To conduct public business.

2. To transact private business with individuals at the request of the captain.

3. To furnish services and supplies that are not available to the personnel of the command or are not available in sufficient quantity.

Fleet and force regulations that restrict casual visiting and the approach of bumboats should be followed with great care. Persons with a legitimate reason to come on board must be received politely. Every person coming on board, even those in uniform or professing official or business connections, should present proper identification. The harder it is to screen visitors, the more important it is to observe precautions.

### Inspection of Packages and Personal Effects

The OOD is required to inspect all parcels, briefcases, and other items carried on board by both visitors and ship's company and, under some circumstances, to inspect those being carried off the ship. The OOD's authority is backed by federal regulation and there are no exceptions to it. Personal effects should be inspected for classified material, contraband, drugs, liquor, and weapons, as well as government property being removed from the ship without authorization. When circumstances dictate, body searches of all or randomly chosen persons may be carried out. If many people are to be inspected at one time, the duty master-at-arms should be called away to assist and to prevent congestion on the quarterdeck.

### Sentries and Guards

When sentries and armed guards are needed, the OOD usually has only to implement existing directives covering the use of forecastle, fantail, and pier sentries. All sentries must know the right way to challenge boats in order to identify their occupants before they come alongside. Forecastle and fantail sentries check mooring lines and make periodic reports to the OOD. Pier sentries control flow of personnel and traffic on the pier. All sentries may be armed when the situation demands. The OOD must be certain that armed sentries or guards are proficient in the use of their weapons and fully qualified in terms of personnel qualification standards and all other shipboard requirements.

### Sneak Attack and Sabotage

Particularly during darkness, ships at anchor or moored are vulnerable to various forms of sneak attack and sabotage conducted by swimmers, people in small boats, or submarines. Limpet mines can be attached to the hull of the ship, explosive charges can be placed below the ship, and mobile limpets can be used. Saboteurs may pose as bumboat crews or visitors, or they may mingle with a returning liberty party. Surreptitious boarding from the shore is possible when ships are moored to a pier. Attack may also consist of contamination of food and water supplies or destruction of vital equipment by explosives or other means.

Where such dangers exist, normal security measures must be increased. The OOD should maintain gangway security by considering all approaching boats, persons, and packages suspect until they have been identified and inspected. All unnecessary lines, fenders, and sea ladders should be taken in. Boats not in use should be hoisted in, and booms should be rigged out of reach of swimmers and boats. Guards should be posted at all topside openings and a party held in readiness to repel boarders. Automatic weapons should be manned and all personnel armed. Unnecessary noise should be avoided. Swimmers and explosive-ordnance-disposal teams may be assigned to inspect the ship's bottom, but only after sonar has been secured and all sentries and boats have been advised so as to prevent the dropping of explosive charges.

In case of attack, the highest degree of material readiness should be set, the rail manned with armed personnel, the SOPA and all ships present notified, and the ship made ready for getting under way immediately.

## INTERNAL SECURITY

The safety of a ship may be threatened by persons or forces within, particularly in times of international tension. The OOD should make sure that required patrols are carried out and reports made in person and on time. In addition to making routine checks of watertight closures and other safety devices, patrols should be alert to fire hazards and to the presence of combustibles that have not been properly stowed.

### Shipyard Security

Except in matters coming within security and safety regulations of the ship, the Commanding Officer shall exercise no control over the officers or employees of a naval shipyard or station where his ship is moored, unless with the permission of the Commander of the naval shipyard or station.

Navy Regulations

A ship under repair and overhaul in a shipyard has particular security problems. All workers coming on board must be identified. If their tools are stowed in racks on deck, they should be safeguarded by ship's sentries. Most shipyard workers are honest, but a small percentage might not be able to resist a souvenir or two, particularly if tools are left adrift. It must be the duty of the watch on deck to see that theft, by both ship and shipyard personnel, is prevented.

Compartments containing classified matter must be secured, either by lock or by sentry. There are times when yard workers have to enter locked spaces, and the OOD can anticipate such occasions by keeping reasonably well informed about the nature and location of the work being done. Fire watches are normally assigned to every welder and burner working on the ship. Another precaution that should be taken during shipyard work is the inspection of spaces after each shift for rubbish and any other material that may create a fire hazard.

### Custody of Keys

Custody of a ship's keys is carefully organized, and the OOD must fully understand how it works. Designated duty personnel have custody of some of the keys to their spaces. OpNavInst 3120.32C states that department heads must maintain a locker containing all the keys to their spaces. It also states that keys to that locker will be available to the OOD at all times for use in an emergency. The OOD must know who the duty keyholders are and what procedures to follow to gain access to secured spaces.

## ANCHORAGE AND MOORINGS

When the ship is anchored, moored, or secured to a pier or wharf, the OOD's greatest responsibilities concern the weather. At sea, the commanding officer makes the big decisions; in port, the OOD must often take action before the commanding officer can be advised of a situation.

Meteorological forecasts are not always available, nor can they be 100 percent accurate. They may even lull inexperienced officers into a false sense of security. The *actual* weather at the ship's position is the important factor, not the weather that is *forecast* for that position. It is advisable for the OOD to know what sort of weather can be expected in a certain area at a certain time of year. Pilot charts are one source of this information. There may be little possibility of winds over forty knots in San Diego Bay at any time, but at Adak, in the Aleutians, the wind can whip up to sixty knots almost any afternoon. Thus the OOD should inspect anchor chains or mooring lines as often as the weather dictates and take appropriate action to avert problems.

## Dragging

The most certain indication of dragging is a change in anchorage bearings, particularly those near the beam. These bearings should be checked at regular intervals even in good weather. Ships sometimes part their chain when letting go the anchor, then drag because only part of the anchor chain is holding. A dragging anchor can be detected by watching the chain or by feeling it on deck. The chain pulsates or jumps when the anchor is dragging, because the flukes are alternately taking hold and being pulled loose.

The major safeguards against collision or grounding caused by dragging are having (1) a second anchor ready to go and (2) steam at the throttle or a gas-turbine engine ready to start, the steering gear ready for use, and the engine room ready to answer bells. The latter course is expensive in personnel hours and fuel and should not be ordered without good cause. However, the OOD should not hesitate to inform the commanding officer of the possibility of dragging. The commanding officer will decide what precautionary measures to take.

A ship secured to a well-anchored mooring buoy by an anchor chain is not likely to be in danger unless the wind is exceedingly high. In severe weather, vessels as big as destroyers have been known to carry away from a mooring, generally because too little scope of chain was allowed. When the scope of chain is not long enough to provide a catenary, the sudden strain as the bow of the ship pitches is sufficient to part the chain or the chain stopper on deck. To counter the yaw that results from a long scope to the buoy, an anchor dropped straight down (under foot) is often useful.

## Heavy Weather

A ship alongside a pier or a wharf, with the standard mooring lines doubled up, is in little danger from high winds except in extreme cases. When heavy seas and high winds are anticipated, the OOD should do the following:

1. Request permission to hoist in all boats in the water, to trice up gangways, and to order boat-pool boats to return to their base or be secured astern on long painters.

2. Establish a special boat watch.

3. Call away the anchor detail and prepare to drop the anchor straight down if directed.

4. Put over storm wires, spring lays, or the anchor chain to augment mooring lines.

5. Try to get any camels that might be holding the ship off the pier removed.

6. Have all loose gear on deck secured and, if the ship is beginning to surge, be prepared to take in the brow.

7. Be prepared to disconnect shore power and shift to ship's power. Shore power cables placed under strain are liable to part, causing fires and explosions.

8. If extreme conditions are forecast, be prepared to light off one or more boilers to get under way when directed.

## HURRICANES AND TYPHOONS

When a hurricane or typhoon is moving into the area, the ship must either put to sea to avoid the storm or remain in port and ride it out. If the ship is to remain in port, she may move to a sheltered anchorage, in which case all preparations for getting under way should be made and the precautions listed above be carried out.

Preparations for riding out a storm, normally prescribed in the SOPA's instructions, include the following:

1. Double up the mooring lines and inspect them frequently.

2. Recall personnel to the ship and place the engineering plant and sea detail on standby.

3. Maintain radio and signal watches, man the radar, and keep a plot of the storm in the combat information center.

4. Police the dock area, secure topside gear, break out heavy-weather gear and flashlights, and inventory rescue-assistance lockers.

5. Maintain a plot of the storm's movements and brief the crew on them.

The anchorage should allow room for the ship to swing with the longest scope of chain available. Main engines should be used to off-set the wind, with revolutions per minute from three to five knots as required.

Bearings on shore, radar, drift lead, continuous echo soundings, and a continuous watch on the chain should all be used to detect signs of a dragging anchor.

## STORES AND FUEL

When stores are to be loaded, the OOD must make certain that the right people have been notified and are in charge. The deck force is responsible for operating gear and tackle, and the OOD should check to see that a competent boatswain's mate is on the job. The supply officer or that person's representative should check the stores aboard and direct their stowage.

When a ship is refueling in port, the OOD has clearly defined responsibilities for both safety and the prevention of spills. In coordination with the engineering officer, he or she should see that the required stations are manned for the detection of spills and that oil-recovery materials are available for use on short notice should a spill occur. The reports required and the telephone numbers to call in case of a fuel spill should be at hand on the quarterdeck. During fueling, the OOD is also responsible for displaying proper signals and passing the word restricting smoking.

## LIBERTY

Crews are granted liberty by sections. When a ship is in a foreign port, forward deployed, or in a high state of readiness, her crew is normally divided into three duty sections, two of which may be on liberty at a given time. This practice is followed because experience has taught that the minimum number of people required to get a ship under way is about one-third of her crew. In home port and when no special conditions of readiness are in effect, most ships have their crews divided into six duty sections, five of which may be on liberty at a given time. Regardless of prevailing conditions, the duty section left on board should always be big enough to fight fires, deal with emergencies, and carry out the ship's routine. If the OOD feels that this condition is not being met, the CDO should be informed immediately.

## Inspection of Liberty Parties

The OOD and the watch team have the primary responsibility for enforcing the Navy's and the ship's standards of dress and grooming. The OOD in port must continually inspect individuals going ashore and judge, using common sense and knowledge of the rules, whether someone should be permitted to go ashore or be turned back.

Fashions and styles of dress change, and considering the range of age groups and interests represented in most ships, it is almost impossible to lay down definitive standards for dress and grooming. However, it is reasonable to assume that the majority of any crew will respect reasonable standards, especially if they are equitably enforced by all deck watchstanders.

In foreign ports, the situation is slightly different. Because a sailor ashore represents his or her country, navy, and ship, the command has every right to expect that he or she will present an appearance that is a credit and not an embarrassment.

The return of liberty parties may be a routine matter or it may be a lively occasion. The OOD usually has only to identify the crew members. If the ship has just made port after a long voyage or is sailing the next day for an extended absence, there may be a few drunk celebrants. A master-at-arms or corporal of the guard should be detailed to get them off the quarterdeck and below quietly. The OOD must remain aloof and let experienced assistants handle most such matters. However, persistent troublemakers may require special attention, and direct orders may be needed to control them. Physical contact should be avoided, and enlisted watchstanders should be left to handle those who will not go below peaccfully. The people most in need of attention are those who are brought aboard apparently drunk. They should be taken to sick bay and examined; they may have head injuries or be under the influence of drugs instead of, or in addition to, being drunk. If necessary, the duty medical officer should be called to examine them. Matters of this sort are recorded fully in the log, together with a written medical report. An extremely drunk sailor should not be sent below without a watch; there is a danger that he or she may choke on vomit while sleeping.

## Loading Liberty Boats

While juniors in the Navy generally embark in boats and vehicles before their seniors, the procedure is sometimes reversed. When liberty parties are being loaded into boats or buses, the chief petty officers go first, followed by the other petty officers in descending order of rank. This practice enhances the prestige of the petty officers and provides them with a convenience that they well deserve. When many officers are waiting to go ashore, some junior officers may have to wait for the next boat to leave room for the senior officers.

## CREW'S MESS

Each meal served in the general mess shall be sampled by an officer detailed by the Commanding Officer for that purpose. Should he or she find the quality or quantity of food unsatisfactory, or should any member of the mess object to the quality or quantity of the food, the Commanding Officer shall be notified and shall take appropriate action.

Navy Regulations

It is normal procedure, when in port, for the CDO or the OOD to eat at least one meal in the crew's mess during the duty day. When under way, one of the watch officers should eat a meal with the crew daily. When an officer eats with the crew, he or she should note not only the quantity and quality of food being served but, equally important, the cleanliness and adequacy of mess gear, the manner in which food is served, and the cleanliness of food handlers. It is not unusual for a commanding officer to make an unannounced visit to the crew's mess and personally check these matters.

## Night Rations

It is customary to serve a night ration ("midrats") to the persons who have the midwatch. This helps them to stay awake and sustains them during tasks that are often just as demanding as those of the day. In cold weather, a warm ration is especially welcome to those going on or coming off watch topside, as well as to those standing watch in the engineering spaces.

## EIGHT O'CLOCK REPORTS

Eight o'clock reports are an important part of a ship's routine. They serve two functions: they confirm that security and damage-control inspections have been made, and they furnish the executive officer with information to make a report to the commanding officer on the condition of the ship at 2000.

The reports made to the executive officer or the CDO by the heads of departments at 2000 are known as eight o'clock reports, *not* twenty hundred reports. On many ships, they are taken at 1930 or even earlier.

## WORKING PARTIES

A ship's schedule often requires large working parties to complete without rest an evolution such as provisioning ship. The necessity is normally accepted by the crew with reasonable understanding. Many times, when only small groups are involved, the OOD can contribute to the well-being of the crew by considering their comfort. Leisure time and meal hours should be respected as much as possible. Crew members whose work is interrupted by a meal should not be required to change into another uniform just to eat, and those who miss a regular meal should have a complete hot meal saved for them. Working parties leaving the ship should be provided with such comforts as rain gear and drinking water if circumstances warrant.

When crew members are required to do work that results in their losing sleep or missing regular meals, it is incumbent upon the officer to see that they get compensatory rest and meals.

## APPREHENSION AND RESTRAINT

An OOD must know the difference between apprehension and the three degrees of restraint: confinement, arrest, and restriction in lieu of arrest. He or she will have occasion to take custody of crew members charged with misconduct. They may be delivered by the shore patrol or an officer or petty officer aboard ship, and they may even deliver themselves for such minor offenses as being out of uniform. It is important that the OOD know the legal meanings of the terms involved and also know what action to take. All officers, petty officers, and noncommissioned officers of any service have authority to apprehend offenders subject to the Uniform Code of Military Justice (UCMJ). Enlisted persons have the same authority when they are assigned such duties as shore patrol and military police.

*Apprehension* means clearly informing a person that he or she is being taken into custody and for what reason. It should be noted that apprehension in the services means the same thing as arrest in civilian life. A police officer informs a citizen that he or she is "under arrest," while a naval officer says that the person is being "apprehended," or taken into custody.

*Custody* is control over the person apprehended until he or she is delivered to the proper authority, who, on board ship, is the OOD. In general, persons who have authority to apprehend may exercise only that force which is necessary. Petty officers should apprehend officers only in unusual circumstances; for example, when an officer is doing something that disgraces the service.

*Restraint* involves some deprivation of free movement. It is never imposed as a punishment, and the degree to which it is imposed should be no greater than what is necessary to ensure the presence of the offender at further proceedings in the case. A suspect need not be restrained at all if his or her presence at future proceedings is assured.

Only the commanding officer may impose restraint on a commissioned officer or a warrant officer. If an officer should be restrained, the commanding officer must be notified. Ordinarily, only officers impose restraint on enlisted men. However, the commanding officer may delegate this authority to warrant officers and enlisted men.

*Confinement* is physical restraint imposed on a serious offender to ensure the presence of the person at future proceedings.

*Arrest* is the restraint of a person, by oral or written order, to certain specified limits, pending the disposition of charges. It is not imposed as punishment. It is imposed only for probable cause based on facts concerning an alleged offense.

One of the disadvantages of placing the accused under arrest is that he or she may no longer be required to perform military duties. Should the accused be required to, arrest is automatically terminated and a lesser form of restraint, *restriction in lieu of arrest,* can be imposed.

A person apprehended on board ship is delivered, together with a misconduct report, into the custody of the OOD. The latter advises the executive officer (or CDO) of the situation and receives instructions regarding the nature of the restraint to be imposed, which depends on the gravity of the offense. If formal restraint, such as arrest, is ordered, the OOD notifies the offender, making sure the offender understands the nature of the restraint and the penalties for violating it. The OOD confirms that the offender has been so notified by having that person sign the misconduct report slip. The OOD then turns the offender over to the master-at-arms. The whole affair must, of course, be entered in the log with full details.

When the offense is relatively minor and it can be assumed that the accused will not attempt to leave the area to avoid trial, no restraint is necessary. Arrest and restriction in lieu of arrest may be lifted only by the authority who ordered the restraint or by that person's superior. Once a person has been confined, he or she can be released only by order of the commanding officer of the activity where the confinement takes place. On board ship, of course, the authority ordering confinement is usually the commanding officer.

## ASYLUM AND TEMPORARY REFUGE

Under the conventions of international law and as a matter of U.S. government policy, certain persons may, in certain circumstances, be granted asylum or temporary refuge on board a naval vessel. The terms and conditions under which asylum or temporary refuge is granted are specified in the Navy Regulations cited below:

1. If an official of the Department of the Navy is requested to provide asylum or temporary refuge, the following procedures shall apply:
    a. On the high seas or in territories under exclusive United States jurisdiction (including territorial seas, the Commonwealth of Puerto Rico, territories under United States administration, and possessions):
        (1) At his or her request, an applicant for asylum will be received on board any naval aircraft or water-borne craft, Navy, or Marine Corps activity or station.
        (2) Under no circumstances shall the person seeking asylum be surrendered to foreign jurisdiction or control, unless at the personal direction of the Secretary of the Navy or higher authority. Persons seeking political asylum should be afforded

every reasonable care and protection permitted by the circumstances.

b. In territories under foreign jurisdiction (including foreign territorial seas, territories, and possessions):

(1) Temporary refuge shall be granted for humanitarian reasons on board a naval aircraft or water-borne craft, Navy or Marine Corps activity or station, only in extreme or exceptional circumstances wherein life or safety of a person is put in imminent danger, such as pursuit by a mob. When temporary refuge is granted, such protection shall be terminated only when directed by the Secretary of the Navy or higher authority.

(2) A request by foreign authorities for return of custody of a person under the protection of temporary refuge will be reported to the CNO or Commandant of the Marine Corps. The requesting foreign authorities will be informed that the case has been referred to higher authorities for instructions.

(3) Persons whose temporary refuge is terminated will be released to the protection of the authorities designated in the message authorizing release.

(4) While temporary refuge can be granted in the circumstances set forth above, permanent asylum will not be granted.

(5) Foreign nationals who request assistance in forwarding requests for political asylum in the United States will not be received on board but will be advised to apply in person at the nearest American Embassy or Consulate. If a foreign national is already on board, however, such person will not be surrendered to foreign jurisdiction or control unless at the personal direction of the Secretary of the Navy or higher authority.

c. The Chief of Naval Operations or Commandant of the Marine Corps, as appropriate, will be informed by the most expeditious means of all action taken pursuant to subparagraphs 1a and 1b above, as well as the attendant circumstances. Telephone or voice communications will he used where possible, but must be confirmed as soon as possible with an immediate precedence message, information to the Secretary of State (for actions taken pursuant to subparagraphs 1b[1] and 1b[5] of this article, also make the appropriate American Embassy or Consular Office an information addressee). If communication by telephone or voice is not possible, notification will be effected by an immediate precedence message, as described above. The Chief of Naval Operations or Commandant of the Marine Corps will cause the Secretary of the Navy and the Deputy Director for Operations of the National Military Command Center to be notified without delay.

2. Personnel of the Department of the Navy shall neither directly nor indirectly invite persons to seek asylum or temporary refuge.

Operational commanders usually require, in addition to the above, a report of the circumstances surrounding a request for asylum or temporary refuge, generally under the operational reporting system.

## REPORTING AND DETACHMENT OF PERSONNEL

An OOD should appreciate that first impressions are important. When new people are being received on board, the provisions of the ship's organization manual should always be followed and every effort made so that a new officer or enlisted person feels at ease. New people, especially those reporting to their first ship from boot camp or school, are likely to be overwhelmed by their surroundings. Their apprehension will be lifted considerably by the knowledge that the ship is interested in their welfare. If a sponsor has not been assigned or is not on board, the OOD and the duty master-at-arms should see that a temporary escort is assigned to give a new crew member help in finding his or her compartment, the mess decks, and the offices into which he or she will have to check.

People being detached should be processed on the quarterdeck as expeditiously as possible, since they may have transportation arrangements to make. If there is to be any sort of departure ceremony, those taking part in it should be standing by on the quarterdeck before the people departing arrive.

## RECEIVING GUESTS AND VISITORS

The OOD is responsible for welcoming all guests and visitors to the ship. He or she usually has advance information as to who is expected, who will meet them on the quarterdeck, and what sort of assistance the watch is to provide. Exercise observers and ship riders are generally met by the cognizant department head or a representative, and VIPs by the commanding officer. When the ship is open to general visiting or to tours by special groups, the OOD should check in advance arrangements prescribed by the ship's visiting bill. Areas of the ship should be roped off as required and tour guides mustered and inspected before the visitors arrive. When large numbers of visitors are expected, arrangements must be made in advance for the provision of local police or guard forces.

# 13

## SAFETY

The Commanding Officer shall require that persons concerned are instructed and drilled in all applicable safety precautions and procedures, that these are complied with, and that applicable safety precautions, or extracts therefrom, are posted in appropriate places. In any instance where safety precautions have not been issued or are incomplete, the Commanding Officer shall issue or augment such safety precautions as are deemed necessary, notifying, when appropriate, higher authorities concerned.

Navy Regulations, Article 0825

Safety must be practiced twenty-four hours a day, because the operation of a naval vessel is dangerous. It involves powerful machinery, high-speed equipment, steam under intensely high temperature and pressure, volatile fuels and propellants, heavy lifts, high explosives, stepped-up electrical voltages, and the elemental forces of wind and wave, which are unpredictable. Inexperienced sailors are inclined to be careless, if not downright reckless. It is a watch officer's responsibility to see that all precautions are observed to protect the lives of the crew and the safety of the ship.

Precautions ensure the safe operation of all equipment. The Naval Ships Technical Manuals contain safety precautions, as do manuals put out by the various bureaus and the Standard Ship's Organization and Regulations Manual (OpNavInst 3120.32C). As new equipment is introduced into the fleet, new safety procedures are generated and old ones modified. Accidents and injuries also lead to a continual updating of precautions, the general trend being toward more detailed descriptions of procedures, checks, and inspections.

Every accident that occurs in a ship should be reported in standard form to the appropriate safety center, so that the condition that caused it can be investigated and corrective action taken. OODs should always be on the alert for dangerous conditions and violations of safety rules and prompt about correcting them.

The OOD, both in port and under way, should see that the following safety regulations and procedures, compiled from OpNavInst 3120.32C, are adhered to. Most ship, fleet, and type commanders supplement these regulations to fit specific situations or requirements. For example, detailed procedures are issued for the guidance of personnel who handle nuclear weapons. The watch officer is also directed to the Navy Occupational Safety and Health (NavOSH) Program Manual for Forces Afloat, NavShips technical manuals, and planned maintenance system (PMS) maintenance requirement cards (MRCs) for detailed guidelines and precautions applicable to their specific situations.

## AMMUNITION

1. All personnel required to handle ammunition must be carefully and frequently instructed in the safety regulations, methods of handling, storage, and uses of all kinds of ammunition and explosive ordnance with which the ship, aircraft unit, or station is supplied.

2. No one is permitted to inspect, prepare, or adjust live ammunition and explosives until he or she thoroughly understands the duties, precautions, and hazards involved and has been properly certified.

3. Only careful, reliable, mentally sound, and physically fit persons are permitted to work with or use explosives or ammunition.

4. All persons who supervise the inspection, care, preparation, handling, use, or disposal of ammunition or explosives must do the following:

   a. Exercise the utmost care that all regulations and instructions are observed, and remain vigilant throughout the operation.

   b. Carefully instruct and frequently warn those under them of the need for constant vigilance.

    c. Before beginning the operation, ensure that all subordinates are familiar with the characteristics of explosive materials and equipment involved, safety regulations to be observed, and the hazards of fire, explosion, or other catastrophe that safety regulations are intended to prevent.

    d. Be alert for hazardous procedures or symptoms of a deteriorating mental attitude, and take immediate action when such are detected.

5. Smoking is not permitted in magazines or in the vicinity of operations involving explosives or ammunition. Matches, lighters, and spark- or flame-producing devices are not permitted in spaces where ammunition or explosives are present.

6. Personnel working with explosives or ammunition are limited to the minimum number required to perform the operation properly. Unauthorized personnel are not permitted in magazines or in the vicinity of operations involving explosives or ammunition. Authorized visitors must always be properly escorted.

7. When fused or assembled with firing mechanisms, mines, depth charges, rockets, projector charges, missiles, and aircraft bombs must be treated as if armed.

8. Live ammunition, rockets, or missiles are loaded into guns or on launchers only for firing purposes, unless personnel are otherwise notified.

9. Supervisors must enforce good housekeeping in explosives spaces. Nothing should be stored in such spaces except explosives, their containers, and authorized handling equipment.

10. No detonator is to be assembled in a warhead in or near a magazine containing explosives. Fusing is to be done at a designated fusing area.

## BOATS

1. In motor launches, only the coxswain and the boat officer or the senior line officer may ride on the coxswain's flat. No more than two persons may be on the deck at one time.

2. Boat crews must keep their stations, especially when weather conditions are unpleasant, for it is usually during these times that vigilance is most needed.

3. Boats must always be properly loaded for the sea state. In heavy weather, the boat is loaded slightly down by the stern and the passengers and crew are kept in life jackets. Boat passengers must remain seated when a boat is under way and keep arms inboard of gunwales.

4. The coxswain, or boat officer when assigned, is responsible to the commanding officer for the enforcement of these regulations.

5. No boat is to be loaded beyond the capacities established by the commanding officer and published in the boat bill.

6. Smoking is forbidden in boats.

7. No persons other than those specifically designated by the engineering officer should operate or attempt to operate a boat engine; test, remove, or charge a boat's battery, or tamper in any way with a boat's electrical system; or fuel a ship's boat.

8. No person is to be assigned as a member of a boat crew unless he or she is a qualified swimmer; has demonstrated a practical knowledge of boat seamanship, the rules of the road, and boat safety regulations; and has duly qualified for his or her particular assignment.

9. All persons in boats being hoisted in or out, or hung in the davits, must wear vest-type, inherently buoyant life preservers properly secured and safety helmets with chin straps.

10. Boats must not be boarded from a boat boom unless someone is standing by on deck or in a boat at the same boom.

11. All members of a boat's crew must wear rubber-soled canvas shoes when embarked in a ship's boat.

12. Fueling instructions must be posted in all power boats, and passengers must be kept clear of a boat that is being refueled.

13. Maximum operating speeds must be posted permanently on the engine cover of all boats.

14. Standard equipment listed in the allowance list must be in boats at all times.

15. Prescribed lights must be displayed by all boats under way between sunset and daylight or in poor visibility.

16. Life buoys must be carried forward and aft in each boat and secured in such a manner that they can be easily broken out for use.

17. All boats leaving the ship should have local charts with courses to and from their destination recorded thereon. Compasses and fog-signaling equipment must be carried on boats.

18. All boats must have life preservers on board to accommodate all persons embarked, and the life preservers must be readily available when rough seas, reduced visibility, or other hazards threaten.

19. No boat should be dispatched or permitted to proceed unless released by the OOD. Release should not be given unless it has been determined that the boat crew and passengers are wearing life preservers, when advisable, and that weather and sea conditions are suitable for small-boat operations.

20. Recall and lifeboat signals must be posted in boats where they can be easily read by the coxswain.

21. A set of standing orders to the coxswain must be prepared and kept in each boat.

## CARGO

1. Open hatches in use should be cleared of any adjacent loose equipment that might fall into them and injure personnel below.

2. Traffic about a hatch is restricted to the side where cargo is not being worked. The area over which loads are traveling is roped off to traffic.

3. Hatch beams or other structures in the way of hatches where cargo is being worked are secured by bolts or removed. Personnel moving hatch beams must wear a safety line, which should be tended at all times.

4. Qualified personnel must always supervise the topping and lowering of booms. Before any repairs are made or any gear is replaced, booms should always be lowered on deck. When life lines are removed for any purpose, officers and petty officers must see that emergency lines are rigged and that everyone is cautioned to keep clear.

## CLOSED COMPARTMENTS

The danger of explosion, poisoning, and suffocation exists in closed compartments or poorly ventilated spaces such as tanks, cofferdams, voids, and bilges. No person should enter any such compartment or space until the space has been declared safe by a qualified gas-free engineer. The following precautions should be observed:

1. The seal around the manhole or other opening should be broken before all hold-down bolts or other fastenings are completely removed, to allow dissipation of pressure that may have built up inside and to make it possible to quickly secure the cover again if gas or water is present.

2. No person should enter any such space without permission from the responsible division officer, who obtains approval from the department head and the gas-free engineer before granting permission.

3. No naked light or spark-producing electrical apparatus should be carried into a closed space.

4. Safety lamps used in closed compartments must be in good operating condition. If a lamp fades or flares up, the space should not be entered.

5. No person should work in such a compartment without a life line attached and a responsible person stationed outside the compartment to tend the line and maintain communications.

## COMPRESSED GAS

Compressed gases used aboard ship include oxygen, acetylene, carbon dioxide ($CO_2$), and plain compressed air. Helium, nitrogen, ammonia, and certain insecticide fogs may also be used. All cylinders are identified in stenciled letters and by color as follows:

*Yellow.* Flammable materials, such as acetylene, hydrogen, and petroleum gases.

*Brown.* Poisonous materials, such as chlorine, carbon monoxide, and sulphur dioxide.

*Green.* Oxidizing material, particularly pure oxygen.

*Blue.* Anesthetics and materials with similarly harmful fumes.

*Gray.* Physically dangerous materials: inert gas under high pressure or gas that would asphyxiate if breathed in confined areas, such as $CO_2$, nitrogen, and helium.

*Red.* Fire-protection materials, especially $CO_2$ and nitrogen.

*Black with Green Striping.* Compressed air and helium-oxygen and oxygen-$CO_2$ mixtures.

All flammable gases, such as acetylene, become highly explosive when mixed in certain proportions with air. Even an inert gas like $CO_2$

can cause an explosion if its cylinder becomes too hot or cracks because of rough handling. The following rules should be obeyed without exception:

1. Gas cylinders and air cylinders must be kept away from high-temperature areas. Oil should never be allowed to come in contact with oxygen cylinder valves because a violent explosion could result.

2. Gas cylinders must not be handled roughly, dropped, or clanked against each other. They should not be handled or transported without their valve caps in place.

3. Flames or sparks should not be permitted in any closed spaces where acetylene or oxygen tanks are stored, for seepage from the tanks may have filled the compartment with a dangerous level of gas or pure oxygen.

4. Caution should be used around cylinders of poisonous gas. There is always the possibility that gas is leaking from a loose valve or seeping through a defective connection.

5. In case of fire or other disaster, gas cylinders should be moved immediately from the danger area and, if necessary, thrown overboard.

## DIVERS

Divers may go below the ship only with the permission of the OOD. The OOD is responsible for seeing that the following safety precautions are observed before granting permission:

1. The location and status of all ship's machinery that might affect a diving area must be determined before diving operations begin. The status of this equipment must not be altered without prior notification by the engineering duty officer and the concurrence of the diving officer.

2. Divers must not enter the water until permission is granted by the OOD and the international signal Code Alfa is flying from the ship and the diving boat.

3. Without the specific knowledge and concurrence of the diving officer,

    a. Main ballast tanks will not be flooded or blown.

    b. Sanitary tanks will not be blown.

   c. Stern planes will not be moved.*

   d. The rudder will not be moved.*

   e. The screw will not be turned. With the concurrence of the diving officer, screws may be turned at minimum jacking speed. In this case, the OOD, via the engineering duty officer, must ensure that screws are turning no faster than the minimum jacking speed.

   f. The mooring will not be adjusted.

   g. The secondary propulsion motors will not be rigged out or trained, nor will the screw be turned except as noted above.*

   h. The MSD system will not be operated.

   i. The anchor and anchor chain will not be manipulated in any way.*

   j. The torpedo tubes will not be exercised.*

   k. Radioactive effluents will not be discharged.

   4. All boats must stay at least fifty yards from the diving area.

   5. Except in an extreme emergency, no diving operation will commence unless four qualified divers are present.

   6. Divers must always dive with one standby diver in a ready condition.

   7. Divers are checked for sickness and injury immediately upon leaving the water.

   8. All ships in a nest must be informed of the presence of divers on any ship in the nest.

   9. When divers are over the side, the word is passed every 30 minutes.

   10. Active sonar must not be operated if divers are anywhere in the nest.

   11. When divers are working in the vicinity of adjacent ships, the regulations set forth in this article apply. The duty officer must clear with the duty officer of the ship in which divers are working before undertaking any evolution prohibited by this article.

## ELECTRICAL AND ELECTRONIC EQUIPMENT

This includes generators, electrically powered machinery and mechanisms, power cables, controllers, transformers and associated

*System must be properly tagged out.

USS _____

1. Diving will be conducted over the side, commencing at _____ (time/date).

2. The following work is to be accomplished by the divers: _____

_____

3. Diving will be in the following location(s): _____

_____

4. Prior to a diver entering the water, accomplish the following:

**Initials**

_____ a. Notify the engineer officer/engineering duty officer of the diving operation. Determine the operating status of sea water systems within the diving area. Direct no alterations of this status (except as described in f. below) without the permission of the engineering duty officer. Inform diving supervisor of systems in operation.

_____ b. Notify reactor officer/radiation control officer (nuclear powered ships only). Ensure divers have radiological protection specified by the reactor officer.

_____ c. DANGER tag-out rudder to ensure no movement and secure and tag-out the cathodic protective source.

_____ d. Ensure that screws are on the jacking gear and locked (screws may be turned at minimum jacking speed with the concurrence of the diving supervisor).

_____ e. Do not permit mooring line adjustment.

_____ f. Do not permit main circulating water system components to be operated.

_____ g. DANGER tag-out anchor windlass and brake to ensure no manipulation in any way.

_____ h. Do not conduct boiler/steam generator blow downs or if a nuclear powered ship, permit no discharge of radioactive effluent.

**Figure 13-1. Check Sheet for Divers over the Side**

equipment, radars, radios, power amplifiers, antennas, electronic warfare equipment, computers, and associated controls.

1. No person is to operate, repair, adjust, or otherwise tamper with any electrical or electronic equipment (unless it is within his or her assignment in the department organization manual to perform a specific function on certain equipment) except in emergencies, and then only when no qualified operator is available.

2. No person is to be assigned to operate, repair, or adjust electrical and electronic equipment unless he or she has demonstrated

_____ i. Keep all small boats outside a 50 yard radius of the diving operations.

_____ j. Do not permit diving unless the required number of qualified divers in accordance with the U.S. Navy Diving Manual are present with one diver out of the water in a ready condition as a standby diver.

_____ k. If equipped with thrusters or electric propulsion motors, tag them out to ensure they are not operated.

_____ l. Do not permit any active sonar to be operated.

_____ m. Notify adjacent ships or other ships in a nest of the diving operations. Request the command duty officers of these ships to not permit active sonar operation.

_____ n. **Fly CODE ALPHA.** Ensure this signal is flying from the diving boat.

_____ o. **Pass the following word prior to the divers entering the water:** "Divers are over the side in the vicinity of _____", and every 30 minutes thereafter.

5. Conditions have been established to permit diving operations.

Command Duty Officer/Time

Diving Commenced _____

Diving Completed _____

Note: Initials certify completion of an item. If an item is not applicable, indicate "NA" on initial line.

## Figure 13-1.—*Continued*

practical knowledge of its operation and repair and of all applicable safety regulations, and then only when duly qualified by the head of the department.

3. No person is to paint over or otherwise mutilate markings, name plates, cable tags, or other identification on any electrical or electronic equipment.

4. No person is to hang anything on, or secure a line to, any power cable, antenna, wave guide, or other piece of electrical or electronic equipment.

5. Only authorized and portable electrical equipment that has been tested by the electric shop is to be used.

6. Electrical equipment must be de-energized (and, if possible, checked with a voltage tester or voltmeter to ensure it is de-

energized) before being serviced or repaired. Circuit breakers and switches of de-energized circuits are to be locked or placed in the "off" position while work is in progress, and a suitable warning tag should be attached.

7. Every effort must be made to insulate a person working on live circuits or equipment, and all other related safety measures should be observed. If possible, rubber gloves should be worn. Another person should be standing by to de-energize the circuit and to render first aid.

8. No personal electrical or electronic equipment should be used aboard ship until it has been approved by the engineering and executive officers.

9. No person should intentionally receive a shock from any voltage whatsoever.

10. Bare lamps or fixtures with exposed lamps must not be installed in machinery spaces. To minimize the hazard of fire caused by flammable fuels making contact with exposed lamps, only enclosed fixtures are to be installed in such spaces.

11. Personnel are not permitted aloft near energized antennas unless it has been determined that no danger exists. If there is any danger from rotating antennas, induced voltages in rigging and superstructure, or high-power radiation that could cause direct biological injury, equipment should be secured and a suitable warning tag should be attached to the main supply switches. These precautions are also observed if any other antenna is in the vicinity, as on an adjacent ship.

12. Department heads must see that electrical and electronic safety precautions are conspicuously posted in appropriate spaces and that personnel are frequently and thoroughly instructed and drilled in their observance.

13. Department heads must ensure that all electrical and electronics personnel are qualified in the administration of first-aid treatment for shock and that emergency resuscitation procedures are posted in all spaces containing electronic equipment.

14. Department heads must make sure that rubber matting is installed in front and in back of propulsion-control cubicles, power and lighting switchboards, IC switchboards, test switchboards, fire-control switchboards, announcing-system amplifiers, and control

panels; areas in and around radio, radar, sonar, and countermeasures equipment spaces that may be entered by personnel servicing or tuning energized equipment; and around workbenches in electrical and electronics shops where equipment is tested or repaired.

## FIRE AND EXPLOSION PREVENTION

The reduction of fire and explosion hazards is the responsibility of every person on board, both individually and collectively. The gravity of these hazards is increased by the configuration of machinery spaces and the presence on board of fuel and heat. The following steps are essential:

1. To the extent possible, eliminate all fire and explosion hazards, including nonessential combustibles.
2. Wherever possible, replace highly combustible materials with less combustible ones.
3. Keep only the minimum required amount of essential combustibles.
4. Stow and protect all combustibles in designated lockers.
5. Avoid the accumulation of oil and other flammable materials in bilges and inaccessible areas. Any excess must be flushed out or removed at the first opportunity.
6. Stow oily rags in airtight metal containers.
7. Stow paint, paint brushes, rags, paint thinner, and solvents in authorized locations.
8. Do not use compressed air to accelerate the flow from containers of oil, gasoline, or other combustible fluids.
9. Make regular and frequent inspections for fire hazards.
10. Train all personnel in fire prevention and firefighting.
11. Enforce sound fire-prevention policies and practices.
12. Maintain damage-control equipment in a state of readiness for any emergency.

## FUEL OIL

1. While oil is being received on board, no naked light, lighted cigarette, electrical apparatus, or anything else likely to spark should

be permitted within fifty feet of an oil hose, tank, or compartment containing the tank or a vent. No one may carry matches or cigarette lighters while loading or unloading oil.

2. No naked light, lighted cigarette, electrical fuse, switch (except the enclosed type), steel tool, or other apparatus liable to cause sparks should be permitted at any time in a compartment that contains fuel-oil tanks, pumps, or piping. Electric lamps used in such a compartment must have gaslight globes. Smoking may be permitted in the engine rooms and the fireroom. The term "naked light" includes oil lanterns as well as open lanterns, lighted candles, and lighted matches. Flashlights must not be turned on or off inside a fuel compartment lest a spark ignite vapors.

3. No person should be allowed to enter a fuel-oil tank until the tank has been freed of vapor, the person has obtained permission from the safety or commanding officer, and the required precautions have been taken. No one should ever enter a fuel-oil tank without wearing a life line attended by someone outside the tank.

4. Compartments and tanks used for the storage of fuel oil should not be painted on the inside.

5. Whenever a fuel-oil tank is to be entered, work is to be done in it, or lights other than portable explosion-proof electric lights are to be used, and whenever work is to be done in the vicinity of an open tank or of pipes, all such tanks and pipes must first be cleared of vapor after the fuel oil has been removed. No person should enter a fuel-oil tank for any purpose without obtaining permission from the safety or commanding officer.

6. Oil fires can be extinguished by smothering and cutting off oxygen. $CO_2$ extinguishers and chemicals or water in the form of fog may be used.

## HAZARDOUS MATERIAL

To attain and maintain operational effectiveness, Navy ships require specified types and quantities of hazardous material (HM). Great care must be taken in handling, using, and storing HM to prevent injury to personnel, damage to equipment, or harm to the environment. Risks associated with HM are greater aboard ship than ashore because of the limited number, confined nature, and "at sea" environment of shipboard spaces. Consequently, special precautions and an effective program to manage HM are both needed. The maintenance of safe and healthful working conditions for HM is a chain of command responsibility. Implementation begins with the commanding officer and extends to the individual sailor. The OOD, particularly in port, has a key role in ensuring HM does not enter or leave the ship in an unauthorized fashion.

Hazardous material (HM) is material that, because of its quantity, concentration, or physical or chemical characteristics, may pose a substantial hazard to human health or the environment when incorrectly used, purposefully released, or accidentally spilled. Subcategories of HM include:

1. Flammable/combustible materials.
2. Toxic materials.
3. Corrosive materials (including acids and bases).
4. Oxidizing materials.
5. Aerosol containers.
6. Compressed gases.

Not included in this definition are ammunition, weapons, explosives, explosive actuated devices, propellants, pyrotechnics, chemical and biological warfare materials, pharmaceutical supplies (if not considered hazardous based on composition, physical form, and review of procedures which may involve the handling/dispensing of the materials), medical waste and infectious materials, bulk fuels, and radioactive materials. Asbestos, mercury, lead, and polychlorinated biphenyls (PCBs) are HM that require special guidance for their handling and control.

Ships are required to transfer used or excess HM to a Navy shore activity to determine if it is suitable for further use. Navy shore activities possess trained personnel who can determine, working with ship's personnel, whether shipboard HM is usable, reusable, or should be disposed of as hazardous waste (HW). The shore activity will act as the HW generator if they determine that the material has no further use and will dispose of it as required by federal, state, and local regulations.

Ships shall develop a spill contingency plan (SCP) in preparation for possible HM spills or releases to the environment. This plan shall include information on spill response team makeup, spill cleanup equipment location, and internal and external spill reporting criteria. The OOD must be well acquainted with this plan, which will be outlined in the ship's SORM.

The Hazard Characteristic Code (HCC) is a two-digit alphanumeric code that is used to provide a means of categorizing hazardous material (HM). HCCs are assigned by trained scientific or engineering personnel, thereby uniformly identifying HM that is managed by all government activities. HCCs allow personnel to properly receive, handle, store, and process HM. In particular, the HCC allows the user to determine which materials are compatible for storage with other materials. In addition, HCCs can be used to simplify spill response and cleanup, processing of HM during recoupment operations, and assist in the identification of potential hazardous wastes. The HCC serves as an identifier for automated processing of HM transactions and space utilization management. The HCCs can be found in OpNavInst 5100.19C.

## HEAVY WEATHER

Safety requires the following precautions in heavy weather:

1. Decks exposed to the sea should be kept clear of all personnel except those on urgent duty. Word to this effect and concerning any other area to which entry is forbidden should be passed periodically.

2. Extra life lines and snaking should be in place, particularly in areas where there are ongoing evolutions such as replenishment or recovery of a person overboard.

## HELICOPTERS

Helicopters on ships are operated with permission from the OOD. The OOD is responsible for seeing that the following precautions are observed before granting permission:

1. All helicopter safety crews (firefighting, pilot-rescue, etc.) must be fully manned, on station, and ready.

2. Only those involved are allowed in the vicinity of helicopter operations, and they must wear safety helmets and vests.

3. A complete and thorough check must be made of the helicopter area for loose gear or objects (foreign object debris or FOD) that could cause injury or damage.

4. All hands topside must remain uncovered.

5. Passengers are led to and from a helicopter by a member of the handling crew or flight crew.

## HELM SAFETY OFFICER

The helm safety officer is a bridge watchstander during special maneuvers when precise shiphandling and control is required. The helm safety officer is usually an OOD-qualified officer whose duty is to monitor the helmsman and lee helmsman, ensuring that all orders from the conning officer are carried out smartly and correctly.

## HOT WORK

Hot work involves welding, flame-cutting, open-flame equipment, and the manipulation of metal with red heat. No person should engage in hot work until the gas-free engineer (or an authorized representative) has inspected the place where it is to be done and indicated that it is free of the danger of poisoning, suffocation, fire, and explosion.

1. No hot work shall be undertaken without the permission of the commanding officer under way or the duty officer in port.

2. When flammable or explosive materials are to be exposed to welding or cutting, a fire watch should be posted in the vicinity. If fire hazards exist on both sides of a deck or bulkhead being worked on, a watch should be posted on each side. Fire watches should remain on station for at least thirty minutes after a job has been completed to ensure that no smoldering fires have started. Suitable fire-extinguishing equipment should be kept near all welding and cutting operations.

3. No welding or burning is permitted in compartments where explosives are stored.

4. Various synthetic materials yield toxic gases when burned or heated. Suitable warning signs must be placed in areas where dangerous vapors can accumulate.

5. Only qualified personnel may operate welding equipment.

## LIFE JACKETS

Life jackets must be worn whenever there is a possibility of personnel slipping, falling, or being carried into the water. The safest life jacket, when properly worn, is the Navy's standard buoyant vest. Life jackets must be worn by the following persons:

1. Those working over the side, in port and at sea, on stages and in boatswain's chairs, boats, or punts. Over the side means any part of the ship outside the life lines or bulwarks.

2. Those going out on weather decks during heavy weather, even if they are to be exposed only long enough to go from one station to another.

3. Those handling lines or other deck equipment during such evolutions as transfers between ships, fueling under way, and towing.

4. Those in boats being raised or lowered, entering boats from a boom or Jacob's ladder, in boats under way, and on the ship in rough water or low visibility. Ring buoys with a line and light attached must be available when a sea ladder or a Jacob's ladder is being used.

5. Those being transferred by highline or helicopter. They must don life jackets before they get into the transfer seat or sling.

## LIFE LINES

1. No person is to lean on, sit on, stand on, or climb over any life line, either in port or at sea. Personnel working over the side in port may climb over life lines when necessary, but only if they are wearing life preservers.

2. No life line is to be dismantled or removed without the permission of the first lieutenant, and even then temporary life lines must be promptly rigged.

3. No person shall hang or secure any weight or line to any life line unless authorized by the commanding officer.

## LIGHTS

When a ship is in port at night, weather decks, accommodation ladders, gangways, and brows must be well lighted.

## LINES AND RIGGING

When work with lines and rigging is being done, the following precautions should be observed:

1. Lines or rigging under heavy strain should be eased to prevent overstress or parting. Personnel must keep clear of heavily stressed line or wire and must under no circumstances stand in the bight of a line or on a taut fall.

2. Heavy loads should not ordinarily be hoisted overhead, but if it is essential, the person responsible must warn everyone away from the area directly below.

3. Boat falls and highlines should be replaced at the first indication of wear or stress.

4. Lines not in use should be carefully made up and stowed clear of walkways and passages.

5. Lines must be made fast not to capstans or gypsy heads but only to fittings provided for that purpose, such as cleats or bitts.

6. Steadying or frapping lines should be used on boat falls and on large lifts to prevent uncontrolled swinging or twisting.

## LINE-THROWING GUN

A line-throwing gun is used in the opening phase of replenishment operations, during which the following safety precautions must always be observed:

1. Members of the line-throwing crew must wear red helmets and highly visible red jackets so that they can be easily identified.

2. The bolo-heaver and line-throwing gunner must be thoroughly trained to place the line within easy reach of the receiving ship's crew, no matter what the conditions of range, wind, and relative motion may be.

3. Bolos and gun lines must be properly prepared for running.

4. When the receiving ship reaches the proper position, both ships pass the word over the bull horn and topside loudspeaker, "Stand by for shot line—all hands take cover."

5. The officer in charge at each replenishment station in the firing ship sounds a one-blast signal on a mouth whistle or passes the

word "Stand by" on the electric megaphone. When he or she is ready to receive the shot line and all personnel in the vicinity have taken cover, the officer in charge of the corresponding station in the receiving ship replies with a two-blast signal on a mouth whistle and passes the word "Ready" on the electric megaphone. After ascertaining that all hands in the vicinity of the target area are under cover, the officer in charge on the firing ship gives the order to fire. The bolo is thrown or the gun is fired only by order of the officer in charge.

6. Only those members of each replenishment station designated by the officer in charge may leave cover to retrieve the bolo or shot line. No one else in the receiving ship may leave cover until all bolos or shot lines are on board and word has been passed on the topside loudspeaker that shot (bolo) lines are secure.

7. The receiving ship, unless she is an aircraft carrier, does not fire her line-throwing guns unless ordered or requested by the delivering ship.

8. All hands must take cover immediately on receipt of the word to do so.

## MACHINERY

Machinery refers to every engine, motor, generator, hydraulic system, and other apparatus that supplies power or motive force.

1. Except in emergencies, and then only when no qualified operator is present, no person should operate, repair, adjust, or otherwise tamper with any machinery unless assigned by the department head to perform a specific function on that machinery.

2. No person should be assigned to operate, repair, or adjust any machinery unless he or she has demonstrated practical knowledge of its operation and repair and of all applicable safety regulations, and then only when certified by the head of the department responsible for such machinery.

3. The power or activation source of machinery undergoing repair should be tagged to that effect to prevent the accidental application of power.

## OPERATIONAL RISK MANAGEMENT (ORM)

ORM is a term with which the OOD should be very familiar, both in port and at sea. It means identifying hazards, assessing risk, evaluating control options, and supervising all activities with an eye toward minimizing risk. It is discussed in OpNavInst 3120.32C, Article 604.7. It is a systematic way of thinking that should be applied to everything under the control of the OOD. It increases awareness of hazards and risks involved in operations.

## PAINTING

Poisoning from paint may be produced by either the vehicle or the pigment. The vehicle is a volatile solvent. Excessive exposure to a vaporized solvent produces irritation of the nose and throat, headache, dizziness, loud or boisterous conversation, loss of memory, and a staggering gait. A person exhibiting such symptoms must be quickly removed from exposure to paint fumes.

The pigment in most paints contains lead, which may be absorbed through the skin or inhaled as particles, particularly if a spray gun is used. The following precautions should be observed:

1. A painter should wear a respirator and change its filter frequently. (Respirators offer no protection against paint fumes.)

2. After painting, workers should wash their hands and clean under their fingernails to protect against pigment poisoning.

3. Soiled clothing should be changed as soon as possible.

4. Personnel regularly employed with or around spray guns should wear face masks.

## PERSONNEL PROTECTION

1. Personnel working on or near rotating machinery must not wear clothing with loose ends or loops that might be caught by moving equipment.

2. Personnel working on steam valves or other hot units must wear leather or other heavy gloves.

3. Personnel working in the vicinity of steam equipment must keep their bodies well covered to reduce the danger of steam burns.

4. Personnel brazing, welding, or cutting must wear protective goggles, a helmet, and leather welding jackets.

5. Personnel must wear goggles whenever they are working with substances corrosive to the eyes.

6. Personnel must wear respirators when working in areas with excessive dust.

## PERSONNEL TRANSFER

Personnel transfer at sea is performed under strict requirements to ensure the safety of those being transferred.

1. The highline may be either three- or five-inch manila or three- or four-inch synthetic, double-braided spun polyester (dacron). The three-inch synthetic and manila highlines have a three hundred-pound weight limit, while the four-inch synthetic and five-inch manila lines have a six hundred-pound weight limit.

2. The highline used for personnel transfer is tensioned by a minimum of twenty-five people. The highline is hand-tended to prevent its parting as a result of ship's movement.

3. A highline that has been tended by a capstan may not be used for personnel transfers.

4. Persons being transferred must wear orange-colored, inherently buoyant life preservers.

5. Boatswain's chairs used in personnel transfers must have a quick-release seat belt. They should also be fitted with a flotation device.

6. Stretchers used to transfer patients must be equipped with flotation gear.

## RADIATION

Radioactive material is present in a nuclear reactor core, in contaminants in the primary coolant, in the sources used for calibration of radiation-monitoring equipment, and in certain electronic tubes.

1. Radiation sources must remain installed in radiation-detection equipment or be stowed in shipping containers in locked storage.

2. Spare radioactive electronic tubes and fission chambers are to be stored in clearly marked containers and locked stowage.

3. All hands must scrupulously obey radiation warning signs and remain clear of radiation barriers.

## SAFETY DEVICES

1. Mechanical, electrical, and electronic safety devices must be inspected at regular intervals and whenever unusual circumstances or conditions warrant. When practical, such devices should be inspected while the equipment or unit to which they apply is in operation. Machinery or equipment must not be operated when their safety devices are not in proper working condition.

2. No person is to tamper with any safety device, interlock, ground strap, or similar device intended to protect operators or their equipment.

## SEMISAFE AND DANGEROUS MATERIALS

Semisafe materials are materials considered safe so long as they are in unopened containers that do not leak—but it is understood that should leakage occur, any spilled material will be cleaned up promptly and the leaking container disposed of. Some more common semisafe materials are diesel oil, grease, lubricating oil, metal polish, paint, safety matches, and wax.

Dangerous materials may or may not be in sealed containers. Some more common dangerous materials are acids, alcohol, anticorrosive paint, bleaching powder (chlorinated lime), calcium hypochlorite, compressed gases, gasoline, kerosene, lacquer, paint thinner, paint-stripping compound, paint drier, rust-prevention compound, storage-battery electrolyte, turpentine, and varnish.

All semisafe and dangerous materials should be stowed in storerooms specially designed for paint and flammable liquids, unless another designated stowage area is provided. Naked lights and spark-emitting devices must not be used in compartments that contain semisafe or dangerous materials.

Calcium hypochlorite and bleaching powder must he stowed in a clean, cool, dry compartment or storeroom not adjacent to a magazine; they must be isolated from flammable materials, acids, and other chemicals. Their containers should be inspected periodically for tight sealing and rust. The contents of defective containers must be used immediately or otherwise disposed of. Bleach in plastic containers must be stowed in a covered metal container.

## SHOES

All persons must wear rubber-soled shoes. Boat crews wear rubber-soled canvas shoes when embarked in ship's boats. Only leather shoes are permitted in engineering spaces. Plastic shoes are forbidden. Safety shoes must be worn in areas designated for foot hazards. Shoes with taps, cleats, or any other metal device on the heels or soles may not be worn on board ship or in ship's boats.

## SMALL ARMS

Small arms are hand-held pistols, rifles, machine guns, line-throwing guns, and flare guns of less than .50-caliber bore diameter.

1. No one is to be issued a small arm unless he or she has demonstrated to the department head or division officer full knowledge of its operation and the safety regulations that pertain to it. This includes applicable personnel qualification standards and classroom instruction, familiarization firing, and qualification firing. A list of qualified individuals is normally maintained at the ship's armory.

2. No one is allowed to insert a clip or otherwise load any small arm unless he or she intends and is required to use the weapon in the performance of duty.

3. Only designated persons may clean, disassemble, adjust, or repair small arms.

4. A small arm must never be pointed at anyone unless its bearer intends to shoot, or in any direction where accidental discharge could do harm.

## SMOKING

Smoking is prohibited in the following areas and during the following evolutions:

1. Holds, storerooms, gasoline-tank compartments, gasoline-pump rooms, voids, trunks, any shop or space where flammable liq-

uids are being handled, ship's boats, bunks or berths, magazines, handling rooms, ready-service rooms, gun mounts or turrets, gasoline-control stations, oil-relay tank rooms, battery and charging rooms, film-projection rooms and the vicinity of motion-picture stowage, photography laboratories, and areas where vinyl or saran paint is being applied.

2. Any area of the ship where ammunition is being handled.

3. When ammunition is being either loaded or unloaded.

4. When fuel oil, diesel oil, aviation gasoline, or other volatile fuel is being received or transferred.

5. During general quarters, general drills, and emergencies, except as authorized by the commanding officer.

6. When word is passed that the smoking lamp is out.

## SPECIAL EQUIPMENT

All personnel concerned with the operation of such equipment as davits, winches, and booms must be thoroughly familiar with the safety precautions peculiar to its use. Applicable safety precautions must be posted in the vicinity of the equipment. Only personnel who have been instructed in the relevant duties and have been authorized by the first lieutenant are permitted to operate cranes, capstans, winches, and windlasses. Except in an emergency, operation of such machinery must be supervised by a responsible officer.

## SYNTHETIC LINES

Nylon, dacron, and other synthetic lines for mooring and rigging have high elasticity and a low coefficient of friction. Therefore, persons working with them should take the following precautions:

1. Give an extra turn when securing synthetic line to bitts, cleats, capstans, and other holding devices.

2. Exercise extreme care when easing out synthetic lines from bitts, cleats, and other holding devices.

3. Make sure no one is standing in the direct line of pull when heavy loads are applied to nylon line. Nylon line stretches to one and a half times its original length, and when it parts, it snaps back with lethal effect.

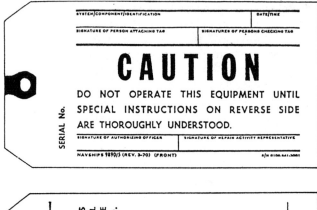

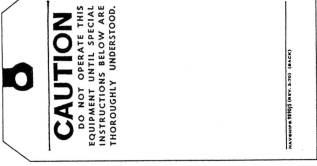

**Figure 13-2a. CAUTION Tags**

**TAG OUT**

The proper tag out of equipment and instruments greatly enhances the safety of both crew and ship. Once a piece of equipment has been tagged, it cannot be untagged, operated, or used without specific directions from a competent authority. General practice is as follows:

1. All tags must be filled out completely, dated, and signed.

2. A proper entry must be made in the tag-out log whenever machinery is tagged in or out.

3. The individual who tags equipment must be notified before any change is made to its status.

Both "danger" tags and "caution" tags can be used (see figure 13-2). Tag out is a fairly complicated process with many built-in safe-

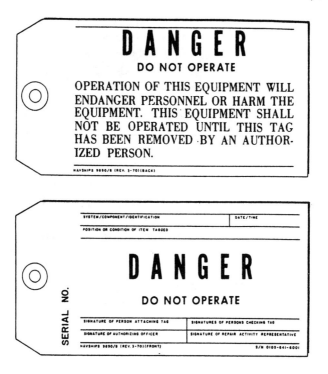

**Figure 13-2b. DANGER Tags**

guards. Details are contained in the Standard Ship's Organization Manual.

## TOOLS

Danger from electric shock, electric shorts, and flying particles accompanies the use of pneumatic or electrically powered tools.

1. No person is to use an electric or pneumatic tool unless specifically authorized to do so by the division officer, and then only after demonstrating that he or she knows how to use it and what safety measures to follow.

2. No electric tool is to be issued unless it has been carefully inspected and checked for resistance to insulation.

3. No electric or pneumatic tool is to be used for any purpose other than those specifically authorized by the department head.

4. No electric tool is to be used unless its housing is grounded to the ship's metal structure, either through a receptacle and plug or by direct connection to the hull.

5. All persons using pneumatic or electrically powered wire brushes, chippers, sanders, and grinders must wear goggles or eye shields and rubber gloves.

## TOXIC MATERIALS

The issue and use of hazardous materials must be strictly controlled by a medical officer or some other designated person.

Methyl alcohol, commonly used in duplicator fluid, paint thinner, cleaners, and antifreeze is hazardous if inhaled, absorbed through the skin, or swallowed. The swallowing of even small amounts can cause permanent blindness or death. Methyl alcohol and products containing it may be released only in the amount required and at the time needed to perform a specific job. It may be used only in well-ventilated spaces and in a manner that prevents it from coming into contact with the skin.

Halogenated hydrocarbons, normally used in gaseous or liquid form as solvents, refrigerants, fumigants, insecticides, paint removers, dry-cleaning fluids, and propellants for pressurized containers, are also hazardous if inhaled, swallowed, or absorbed by the skin. They may be used only where there is adequate ventilation, by authorized personnel under close supervision, and in such a way that they do not come into contact with the eyes or skin.

## UNDERWAY REPLENISHMENT

In this operation, speed is important but must never be attained at the price of safety. It is impossible to anticipate all the hazardous situations that could arise. The following precautions, which should always be reviewed before an operation begins, are a start:

1. Only essential personnel should be allowed in the vicinity of a transfer station.

2. Life lines should be lowered only when absolutely necessary, and if they are, temporary ones must be rigged.

3. When line-throwing guns or bolos are used, all hands on the receiving ship must take cover (see Line-Throwing Gun, page 233).

4. Topside personnel engaged in handling stores and lines must wear safety helmets and orange-colored, inherently buoyant, vest-type life preservers. If safety helmets have quick-acting break-away devices, the chin strap must be fastened and worn under the chin. If helmets are not so equipped, the chin strap must be fastened behind the head or worn unbuckled. Between-ship phone talkers must not secure neck straps around their necks lest they be dragged over the side by the telephone lines.

5. Line-handlers must use the hand-over-hand method of hauling in a line. They should not hold a line and run with it to provide extra pull.

6. Cargo-handlers must wear safety shoes, and those handling wire-bound or banded cases must wear work gloves.

7. All hands must keep clear of bights and handle lines from the inboard side, and stay at least six feet away from any block through which lines pass. Personnel must also keep clear of suspended loads and rig-attachment points until loads have been landed on deck.

8. Care must be taken to prevent the shifting of cargo. No one should get between any load and the rail.

9. Deck space in the vicinity of transfer stations must be covered with a slip-resistant material.

10. A life-buoy watch must be stationed well aft on the engaged side, and provisions made for rescuing anyone who falls overboard. If a lifeguard ship is not available a boat must be kept ready.

11. Suitable measures must be taken to avoid the hazards associated with high-energy radio transmissions. This is especially important when ammunition, gasoline, and other petroleum products are handled.

12. Dangerous materials, such as acids, compressed gases, and hypochlorites, must be transferred separately from one another and from other cargo. The delivery ship must notify the receiving ship of the type of dangerous material in each load before transferring it. The receiving ship must keep dangerous materials separated and stow them in designated storerooms as soon as possible.

13. When fuel oil is being received or transferred, naked lights and electrical or mechanical apparatus likely to spark may not be

within fifty feet of an oil hose in use, an open fuel tank, the vent terminal from a fuel tank, or an area where fuel oil or fuel-oil vapors are or may be present. The term "naked light" includes all oil and gas lanterns, lighted candles, matches, cigars, cigarettes, cigarette lighters, and apparatus for flame welding or arc welding and cutting. Portable electric lights for fueling must have explosion-proof protected globes, be thoroughly inspected for proper insulation, and be tested before they are used. When a ship is being fueled, portholes on the side where she is being fueled must be closed and secured. Fuel-tank overboard discharges must be monitored by personnel in direct communication with the fuel-control station. All scuppers and deck drains around the fueling station should be blocked to prevent fuel spills.

14. When gasoline is being transferred, a ground wire must be connected between the two ships before the hose is brought aboard, and the wire must be left in place until the hose is clear. Gasoline hoses must be blown down by an inert gas after the completion of every transfer.

### VOLATILE FUELS

Aviation gasoline, motor gasoline, JP-4, and JP-5 are highly volatile liquids. They give off a vapor that, when combined with the proper proportion of air, forms an explosive mixture that can be set off by a slight spark or flame. Furthermore, the vapor can travel along an air current for a considerable distance and then be ignited, the flash traveling back to the source of supply and causing an explosion or fire.

1. All spaces into which the vapors of volatile fuel issue must be constantly and thoroughly ventilated.

2. No smoking and no naked lights (see no. 13 above) are permitted in the vicinity of volatile-fuel tanks or filling connections, drums, cans, stowage, piping, or spaces through which such piping passes.

3. Care must be taken to prevent the striking of sparks in places where the vapors of volatile fuels may collect. Only sparkproof tools should be used.

4. When gasoline is carried in cans for a ship's use, it must be stowed in the storeroom for paint and flammable liquids. If there is

no such storeroom, it should be stowed on the weather deck so that the containers may be readily thrown overboard.

5. Gasoline may be issued only under the supervision of a reliable person, who must make sure that all containers are securely closed and all safety regulations observed.

6. The metal nozzle at the end of a fuel hose must be properly grounded to prevent sparks from static electricity (see page 244, no. 14).

7. Gasoline may not be used for cleaning purposes under any circumstances.

8. Upon completion of loading or delivery, piping and hoses must be carefully drained back into the ship's tanks or into containers that can be closed and sealed.

## WHALES

An emerging area of safety concern is protecting whales in the marine environment. OpNavInst 5090.1B, Environmental and Natural Resources Program Manual, contains the important references. Additionally, the type commanders on both coasts have issued guidance. In the Atlantic fleet, there is particular concern about the calfing season of the whales, from December through March. The critical habitat is located off the Atlantic coast, from Georgia to Florida. For the Pacific fleet, there is particular concern during the gray whale's migration season, from January through April. In both cases, if a whale strike occurs, there are specific reports that must be made. While transiting through the key areas during the whale season, it is prudent from a safety standpoint to brief watch teams, proceed at a safe speed (around fifteen knots), and if sighting a whale slow to five to eight knots. You should never approach a whale head on or come closer than five hundred yards.

## WORKING ALOFT

Personnel may go aloft only to perform work or duty, and then only with the permission of the OOD. Before granting permission, the OOD is responsible for seeing that the following safety precautions are observed:

USS _____                                  Time/Date _____

1.  Personnel will be going aloft at (location) _____ for
    accomplishing the following work _____
    _____

2.  Prior to allowing personnel to go aloft, accomplish the following:

**Initials**

_____  a.  If underway, obtain the commanding officer's permission.

_____  b.  DANGER tag-out all rotating equipment, such as radar antennas, in the
            vicinity of the work area.

_____  c.  Place a sign on all HF, MF, and LF transmitters and all radars whose
            danger zone encompasses the work area.  The sign should read:
                        SECURED.  PERSONNEL ALOFT
            DATE_____  TIME_____  INITIALS_____

_____  d.  Ensure personnel going aloft are wearing a parachute type safety
            harness with a Dyna-Brake⁰ safety lanyard, working lanyard, and
            climber safety device (if a climber safety rail is installed).
            Ensure that PMS has been accomplished on all equipment prior to use.

_____  e.  Notify the engineering officer of the watch/engineering duty officer
            to ensure that safety valves are lifted only in an emergency when
            personnel are aloft (main control should notify the officer of the
            deck of an impending emergency as soon as possible to permit warning
            of personnel aloft).

_____  f.  If work is to be accomplished on or in the vicinity of the whistle,
            secure power to the whistle (steam, air, electricity) and DANGER tag-
            out.

_____  g.  Ensure that personnel are briefed on safety prior to going aloft.
            This should include, as a minimum, keeping the lanyard attached with
            a minimum of slack to a fixed structure at all times; changing the
            lanyard connection point as work progresses; keeping good footing and
            grasp at all times.

_____  h.  Ensure all tools are attached to personnel with preventer lines; or,
            if passed up, have lanyards attached which are firmly secured before
            removal from the bucket.

## Figure 13-3. Check Sheet for Working Aloft

1. The power on all radio-transmitting antennas and radar antennas in the vicinity has been secured, and power switches have been tagged out.

2. The engineering officer has been instructed not to lift safety valves and, if personnel are to work in the vicinity of the whistle, to secure steam to the whistle.

3. Personnel, if they are to work in the vicinity of stack gases, have protective breathing masks and have been instructed to remain there for only a brief time.

_____ i. Ensure that assistance is provided to keep areas below the working area clear and for passing tools or performing rigging.

_____ j. Ensure that personnel working in the vicinity of stacks, or other areas where they may be subjected to exhaust fumes, are wearing proper respiratory protection equipment.

_____ k. Do not permit work aloft, except in an emergency, if wind speed is greater than 30 knots, roll is in excess of 10°, pitch is in excess of 6°, or if ice or thunder storms threaten.

_____ l. If in port, notify officers of the deck/command duty officers of adjacent ship(s) to ensure that high-powered radio and radar transmitters will not be energized and endanger personnel going aloft.

_____ m. Fly the KILO or KILO THREE flag, as appropriate, if in port.

_____ n. Prior to personnel going aloft, have the following passed over the 1MC: "DO NOT ROTATE OR RADIATE ANY ELECTRICAL OR ELECTRONIC EQUIPMENT WHILE PERSONNEL ARE WORKING ALOFT".

_____ o. If a crane is used to suspend personnel, ensure that the crane has a current certification and the work platform is approved by NAVSEA for handling personnel.

3. Conditions have been established to permit personnel working aloft.

_____
Command Duty Officer/Officer of the Deck/Time

Working Aloft Commenced _____

Working Aloft Completed _____

Note: Initials certify completion of an item. If an item is not applicable, indicate "NA" on initial line.

**Figure 13-3.—*Continued***

4. Personnel have an approved safety harness, which should be attached to the ship's structure at the level where they will be working.

5. All tools, buckets, paint pots, and brushes have lanyards with which they can be secured when used for work on masts, stacks, upper catwalks, weather decks, or sponsons that overhang areas where other personnel may be.

6. An announcement has been made over the 1MC concerning the operation aloft and any applicable restrictions, to prevent inadvertent changes in the status aloft.

7. The OODs of adjacent ships have been alerted so that high-powered radio and radar equipment in their ships will not be energized or present a danger to personnel going aloft.

USS _____     Time/Date _____

1.  Personnel (number) _____ will be going over the side at (location) _____
    _____ for accomplishing the following work _____
    _____

2.  Prior to allowing personnel to work over the side, accomplish the following:

**Initials**

_____   a.  If underway or in dry dock, obtain the commanding officer's
            permission.

_____   b.  Ensure that personnel working over the side wear a parachute type
            safety harness with Dyna-Brake® safety lanyard and working lanyard,
            wear an inherently buoyant lifejacket modified with a button hole in
            the back to wear with the safety harness, and wear a hard-hat with a
            chin strap.  Appropriate PMS shall be performed on harness, safety
            lanyard, and lifejacket prior to use.  (Note:  If working from a
            float or punt in the water, safety harness and safety lanyard are not
            required.  Lifejackets and hard hat shall be worn.  If in a dry deck
            without water, the life jacket is not required.)

_____   c.  Each person working over the side has an assistant to tend lines.
            (Note:  If working from a punt or float, at least one assistant shall
            be provided on the deck or pier.  If in a dry dock without water, a
            tending line is not required.)

_____   d.  Ship's propellers are stopped and overboard discharges in the area of
            personnel working over the side are secured and DANGER tagged.

_____   e.  If work is to be accomplished in port between the ship and a pier or
            between the ship and other ships, a camel is in place.

_____   f.  Power tools, if in use, are pneumatic.  NO electric powered tools
            shall be used.

**Figure 13-4. Check Sheet for Working over the Side**

8. If the ship is in port, the "kilo" flag has been hoisted to indicate personnel working aloft.

## WORKING OVER THE SIDE

Personnel assigned to work over the side must be instructed in all safety precautions by their division officers before they can be permitted on scaffolding or stages or in boatswain's chairs. The following precautions must be observed:

1. Personnel working over the side must be supervised by a competent petty officer, and only qualified personnel should be assigned to tend safety lines.

_____ g. Ensure that an experienced, senior person has checked the rigging of the bosun chair or staging prior to use.

_____ h. Ensure that personnel working over the side are briefed on safety prior to working over the side.

_____ i. Do not permit working over the side, except in an emergency, if wind speed is greater than 30 knots, roll is in excess of 10°, pitch is in excess of 6°, or if ice or thunder storms threaten.

_____ j. Ensure that a petty officer in charge of work is stationed. Ensure PO in charge is alert for anything which would cause an increase in ship's motion or for the possibility of a collision.

_____ k. If in port, notify officers of the deck/command duty officers of ships alongside.

_____ l. Fly the KILO ONE or KILO THREE flag, as appropriate, if in port.

_____ m. If a crane is used to suspend personnel over the side, ensure that the crane has current certification and that the work platform is approved by NAVSEA for handling personnel.

3. Conditions have been established to permit personnel working over the side.

_____
Command Duty Officer/Officer of the Deck/Time

Working Over the Side Commenced    _____

Working Over the Side Completed    _____

Note: Initials certify completion of an item. If an item is not applicable, indicate "NA" on initial line.

**Figure 13-4.—*Continued***

2. All personnel working on stages, in boatswain's chairs, or in boats alongside the ship must wear inherently buoyant life preservers. With the exception of personnel in boats, they must also wear approved safety harnesses with shock-absorbing inertial attachment points and be equipped with safety lines tended from the deck above.

3. All tools, buckets, paint pots, and brushes used by personnel working over the side must be secured by lanyards to prevent their loss overboard and injury to personnel below.

4. Any person assigned to do work over the side of the ship while she is under way must have the permission of the commanding officer.

# 14

## BOATS AND VEHICLES

Small-boat operation requires particular attention from the watch officer. Today's sleek and powerful boats are valuable assets to their parent ships. They provide the means of immediate response to emergency situations at sea and may serve as the primary connection with the beach, especially in some foreign ports. It is as true now as it was in the past—a ship is judged by the appearance and performance of her boats and crew.

The watch officer should always remember that boat operation has the potential for catastrophe. The improper preparation and poor handling of boats have caused many accidents and much loss of life. Responsibility for the safety of a ship's boats and embarked passengers cannot be taken lightly. The complex coordination required to ensure safe, smart performance dictates that boat operation be carefully supervised by both the command duty officer (CDO) and the OOD.

### UNDER WAY

During operations at sea, the OOD must be concerned with the readiness and security of the boats. OpNavInst 3120.32C requires that at least one motor whaleboat, if available, be prepared for lowering at all times and that at least one complete boat crew be assigned to rescue and assistance. The duty coxswain must conduct an inspection of the rescue boat at the beginning of each watch and report to the OOD on its readiness for service. The OOD should know the coxswain's qualifications and those of the crew, as well as where they are stationed and how long it would take to assemble them. He or she should also know which personnel will lower the boats in an emergency, who will be in charge of the operation, and how long it will take to lower the boats. The first lieutenant is responsible for providing qualified individuals for boat crews and ensuring that all personnel engaged in small-boat operations are adequately trained for this duty.

The readiness of boat engines, the amount of fuel in boats, and rescue equipment are other matters of interest to the OOD. In cold weather, precautions must be taken to keep the engines warm, either by starting them frequently or with heaters. It goes without saying that, at sea, boats should be fueled to capacity. When lowering and recovering a boat, the OOD must be particularly concerned with safety. A boat should not be lowered in a trough or in waters too rough for recovery, and the ship should not exceed five knots even under the calmest of conditions, though a slight amount of headway is desirable during recovery for ease in hooking the boat to the falls. A course should be selected that gives the ship a minimum roll and provides a lee on the side of the ship where the evolution is taking place. The OOD should also try not to pick up a boat with sternway on the ship; if this is absolutely necessary, he or she should ensure that the falls are hooked or unhooked in reverse of normal order. A boat should not be lowered or hoisted with nonessential personnel on board. Everyone in the boat during its raising or lowering must wear a hard hat, safety shoes, and a life jacket. They must grip the lines as the boat goes up or down. If practical, personnel other than the regular crew should enter or leave the boat only while it is waterborne. When not conducting boat operations, the OOD must be concerned with the security of the boat in its stowage. It is prudent to have a designated watchstander check boats once an hour, more often during heavy weather. When heavy weather is expected, the OOD should inform the first lieutenant so that he or she may take extra precautions to ensure the security of the boats. Any deficiencies in the condition of the boats, their readiness for operation, or the readiness of their crew should be brought to the attention of the first lieutenant and the commanding officer immediately.

All these matters are part of the routine of a well-run ship, but the OOD cannot afford to assume that all is well. If a lifeboat is not ready when needed or is launched with a green crew, the OOD is certain to be held responsible.

## IN PORT

In port, the operation, appearance, and security of boats and vehicles are the responsibility of the OOD. OpNavInst 3120.32C, Article 630.1C, directs the OOD to perform the following duties:

    1. Directly supervise ship's boats, and comply with the boat schedules published by the executive officer and other proper authority.

    2. Make sure boats are operated safely and that all relevant safety regulations are observed.

    3. See that boats are not overloaded, and that loading capacity is reduced to a safe margin when weather conditions require.

    4. Use boat officers under such conditions as:

        a. Foul weather or reduced visibility (existing or expected) and on long trips.

        b. First boat trips in foreign or unfamiliar harbors and when required by local regulations.

        c. Returning large liberty parties after sunset, especially prior to sailing.

    5. Require all boat passengers and crew to wear life jackets when weather or sea conditions are hazardous.

    6. Ensure that coxswains understand the information provided by the navigator.

    7. See that designated engineering department personnel fuel and inspect the boats prior to 0800 daily, that the boats are clean and smart, and that the crew is in proper uniform.

    8. Assign one member of the boat crew as a bow lookout. This requirement is particularly important in boats such as LCMs where the coxswain's forward vision is severely limited.

    9. Give coxswains their trip orders and their orders to shove off.

10. Notify the CDO when weather conditions make the suspension or resumption of boating advisable.

11. Inspect boats secured alongside hourly. If weather or sea conditions hinder safety, hoist boats in or send them to a safe haven.

12. In port, have the coxswain of the lifeboat(s) inspect and report daily at sunset the readiness of those boat(s). At sea, have a similar inspection and report done at the beginning of each watch.

Calling away, dispatching, fueling, and receiving boats and vehicles can be complicated and harassing for an OOD who has not organized the watch. A status sheet is mandatory to keep track of the boats and vehicles on so many missions. Even when an assistant is maintaining a record of missions and conditions of readiness, intelligent supervision by the OOD is still needed. Boats and vehicles should be inspected for appearance, and their equipment should be checked. If the instructions to be given a coxswain or driver are complicated, it is best to send for that person and discuss them. If there is any doubt about a person's memory, he or she should be given instructions in writing, and they should be short, complete, and reasonable. The coxswain must be given a section of the harbor chart showing the ship's berth, other occupied anchorages, all commonly used landings and compass courses thereto, and a copy of local traffic rules and navigational dangers and aids. Tracks to and from the boat's destination should also be clearly marked. A boat or vehicle should never be sent to wait for someone indefinitely; if the passenger or passengers should fail to show up, the services of the boat or vehicle are lost until word can be gotten to the coxswain or driver, and that might take hours. The proper procedure for all boats and vehicles, except, of course, a gig, a barge, or some equivalent vehicle, is to direct them to wait for someone a certain length of time or until a specified hour.

## APPEARANCE

The appearance and smartness of a ship's boats and vehicles are important to officers and enlisted personnel who take pride in their ship and in their service. A smart boat is often the criterion by which a ship and her crew are evaluated. Fresh, neat paintwork and fancy knotwork make a good impression, but the manner in which a boat is handled is even more significant. The OOD is responsible for ensuring that coxswains have good sea manners, which includes rendering proper courtesies to passing boats and avoiding hot-rod landings and excessive wake.

The OOD can be a major factor in maintaining high standards for a ship's boats. His or her critical appraisal of a boat and its crew as it comes alongside is the first step. If the OOD then corrects any deficiencies, he or she will have done much to ensure that the ship is well represented by her boats.

## BOAT GONGS

Many ships customarily use boat gongs to indicate that liberty boats will soon depart. Gongs are sounded over the ship's general announcing circuit, their meaning varying as follows:

| Number of Gongs | Meaning |
|---|---|
| 3 | Boat departs in ten minutes |
| 2 | Boat departs in five minutes |
| 1 | Boat departs in one minute |

## CAPACITY AND LOADING

The capacity of a naval boat is indicated on a label plate affixed to it during construction. The figure shown on the plate indicates maximum capacity under good conditions; capacity is always reduced in rough weather or when cargo is carried along with passengers.

It is worth an OOD's time to learn the technique of loading a large liberty boat, because doing it properly is one of those small but significant signs that a ship is smartly run and has an efficient OOD. After the chief petty officers have embarked, other personnel should load from fore to aft. A little supervision may be required to prevent the center section from filling up first, which results in people climbing over each other or walking along the gunwales, a dangerous practice.

## CREWS

The first lieutenant is responsible for training the boat crew, but it is the OOD's responsibility to ensure that those who operate boats during his or her watch are qualified. The OOD must be especially diligent in this, because the potential for disaster is proportional to the crew's inexperience. The OOD's responsibility for safety dictates that he or she allow only fully qualified crew members to operate the boat. Inexperienced personnel may be allowed to go along for instruction if they wish but never as substitutes for fully qualified people. There can be no compromise when safety is involved.

## EQUIPMENT

Compasses, life jackets, and other pieces of boat equipment must be checked by the OOD as circumstances warrant. When a long boat passage is to be taken or visibility is likely to be low, a chart or compass-book entry showing heading and time on each course should be prepared for guidance and reference. Life jackets, foul-weather clothing, harbor charts, and firefighting equipment are other items with which the OOD should be concerned. Life jackets should be checked and crews and passengers directed to wear them when weather or sea conditions warrant. The number of people allowed in a boat should not exceed the number of life jackets in the boat. It should never be assumed that boats belonging to other units are properly equipped; the OOD should have them inspected if they are to be used by his or her ship.

## INSPECTION

The engineering officer designates a qualified petty officer to make a daily check of boats' engines, and the first lieutenant makes periodic checks on the condition of each boat and the equipment it carries. While these inspections are usually thorough, they do not guarantee that certain equipment will be in a certain boat at a particular time, nor do they relieve the OOD of exercising the prudence and foresight expected of a good seaman.

## ORDERS

Orders to the coxswain of a boat should be given in a seamanlike and explicit manner. An unseamanlike order might be "All right, coxswain, shove off and get the navigator at the Dock Street landing." A seamanlike and explicit order would be "Coxswain! When told to shove off, go to the Dock Street landing and bring off the navigator, Lieutenant Commander Jones. If he does not show up by ____ o'clock, return to the ship. Do you understand?" If the coxswain answers in the affirmative, the OOD would say, "Shove off and carry out your orders." It should be remembered that a boat "hauls out" to the boom, it does not "tie up" or "secure" to the boom. A ship "makes fast" to a pier, while a boat "makes fast" to the accommodation ladder (not to the gangway). A boat may be "secured," but this means a longer-lasting fastening than "made fast."

## SAFETY

The safest way to secure boats is to hoist them in at night or in bad weather. When this procedure is not practical, they should be hauled out to the boom and kept under surveillance. Boats usually ride well at the boom, but the practice of making fast astern is risky in bad weather. Boatkeepers or boat sentries are usually posted when the weather threatens ship's boats. Boats should never lie unattended at the accommodation ladder.

If a boat is to be left in the water for a long time, the OOD should make a visual inspection of it at least once an hour and should direct all roving security patrols to check it as well. This is to prevent unauthorized use or theft or to discover a flooding problem quickly. (For detailed safety precautions governing boat operations, see chapter 13.)

## SCHEDULES

The executive officer generally prescribes boat schedules, and they should be followed meticulously by the OOD. Only the most unusual circumstances should be allowed to cause cancellation of a scheduled boat, particularly at night when people ashore may be planning to return to the ship in that boat. If a scheduled boat trip must be canceled, permission for the cancellation is obtained from the executive officer or CDO, and the word must be passed.

When, as often happens, officers and enlisted personnel waiting to leave the ship are going to the same destination as the senior officer, that person usually allows them to embark in his or her gig or barge. The OOD should find out whether the senior officer concerned follows this practice and, if so, embark the people before he or she comes onto the quarterdeck. If doubt exists, there is nothing wrong with asking the senior officer whether he or she is willing to take crew members along. If the answer is affirmative, as is almost always the case, every effort must be made to expedite the loading of the boat. Juniors normally enter boats (and vehicles) first and leave them last.

## SECURITY

One way to ensure the safe and efficient operation of boats is to provide a boat officer. This is true, of course, only if the officer is qualified.

A boat officer can wear a web belt, which is a badge of authority and distinguishes him or her from passengers who are officers. When there are not enough commissioned or warrant officers to act as boat officers, it is customary to assign chief petty officers of deck ratings.

For a more thorough study of small-boat operations, the reader is referred to *The Boat Officer's Handbook* (Naval Institute Press), and OpNavInst 3120.32C, Article 630.1.

## VEHICLES

Ships in port are assigned vehicles to assist in carrying out daily business. The OOD is usually tasked with keeping track of these vehicles and seeing that they are always ready for use. Losing track of the status of a ship's vehicles can significantly hamper a ship's in-port operation and is certain to ruin the OOD's day. The wise OOD will have direct control of all vehicle keys. He or she will give them only to authorized users and require that they be turned back. Ship's vehicles should be parked within sight of the quarterdeck to prevent theft or damage. The OOD should keep notes on who is using vehicles, who will require them and why, and how long trips will take. Priorities must be established, and the OOD may end up making unpopular decisions. Common sense is usually the rule. Often the consolidation of several trips can make for more efficient use of a vehicle. The name and whereabouts of the duty driver are also of concern to the OOD.

The OOD must make sure that the duty driver is on station, in the correct uniform, and ready for an appointment ahead of schedule. Upon return of a vehicle's keys, the OOD should ascertain the fuel status of the vehicle and have it refueled if necessary.

Any number of things can go wrong with ship's vehicles, all of which spell trouble for the OOD. He or she can avoid most of this trouble by requiring a face-to-face turnover of keys before and after each use. The OOD should not lose track of a vehicle and should ensure that every vehicle is used for ship's business only.

Keep a separate log book to record vehicle status.

**Vehicle Security**

Marked government vehicles or vehicles carrying uniformed passengers are possible targets for terrorists. The OOD must always be alert to the possibility of a local terrorist threat and must take appropriate precautions. He or she must always consult the CDO for special precautions and instructions.

## WASTE, FRAUD, AND ABUSE

Ship's vehicles and boats should be used only for official purposes. They should not make unofficial stops, for example, at a restaurant or shopping mall, while conducting official business. Misuse can lead to complaints against the command, especially when a vehicle or boat carries official Navy or command-specific markings. Always check any questionable requests for vehicles or boats with the CDO or executive officer. Review OpNavInst 3120.32C, Article 510.34.

# 15

# HONORS AND CEREMONIES

Honors and ceremonies are based on customs and a long-established code of agreements and regulations, most of which are common to all navies. With some exceptions, honors and ceremonies take place in port, and the manner in which they are rendered or carried out under the supervision of the OOD does much to give a ship a reputation for smartness. It is important that they be conducted in a manner that also reflects credit on the U.S. Navy and the United States.

The governing source for appropriate honors is U.S. Navy Regulations (1990). The OOD need not commit regulations to memory. For convenience, he or she should memorize some honors, but most situations allow time for preparation. To aid the OOD, some ships keep a table of honors posted on the quarterdeck for ready reference.

With honors and ceremonies, as with nearly all other activities, an OOD must look ahead. He or she should be able to estimate the degree of readiness required at any given time. For example, if the ship is anchored at an advanced base, the weather is bad, and there is a possibility of air attack, the OOD is not likely to need side boys standing by. On the other hand, circumstances might be such that the OOD should have the full guard ready at a moment's notice.

The following pages contain enough information from Navy Regulations to enable the OOD, under normal conditions, to discharge his or her duties. On special occasions, such as the death of an important person, the OOD will have to refer to Navy Regulations.

## THE QUARTERDECK

The Commanding Officer of a ship shall establish the limits of the quarterdeck and the restrictions as to its use. The quarterdeck shall embrace so much of the main or other appropriate deck as may be necessary for the proper conduct of official ceremonial functions.

Navy Regulations, Article 1256

The quarterdeck functions as the command and control center for a ship's daily administrative activities and for the conduct of the ship's in-port routine. It is whatever part of the ship the commanding officer designates. It is normally on the main deck near the brow, making it the first line of security for the ship. It may be marked off by appropriate lines, deck markings, cartridge cases decoratively arranged, or fancy work. It is always kept clean and shipshape. Personnel not on duty should not be allowed on or near the quarterdeck. The dignity and appearance of the quarterdeck reflect the professional and seamanlike attitude of a ship and her crew. The OOD should be zealous in upholding this dignity and appearance, together with the highest standards of smartness on the part of the personnel.

The brow should always be tended by the OOD or an assistant, for reasons of both security and courtesy. Every person who comes aboard should be greeted immediately by a member of the watch. His or her business should then be ascertained and credentials examined. If all is in order, appropriate steps must be taken to have the guest escorted below or to send for the person he or she wishes to see. Officers' guests should be taken to the wardroom.

When an officer comes aboard, his or her boat usually lies alongside the accommodation ladder until it receives its orders. The OOD should ask the visitor or an aide what orders are desired for his or her boat, gig, or barge.

### Side Boys

Side boys, being the first members of the crew to come under the observation of an important visitor, should be particularly smart, their shoes polished and their uniforms immaculate. They should be kept together under the eye of a petty officer and not employed in any activity that might spoil their appearance or remove them from the quarterdeck. The OOD should see that they are properly instructed and can fall in without confusion. Similar care should be taken with the guard and band. Generally, side boys are not paraded or required on any occasion other than a prearranged visit by a flag officer or a VIP.

### Piping the Side

The call "Alongside" is timed to finish just as a visitor's boat reaches the accommodation ladder. During this call, the side boys and the boatswain's mate stand at attention but do not salute.

For a visitor approaching by way of an accommodation ladder, the call "Over the side" starts just as his or her head appears at quarterdeck level. For a visitor approaching over a brow, it starts when he or she arrives at a designated point at the outboard end of the brow. Side boys and boatswain's mate salute on the first note and drop their hands from salute on the last note. The boatswain's mate may salute with the left hand. The saluting and piping procedure is reversed when a visitor leaves.

### Official Visits

When the OOD is notified that an official visit is to be paid to the ship, he or she should take these steps:

1. Consult the table of honors in Navy Regulations.
2. Notify the admiral, chief of staff, commanding officer, executive officer, command duty officer, navigator, senior watch officer, flag lieutenant, and commanding officer of the marine detachment.
3. Have on deck a qualified boatswain's mate and a quartermaster.
4. Inspect and rehearse the side boys.
5. Inspect the quarterdeck for appearance.
6. Station an alert lookout, notify the signal bridge to be prepared, and have the visitor's personal flag ready.
7. Notify the band.
8. If a gun salute is required, notify the combat systems officer.

## SALUTES AND HONORS

The following extracts from Navy Regulations provide a ready reference for the OOD.

### Morning and Evening Colors

1. The ceremonial hoisting and lowering of the national ensign at 0800 and sunset at a naval command ashore or aboard a ship of the Navy not under way shall be known as Morning Colors and Evening Colors, respectively, and shall be carried out as prescribed in this article.

2. The guard of the day and the band shall be paraded in the vicinity of the point of hoist of the ensign.

3. "Attention" shall be sounded, followed by the playing of the national anthem by the band.

4. At Morning Colors, the ensign shall be started up at the beginning of the music and hoisted smartly to the peak or truck. At Evening Colors, the ensign shall be started from the peak or truck at the beginning of the music and the lowering so regulated as to be completed at the last note.

5. At the completion of the music, "Carry on" shall be sounded.

6. In the absence of a band, an appropriate recording shall be played over a public address system. "To the Colors" shall be played by the bugle at Morning Colors and "Retreat" at Evening Colors and the salute shall be rendered as prescribed for the National Anthem.

7. In the absence of music, "Attention" and "Carry on" shall be the signals for rendering and terminating the salute. "Carry on" shall be sounded as soon as the ensign is completely lowered.

8. During colors, a boat under way within sight or hearing of the ceremony shall lie to, or shall proceed at the slowest safe speed. The boat officer, or in his absence the coxswain, shall stand and salute except when dangerous to do so. Other persons in the boat shall remain seated or standing and shall not salute.

9. During colors, vehicles within sight or hearing of the ceremony shall be stopped. Persons riding in such vehicles shall remain seated at attention.

10. After Morning Colors, if foreign warships are present, the national anthem of each nation so represented shall be played in the order in which a gun salute would be fired to, or exchanged with, the senior official or officer present of each such nation; provided that, when in a foreign port, the national anthem of the port shall be played imme-

diately after Morning Colors, followed by the national anthems of other foreign nations represented. Article 1206

## Salutes to the National Ensign

1. Each person in the naval service, upon coming on board a ship of the Navy, shall salute the national ensign if it is flying. He or she shall stop on reaching the upper platform of the accommodation ladder, or the shipboard end of the brow, face the national ensign, and render the salute, after which he or she shall salute the officer of the deck. On leaving the ship, he or she shall render the salutes in inverse order. The officer of the deck shall return both salutes in each case.

   a. After rendering the appropriate salute to the national ensign, an officer coming on board a ship to which he or she is attached shall report his or her return. An officer coming on board a ship to which he or she is not attached shall request permission to come on board and shall state his or her business. An enlisted person shall request permission to come on board, and shall state his or her business if the ship is not the one to which her or she is attached.

   b. After rendering the appropriate salute to the officer of the deck, an officer shall state that he or she has permission to leave. An enlisted person shall request permission to leave.

2. A member not in uniform shall render appropriate honors to the national ensign by facing the flag and standing at attention with the right hand over the heart. If covered, men shall remove their headdress with the right hand and hold it at the left shoulder, the hand being over the heart.

3. Each person in the naval service in uniform, upon being passed by or passing a military formation carrying the national ensign uncased shall render the hand salute. A member not in uniform being passed by or passing such a formation shall face the flag and stand at attention with the right hand over the heart. If covered, men shall remove the headdress and hold it at the left shoulder, the hand being over the heart. Persons in vehicles or boats shall follow the procedure prescribed for such persons during colors.

4. The salutes prescribed in this article shall also be rendered to foreign national flags and ensigns and aboard foreign men-of-war, unless to do so would cause embarrassment or misunderstanding. Aboard foreign men-of-war, the practice of the host nation may be followed, if known. Article 1207

**Table 15-1. Passing Honors between Ships, Sequence**

| OOD OF JUNIOR SHIP | OOD OF SENIOR SHIP | BUGLE CALL | BATTERY WHISTLE |
|---|---|---|---|
| 1. Sounds "Attention" starboard (port) | | "Attention" starboard (port) | 1 whistle starboard, 2 whistles (port) |
| | 2. Sounds "Attention" starboard (port) | | |
| 3. Sounds "Hand salute" (guard presents arms and band sounds off if required) | | 1 short note | 1 short whistle |
| | 4. Sounds "Hand salute" (guard presents arms and band sounds off) | | |
| | 5. Sounds "TWO" (in 3 seconds or after band sounds off) | 2 short notes | 2 short whistles |
| 6. Sounds "TWO" | | | |
| | 7. Sounds "Carry on" | "Carry on" | 3 short whistles |
| 8. Sounds "Carry on" | | | |

**Table 15-2. Passing Honors between Ships, Protocol**

| OFFICIAL | UNIFORM | RUFFLES AND FLOURISHES | MUSIC | GUARD | REMARKS |
|---|---|---|---|---|---|
| President | As prescribed by senior officer present | 4 | National anthem | Full | Man rail, unless otherwise directed by senior officer present |
| Secretary of state when special foreign representative of the president | Do | 4 | Do | Do | Crew at quarters |
| Vice president | Of the day | — | "Hail Columbia" | Do | Do |
| Secretary of defense, deputy secretary of defense, secretary of the Navy, or under secretary of defense | Do | — | National Anthem | Do | Do |
| Assistant secretary of defense, under secretary or assistant secretary of the Navy | Do | — | Do | Do | Do |

**Table 15-3. Passing Honors to Officials and Officers Embarked in Boats**

| OFFICIAL | RUFFLES AND FLOURISHES | MUSIC | GUARD | REMARKS |
|---|---|---|---|---|
| President | 4 | National anthem | Full | "Attention" sounded, and salute by all persons in view on deck; if directed by the senior officer present, man rail[1] |
| Secretary of state when special foreign representative of president | 4 | Do | Do | "Attention" sounded, and salute by all persons in view on deck |
| Vice president | 4 | "Hail Columbia" | Do | Do |
| Secretary of defense, deputy secretary of defense, secretary of the Navy, under secretary of defense, an assistant secretary of defense, under secretary or assistant secretary of the Navy | 4 | Admiral's march | Do | Do |
| Other civil official entitled to honors on official visit | — | — | — | Do |

1. Those who man the rail salute on signal.

## Saluting Ships and Stations

Saluting ships and stations of the naval service are those designated as such by the Secretary of the Navy or by the Secretary's duly authorized representative. The gun salutes prescribed in these regulations shall be fired by such ships and stations. Other ships and stations shall not fire gun salutes, unless directed to do so by the senior officer present on exceptional occasions when courtesy requires.                Article 1212

## "Passing Honors" and "Close Aboard" Defined

"Passing honors" are those honors, other than gun salutes, rendered on occasions when ships of embarked officials or officers pass, or are passed, close aboard. "Close aboard" shall mean passing within six hundred yards for ships and four hundred yards for boats. These rules shall be interpreted liberally, to insure that appropriate honors are rendered.

Article 1227

## Passing Honors between Ships

1. Passing honors, consisting of sounding "Attention" and rendering the hand salute by all persons in view on deck and not in ranks, shall be exchanged between ships of the Navy, and between ships of the Navy and the Coast Guard, passing close aboard. [See table 15-1 for correct sequence.]
2. In addition, the honors prescribed in [table 15-2] shall be rendered by a ship of the Navy passing close aboard a ship or naval station displaying the flag of the official indicated therein; and by naval stations, insofar as practicable, when a ship displaying such flag passes close aboard. These honors shall be acknowledged by rendering the same honors in return.                Article 1228

## Passing Honors to Officials and Officers Embarked in Boats

1. The honors prescribed in [table 15-3] shall be rendered by a ship of the Navy being passed close aboard by a boat displaying the flag or pennant of the . . . officials and officers listed [in table].
2. Persons on the quarterdeck shall salute when a boat passes close aboard in which a flag officer, a unit commander, or a commanding officer is embarked as indicated by a display of a personal flag, command pennant, commission pennant, or a miniature thereof.

Article 1229

## Passing Honors to Foreign Dignitaries and Warships

1. The honors prescribed for the President of the United States shall be rendered by a ship of the Navy being passed close aboard by a

ship or boat displaying the flag or standard of a foreign president, sovereign, or member of a reigning royal family, except that the foreign national anthem shall be played in lieu of the National Anthem of the United States.

2. Passing honors shall be exchanged with foreign warships passed close aboard and shall consist of parading the guard of the day, sounding "Attention," rendering the salute by all persons in view on deck, and playing the foreign national anthem.          Article 1230

### Sequence in Rendering Passing Honors

1. "Attention" shall be sounded by the junior when the bow of one ship passes the bow or stern of the other, or, if a senior is embarked in a boat, before the boat is abreast, or nearest to abreast, the quarterdeck.
2. The guard, if required, shall present arms, and all persons in view on deck shall salute.
3. The music, if required, shall sound off.
4. "Carry on" shall be sounded when the prescribed honors have been rendered and acknowledged.          Article 1231

### Dispensing with Passing Honors

1. Passing honors shall not be rendered after sunset or before 0800 except when international courtesy requires.
2. Passing honors shall not be exchanged between ships of the Navy engaged in tactical evolutions outside port.
3. The senior officer present may direct that passing honors be dispensed with in whole or in part.
4. Passing honors shall not be required by nor required of ships with small bridge areas, such as submarines, particularly in restricted waters.          Article 1232

### Crew at Quarters on Entering or Leaving Port

The crew shall be paraded at quarters during daylight on entering or leaving port on occasions of ceremony except when weather or other circumstances make it impracticable or undesirable to do so. Ordinarily occasions of ceremony shall be construed as visits that are not operational; at homeport when departing for or returning from a lengthy deployment; and visits to foreign ports not visited recently; and other special occasions so determined by a superior. In lieu of parading the entire crew at quarters, an honor guard may be paraded in a conspicuous place on weather decks.          Article 1233

## Side Honors

1. On the arrival and departure of civil officials and foreign officers, and of United States officers when so directed by the senior officer present, the side shall be piped and the appropriate number of side boys paraded.

2. Officers appropriate to the occasion shall attend the side on the arrival and departure of officials and officers.           Article 1249

## Dispensing with Side Boys, Guard, and Band

1. Side boys shall not be paraded on Sunday, or on other days between sunset and 0800, or during meal hours of the crew, general drills and evolutions, and period of regular overhaul; except in honor of civil officials or foreign officers, when they may be paraded at any time during daylight. Side boys shall be paraded only for scheduled visits.

2. Except for official visits and other formal occasions, side boys shall not be paraded in honor of officers of the armed services of the United States, unless otherwise directed by the senior officer present.

3. Side boys shall not be paraded in honor of an officer of the armed services in civilian clothes, unless such officer is at the time acting in an official civil capacity.

4. The side shall be piped when side boys are paraded, but not at other times.

5. The guard and band shall not be paraded in honor of the arrival or departure of an individual at times when side boys in his or her honor are dispensed with, except at naval shore installations.

           Article 1250

## Honors at Official Inspection

1. When a flag officer or unit commander boards a ship of the Navy to make an official inspection, honors shall be rendered as for an official visit, except that the uniform shall be as prescribed by the inspection officer. The inspecting officer's flag or command pennant shall be broken upon his arrival, unless otherwise prescribed in these regulations, and shall be hauled down on his departure.

2. The provisions of this article shall apply, insofar as practicable and appropriate, when a flag or general officer, in command ashore, makes an official inspection of a unit of the command.

           Article 1254

# 16

## FLAGS, PENNANTS, AND BOAT HAILS

The watch officer should be aware that the displaying of flags and pennants, like execution of honors and ceremonies, represents a highly visible evolution that will either enhance or detract from a ship's reputation for smartness or efficiency. This is not an area to be given only cursory attention. The watch officer should see that each action is carried out in a precise, professional manner. This chapter contains the most basic information on the usage of flags and pennants. It is derived from Flags, Pennants, and Customs (NTP-13) and U.S. Navy Regulations. The former publication should be studied by every officer who stands deck watches.

Many countries have variations of their national flag authorized for specific uses. The national flag used by men-of-war is the ensign; that used by merchant ships is the merchant flag. The United States of America has only one flag, the colors, which is used for all purposes and may properly be called the ensign when used in the Navy. A union jack is the union, or inner upper corner of a national flag. The U.S. union is, of course, a blue field with fifty white stars on it.

## GENERAL RULES FOR DISPLAY

The distinctive mark of a naval ship or craft in commission is an officer's personal flag, a command pennant, or a commission pennant. The distinctive mark of a naval hospital ship, such as the *Comfort* or the *Mercy,* is the Red Cross flag. Not more than one distinctive mark is displayed at the same time. Except as prescribed in Navy Regulations for certain occasions of ceremony and when civil officials are embarked, one of the distinctive marks mentioned above is displayed day and night at the after masthead or, in a mastless ship, from the most conspicuous hoist.

When a ship is not under way, the ensign and the union jack are displayed from 0800 until sunset from the flagstaff and the jackstaff, respectively. When a ship has entered port at night, at daylight she displays the ensign from the gaff, if appropriate, for a time sufficient to establish her nationality; it is customary for other ships of war to display their ensigns in return. When mooring or unmooring, the colors are shifted from the gaff to the flagstaff on the stern or the other way around, and the union jack is raised or lowered on the bow. The instant the last mooring line leaves the pier or the anchor is aweigh, the boatswain's mate of the watch sounds a blast on a hand-held whistle and passes the word over the 1MC "Under way, shift colors." This enables the lowering and raising of the flags to occur simultaneously. The jack on the jackstaff forward and the national ensign on the flagstaff aft, if flying, are hauled down smartly. At the same instant, the steaming ensign is hoisted on the gaff and the ship's international call sign and other pertinent signal flags are hoisted or broken. On mooring, the instant the anchor is let go or the first line is made fast to the pier, the boatswain's mate performs the same actions as for unmooring. At this signal, the ship's call sign and steaming ensign are hauled down smartly and the jack and national ensign run up.

Unless otherwise directed by the senior officer present, a ship displays the ensign during daylight from her gaff under the following circumstances:

1. Getting under way and coming to anchor.
2. Falling in with other ships.

3. Cruising near land.
4. In battle (when a special, larger battle ensign is displayed).

## RULES FOR THE U.S. ENSIGN

### During Gun Salutes

A ship of the U.S. Navy displays the ensign at a masthead while firing a salute in honor of a U.S. official or national anniversary, as follows:

1. At the main during the national salute prescribed for the third Monday in February and the 4th of July.
2. At the main during a 21-gun salute to a United States civil official, except by a ship displaying the personal flag of the official being saluted.
3. At the fore during a salute to any other United States civil official, except by a ship which is displaying the personal flag of the official being saluted. Navy Regulations, Article 1261

During a gun salute, the ensign must also remain displayed from the gaff or the flagstaff.

### In Boats

The national ensign is displayed from waterborne boats of the naval service as follows:

1. When under way during daylight in a foreign port.
2. When ships are required to be dressed or full-dressed.
3. When going alongside a foreign vessel.
4. When an officer or official is embarked on an official occasion.
5. When a flag or general officer, a unit commander, a commanding officer, or a chief of staff, in uniform, is embarked in a boat of the command or in one assigned to the personal use of such an officer.
6. At such other times as may be prescribed by the senior officer present. Navy Regulations, Article 1262

### Dipping

When a vessel under U.S. registry, or under the registry of a nation formally recognized by the government of the United States, salutes a ship of the U.S. Navy by dipping her ensign, she is answered dip for dip. If the ensign is not already being displayed, it is hoisted, the dip is returned, and after a suitable interval, it is hauled down. An ensign being displayed at half-mast is hoisted to the truck or peak for the purpose of answering a dip.

Ships of the U.S. Navy dip the ensign only in return for such compliment.

Submarines are not required to dip the ensign.

## Half-Masting

When an ensign that is not already being displayed is to be flown at half-mast, it must be hoisted to the truck or peak before being lowered to half-mast. Similarly, before the ensign is lowered from half-mast, it must be hoisted to the truck or peak.

When the ensign is half-masted, the union jack, if displayed from the jackstaff, must also be half-masted.

Because small boats are a part of a vessel, they follow the procedures of the parent vessel as regards the half-masting of colors.

## Following Motions of Senior Officer Present

Whenever the ensign is to be hoisted, lowered, or half-masted, the motions of the senior officer present are followed, except as prescribed for answering a dip or firing a salute.

A ship displaying the flag of the president, secretary of defense, deputy secretary of defense, secretary of the Navy, an assistant secretary of defense, an under secretary of the Navy, or an assistant secretary of the Navy is regarded as the ship of the senior officer present.

## DISPLAY OF FOREIGN ENSIGNS DURING GUN SALUTES

When a ship is firing a salute to a foreign nation in one of that nation's ports, returning a salute fired by a warship of that nation, or firing a salute on the occasion of a celebration or ceremony of that nation, she displays the ensign of the foreign nation at the main truck.

When a ship is firing a salute to a foreign dignitary or official entitled to twenty-one guns, she displays the national ensign of that dignitary or official at her main truck. When firing a salute to a foreign official entitled to less than twenty-one guns, or to a foreign officer, or when returning a salute fired by a foreign officer, she displays the national ensign of the foreign official or officer at her fore truck.

## DISPLAY OF THE UNITED NATIONS FLAG

The following policy concerns the display of the United Nations flag:

1. The United Nations flag will be displayed at installations of the armed forces of the United States only upon occasion of visits of high dignitaries of the United Nations while in performance of their official duties with the United Nations, or on other special occasions in honor of the United Nations. When so displayed it will be displayed with the United States flag, both flags will be of the same approximate size and on the same level, the flag of the United States in the position of honor on the right (observer's left).

2. The United Nations flag will be carried by troops on occasions when the United Nations or high dignitaries thereof are to be honored. When so carried, the United Nations flag will be carried on the marching left of the United States flag and other United States colors or standards normally carried by such troops.

3. On occasions similar to those referred to in paragraph 2, above, U.S. Naval vessels will display the United Nations flag in the same manner as is prescribed for a foreign ensign during visits of a foreign President or Sovereign.

4. Except as indicated in paragraphs 1, 2, and 3, above, the United Nations flag will be displayed by United States Armed Forces only when so authorized by the President of the United States.

Department of Defense, Directive 1005.1

U.S. naval vessels authorized to display the United Nations flag display it in the same manner as that prescribed for a foreign ensign during visits of a foreign president or sovereign.

## PERSONAL FLAGS AND PENNANTS

### Afloat

Except as otherwise prescribed in Naval Regulations, a flag officer or a unit commander afloat displays a personal flag or command pennant from the flagship. It should never be displayed from more than one ship.

When a flag officer eligible for command at sea is embarked for passage in a naval ship, that ship displays his or her personal flag, unless the ship is already displaying the flag of an officer who is senior.

Flags or pennants of officers not eligible for command at sea are not displayed from ships of the U.S. Navy.

## Broad and Burgee Command Pennants

Broad and burgee command pennants are the personal pennants of officers, not flag officers, commanding units of ships or aircraft. The broad command pennant indicates command of the following:

1. A division of aircraft carriers or cruisers.
2. A force, flotilla, or squadron of ships or craft of any type.
3. An aircraft wing.

The burgee command pennant indicates command of the following:

1. A division of ships or craft other than aircraft carriers or cruisers.
2. A major subdivision of an aircraft wing.

The broad and burgee command pennants are surcharged with numerals to indicate the organizational number within a ship type. When two commanders within a type are entitled to display the same command pennant and have the same organizational number in different echelons of command, the commander in the higher echelon uses Roman numerals in the surcharge. In all other cases, Arabic numerals are used. Blue numerals are used on board command pennants, red numerals on burgee command pennants.

Burgee command pennants are rarely seen.

## Bow and Flagstaff Insignia for Boats

A boat regularly assigned to an officer for personal use must carry insignia on each bow as follows:

1. For a flag or general officer, the stars of rank, as arranged on his or her flag.
2. For a unit commander who is not a flag officer, a replica of his or her command pennant.
3. For a commanding officer or a chief of staff not a flag officer, an arrow.

In a boat assigned to the personal use of a flag or general officer, unit commander, chief of staff, or commanding officer, or in which a civil official is embarked, flagstaffs for the ensign and for a personal flag or pennant must be fitted at the peak with devices as follows.

| | |
|---|---|
| Spread Eagle: | For an official entitled to a salute of nineteen or more guns |
| Halberd: | For a flag or general officer whose official salute is less than nineteen guns; for a civil official entitled to a salute of eleven or more guns but less than nineteen guns |
| Ball: | For an officer of the grade, or relative grade, of captain in the Navy; for a career minister, a counselor or first secretary of embassy or legation, or a consul |
| Star: | For an officer of the grade, or relative grade, of commander in the Navy |
| Flat Truck: | For an officer below the grade, or relative grade, of commander in the Navy; for a civil official not listed above, and for whom honors are prescribed for an official visit |

## Personal Insignia at the Masthead

When the president's flag is displayed at a masthead where an ensign is required to be displayed during an official visit or during periods of dressing or full-dressing ship, it shall remain at that masthead to port of the U.S. ensign and to starboard of a foreign ensign.

Except as provided above, a personal flag or command pennant is not displayed at the same masthead with a national ensign. When both are to be displayed, the personal flag or command pennant should be displayed as follows:

1. During a gun salute, it should be lowered clear of the ensign.
2. During an official visit, it should be shifted to the starboard yardarm in a single-masted ship and to the fore truck in a two-masted ship.
3. During periods of dressing or full-dressing ship:
   a. If displayed from the fore truck or from the masthead of a single-masted ship, it should he shifted to the starboard yardarm.

b. If displayed from the main truck, it should be shifted to the fore truck in lieu of the ensign at that mast.

c. If displayed from the after truck of a ship with more than two masts, it should remain at the after truck in lieu of the ensign at that mast.

## Flags or Pennants in Boats and on Automobiles

When embarked in a boat of the naval service on an official occasion, an officer in command, or an acting chief of staff, displays a personal flag or command pennant or, if not entitled to either, a commission pennant from the bow.

When embarked in a boat of the naval service on other than official occasions, an officer entitled to display a personal flag or command pennant may display a miniature of the flag or pennant in the vicinity of the coxswain's station.

When riding in an automobile on an official occasion, an officer entitled to display a personal flag or command pennant may display the flag or pennant forward on the vehicle.

All flag officers are authorized to show the stars of their rank on automobiles assigned to them. These stars may be displayed only on six-by-twelve-inch plates attached to or in the vicinity of the license plates. Stars or replicas of personal flags may not be painted on automobiles.

## Half-Masting

Personal flags, command pennants, and commission pennants should be half-masted for deceased officials or officers only as prescribed in Navy Regulations.

## Civil Officials in Boats

When a U.S. civil official is embarked in a naval boat on an official occasion, a flag should be displayed in the bow as follows:

1. A union jack for a diplomatic representative of or above the rank of chargé d'affaires, within the waters of the country to which he or she is accredited; and a governor general or governor commissioned by the president, within the area of his or her jurisdiction.

2. A consular flag for a consular representative.

3. A personal flag for other civil officials when they are entitled to the display of a personal flag during an official visit.

## Officials of the United Nations and the
## North Atlantic Treaty Organization

When an official of the United Nations or the North Atlantic Treaty Organization is embarked in a U.S. naval vessel, that person is not entitled to have a personal flag displayed unless he or she is a U.S. Navy flag officer eligible for command at sea.

## MISCELLANEOUS FLAGS AND PENNANTS

### Absence Indicators

The absence from his or her ship of a flag officer, unit commander, chief of staff, or commanding officer is indicated from sunrise to sunset by the display of an absence indicator, as prescribed in table 16-1. Substitute pennants, as shown in the signal book, are used as follows:

| | |
|---|---|
| First | Flag officer or unit commander |
| Second | Chief of Staff |
| Third | Captain |
| Fourth | Other embarked |

When a commanding officer acting as a temporary unit commander is absent from the ship, both absence pennants should be displayed.

### Intention to Depart

The hoisting of the speed pennant where best seen (in port) indicates that the official or officer whose personal flag or command pennant is displayed will leave the ship officially in about five minutes. The hauling down of the speed pennant means that the official or officer is departing.

The following procedure is used when a flag officer shifts his or her flag:

1. Five minutes before departure, the flagship hoists the speed pennant at the main truck, below the personal flag.

2. As the officer departs, the flagship hauls down the speed pennant and hoists the appropriate absence pennant.

## Table 16-1. Use of Substitute Pennants

| Sub. | Indication | Where Normally Displayed | Absentee |
|------|-----------|--------------------------|----------|
| 1st | Absence of an official from his or her ship for a period of 72 hours or less | Starboard main yardarm (outboard) | A flag officer or unit commander whose personal flag or command pennant is flying in this ship |
| 2nd | Same as 1st substitute | Port main yardarm (inboard) | A chief of staff |
| 3rd | Same as 1st substitute | Port main yardarm (outboard) | A captain (executive officer if captain is absent for a period exceeding 72 hours) |
| 4th | Same as 1st substitute | Starboard main yardarm (inboard) | A civil or military official whose flag is flying in this ship |

3. When the officer arrives in the new flagship, that ship breaks his or her flag at the main truck.

4. During the breaking of a personal flag in a new flagship, the former flagship hoists a commission pennant and hauls down the personal flag and the absentee pennant.

### Church Pennant

Public law authorizes the use of the church pennant above the ensign "during church services conducted by naval chaplains at sea." The words "at sea" are interpreted for U.S. Navy purposes as meaning "on board a naval vessel." Shore stations are not authorized to display the church pennant above the ensign, but they may display it separately, if desired.

If divine services are being conducted at the time of morning colors, or if they begin at that time, the ensign is hoisted to the peak at the time prescribed for it. The church pennant is then hoisted and the ensign dipped just clear of it.

Should the time of evening colors occur while divine services are being conducted, the church pennant is hauled down and the ensign hoisted to the peak just before the time for colors; the ensign is then hauled down at the prescribed time.

Should the ensign be displayed at half-mast, the church pennant should be hoisted just above it.

## Battle-Efficiency Pennant (Meatball)

The battle-efficiency pennant, known as the meatball, is flown at the fore truck during the period provided in Awards for Intra-Type Competition when not under way.

When a guard flag, ready-duty flag, or Presidential Unit Citation pennant is displayed at the fore truck with the battle-efficiency pennant, the latter should be flown below the other flag.

## Homeward-Bound Pennant

Specifications for the design of and rules for the use of the homeward-bound pennant have never been firmly established. The usage set forth in NTP-13 is believed to conform with tradition.

## POW/MIA Flag

When prescribed by the senior officer present, the POW/MIA flag shall be flown from 0800 until sunset. Ships under way must not fly the POW/MIA flag. The point of display on board ships in port is the inboard halyard, port signal yardarm. The POW/MIA flag flies beneath the national ensign at shore activities. Additionally, shore activities may display the POW/MIA flag indoors to enhance commemoration ceremonies.

## PUC, NUC, and MUC Pennants

Ships that have been awarded the Presidential Unit Citation, the Navy Unit Commendation, or the Meritorious Unit Commendation should fly the appropriate pennant, described in NTP-13, at the fore truck from sunrise to sunset when not under way.

## Special Flag-Hoist Signals

Instructions from the senior officer present may prescribe certain flag hoists for local use, such as a request for the garbage or trash lighter or the water barge.

## DRESSING AND FULL-DRESSING SHIP

Ships not under way are dressed or full-dressed from 0800 until sunset when prescribed or when directed. Ships under way are never dressed or full-dressed.

When full-dressing is prescribed, the senior officer present may order that dressing be substituted for it if, in his or her opinion, the weather makes it advisable. That officer may also, under such circumstances, direct that the ensigns be hauled down from the mastheads after being hoisted. See NTP-13 for details of dressing and full-dressing, including the specified sequence of signal flags and pennants to be hoisted.

## BOAT HAILS

### Night

All boats approaching a ship at night should be hailed as soon as they are within hearing distance. The watch on board ship should call out, "Boat ahoy!" and the coxswain should indicate the rank or rate of the senior person in the boat by replying as follows:

| Rank or Rate | Coxswain's Reply |
|---|---|
| President or vice president of the United States | "United States" |
| Secretary of defense, deputy or assistant secretary of defense | "Defense" |
| Secretary, under secretary, or assistant secretary of the Navy | "Navy" |
| Chief of naval operations, vice chief of naval operations | "Naval operations" |
| Fleet or force commander | Fleet, or abbreviation of administrative title |
| General officer | "General officer" |
| Chief of staff | "Staff" |
| Squadron commander | ____ Ron ____ (the type and number of abbreviation used is, for example, "DesRon-21") |

| Marine officer commanding a unit, i.e., battalion | "Battalion commander" |
| Commanding officer of a ship | Name of ship |
| Other commissioned officer | "Aye, aye" |
| Noncommissioned officer | "No, no" |
| Enlisted personnel | "Hello" |
| Boat not intending to come alongside, regardless of rank or rate of senior passenger | "Passing" |

### Day

During hours when honors are rendered, the OOD should challenge an approaching boat as soon as possible by raising an arm with a closed fist in the direction of the boat and training a long glass or binoculars on the coxswain. The coxswain should reply by holding up the number of fingers corresponding to the number, if any, of side boys standing by to honor the officer in his or her boat. A wave-off from the coxswain indicates that no side boys are required.

### SIGNAL FLAGS

The following signals from the International Code of Signals (H0102) are of general interest to the OOD. They may be flown when preceded by the signal flag code as follows:

Code A: I have a diver down; keep well clear at slow speed.

Code B: I am taking in, discharging, or carrying dangerous goods (such as explosives or fuel).

Code H: I have a pilot on board.

Code P: All persons should report on board, as the vessel is about to get under way.

Code Q: My vessel is "healthy" and I request free pratique.

Other signal flags from ATP-1 should be committed to memory by qualified in-port OODs.

# 17

## THE WATCH IN THE COMBAT INFORMATION CENTER

The Ops Room of a modern warship, with everyone at their computers and controls, is to any visiting stranger one of the weirdest places on earth.

Admiral "Sandy" Woodward

The CIC Watch Officer is a representative of the CIC Officer and supervises the operation of the CIC during the watch period.

OpNavInst 3120.1C

Up until this point, we have been primarily concerned with standing the watch either on the bridge or on the quarterdeck. In this chapter, we will focus on some of the unique aspects of watchstanding in the combat information center (CIC)—also known as the command and decision center (CDC) on some ships or an operations center (OPS CTR) in the commonwealth navies.

### PREPARING FOR WATCH IN THE CIC

You must be well rested prior to assuming the watch in the CIC, and you should also ensure you are well fed. Many key mistakes are the result of hungry and tired watchstanders. Also, you should take the opportunity to pass through the ship's combat systems maintenance center on your way to taking the watch in the CIC. This will give you the best possible appreciation for the current state of the sensors and weapons systems in the ship. Additionally, you should stop through the ship's intelligence center and have a quick discussion with the ship's intelligence officer or enlisted intelligence specialist prior to assuming the watch. Finally, it is advisable to make a quick stop through the bridge. This gives you an invaluable sense of the environmental conditions facing the bridge team, such as the weather, sea state, and lighting.

## WATCH STATIONS IN THE CIC

The key watch station in the CIC is the combat information center watch officer (CICWO). This officer's job is to back up the bridge watch team in all aspects of navigational safety, maneuvering of the ship, communications, and sensor management. As the name of the watch implies, the CICWO is required to maintain an accurate flow of information from the ship's electronic sensors to the ship's bridge. In this chapter, we will focus on the work of the CICWO, although it is important to understand some of the other key watchstanders in the CIC.

The CICWO also supports the other watchstanders in combat, including the following:

*Tactical Action Officer* (TAO). The ship's TAO is the senior watchstander in the CIC, and is the commanding officer's direct representative in the employment of the ship's weapons system. He or she directs the action of all members of the CIC team and further guides the officer of the deck in the overall employment of the ship. The TAO is in charge of the tactical employment and the defense of the ship.

*Combat Systems Warfare Coordinators.* On many ships, various officers stand watch as warfare coordinators for air, surface, subsurface, and electronic warfare. They work directly for the TAO and interact with the CICWO in the overall operation of the ship.

*Communication Watch Officer* (CWO). The CWO is in charge of the radio communications, normally assigned to the area in which the majority of radio receivers and switching equipment is located, that is, radio central. He or she will work closely with the CICWO on all matters related to communications effectiveness.

***Combat Systems Officer of the Watch*** (CSOOW). This individual may be located within the CIC or in a dedicated combat systems maintenance central. He or she is in charge of the overall operation of the ship's combat system, reporting normally to the TAO when that watch is being stood. As CICWO you will work closely with the CSOOW on all sensors and communications equipment in the CIC.

## KEY RESPONSIBILITIES OF THE CICWO

The first and most important responsibility of the CICWO is to supervise the personnel on watch in the CIC, working hard to make sure that all contacts—surface, subsurface, and air—are reported. Performing this important duty effectively means understanding exactly the jobs of all the watchstanders in the CIC. The best way to gain this appreciation is to stand a series of watches with each of them during your own training period before you begin assuming the watch. Another effective means of gaining an appreciation of their job is to study the qualification books associated with each of the key watch positions in the CIC. You should also understand the basics of the jobs undertaken by the other senior watch stations in the CIC, for example, the TAO and warfare coordinators. Remember also that supervising these highly trained watchstanders is a distinct leadership challenge—you are very much an example when you walk into the CIC and should be prepared to take charge and act with extreme professionalism from the moment you walk into the space.

A second key challenge for the CICWO is maintaining accurate summary and geographic plots, status boards, and watch information. This might be termed the "housekeeping" function of the CICWO. A clean, well-organized, and neatly arranged watch space always outperforms a sloppy space with loose papers lying around. Make your watch team keep everything in organized, tabbed binders; file messages immediately in the appropriate binders. Keep the watch station notebooks updated. Check status boards once an hour and give them a "common sense" readability test. A good policy is that when you leave watch, the entire CIC should have improved in neatness and organization. This sounds mundane, but it is important!

The third key function of the CICWO is ensuring that communications circuits are correctly set up and manned by well-trained operators, and that correct procedures and terminology are used. You must be the expert in communications procedures. This can be reviewed quickly prior to each watch until it becomes second nature. A ship is judged by the quality of its communications—it is an obvious measure of effectiveness that will be commented upon by everyone in your battle group.

Evaluating the mass of information received is a fourth key function of the CICWO. You will receive a vast amount of data through the systems that are in place in your ship. These include voice, radio, radar, sonar, electronic-warfare support measures, visual lookouts, direction finders, intelligence, messages—at times, the sheer volume of information can seem overwhelming. Your job is to bring order from the chaos. This is largely a matter of experience, but gradually you will be able to discern patterns and important pieces of the puzzle that can be extracted from the mass of information and fused together for dissemination to your shipmates. Start, obviously, by focusing on anything that relates directly to your ship. Your captain's standing orders will establish procedures for distances in which you should focus around your ship; as a rule of thumb, anything within about two hundred nautical miles for air activity, one hundred miles for surface activity, and thirty miles for subsurface activity is germane. Additionally, you should focus on information that relates to the significant mission your ship is executing at any given moment. As an example, if you are charged with undersea defense of the carrier, you should be paying particular attention to the prediction ranges for subsurface contacts generated by sonar control. You will quickly develop a sense of what information is critical, what is important, and what is "nice to know" at any given moment.

Once you have set up the watch properly, gathered the information, and evaluated it, your job is really just beginning. The fifth task before you as CICWO is to disseminate effectively and quickly the evaluated information to appropriate control stations throughout the ship. These include the bridge, flag plot (if a destroyer squadron commander, amphibious squadron commander, or flag officer is embarked), war room, strike operations center, air operations, air intelligence, and weapons-control stations. Dissemination can take a variety of forms, from a phone call to the OOD stationed on the bridge to forwarded e-mail to the battle watch captain. It may be verbal, electronic, or written. Your ship will have set procedures in place to accomplish this dissemination of information, but you should be creative and aggressive in sending information around the ship.

The sixth important function of the CICWO is to keep the OOD informed of the CIC's recommendations for maintaining station, avoiding navigational hazards and collisions, and general safe maneuvering of the ship. In most situations, this is your single most important duty. Throughout every watch you stand, you should keep the safety of the ship in the forefront of your mind. Things can get very confusing on the bridge, and your job is to back up the bridge watchstanders at all times. Be proactive in this regard. If there is a disconnection between your team in the CIC and the folks on the bridge, it is up to you to go to the bridge and resolve it. If you ever feel the ship is standing into danger and your recommendations are not being followed, immediately contact the commanding officer, executive officer, or senior watch officer to help resolve the dispute. Every time the ship maneuvers—whether for changing station, adjusting PIM, or any other purpose—you should provide the bridge a coherent recommendation by the fastest clear means. This may be the 21MC, a phone talker, a telephone call from you to the OOD, or any other means appropriate to the configuration of your ship. The key is that you as CICWO and the OOD on the bridge have minute-to-minute access to each other to compare your solutions and achieve concurrence before maneuvering the ship.

A seventh mission of the CICWO is to control the use of radar, sonar, electronic-warfare support measures, and voice circuits. This is, of course, done through the watchstanders working those particular stations. You cannot simultaneously supervise all of them, but it is a good practice to spend a moment or two with each operator at least once an hour. This gives you the chance to judge their general proficiency, state of alertness, tactical knowledge, and situational awareness. It will also give you a chance to impart some of the "big picture" to them. Try not to focus on a single piece of the puzzle; your job is to cycle from station to station and maintain overall control of the ship's systems.

There is an eighth requirement for the CICWO: keeping up with what might be termed the "paperwork" of the watch. This means you need to be familiar with the operational plans, orders, tactical publications, directives, and regulations of higher authority that affect the watch or the operation of the CIC. You must also ensure the highest standards are followed in the preparation of the watch logs. This may require some off-watch study, as well as occasionally spot-checking the log keepers. You may want to experiment with some of the new software programs that permit a watchstander to simply "talk into the computer" and produce written copy. Another alternative is to use hand-held tape recorders for particularly important periods.

Finally, the CICWO must also be prepared to execute a series of operational tasks, including initiating search and rescue (SAR) procedures, assuming duties as a warfare commander if so directed, controlling the combat direction system if no TAO is posted, reporting all landfalls, maintaining a competent navigation track and position record of the ship's movements, and supervising the work of the ship's lookouts. These are all important duties and should receive your attention in the course of the watch.

This is a long list of duties, and the new CICWO may justifiably ask, "Where do I put my emphasis?" The answer to this question is fairly straightforward. Your task is to support the officer of the deck in the safe maneuvering of the ship. If you take as your charter the role of backup to the OOD, you will succeed as the CICWO. Everything falls out from this vital duty. Pay close attention to it, and you will do just fine.

## SUPPORTING THE EMBARKED STAFF

As a watch officer in the CIC, you may be very involved in supporting an embarked staff. On a destroyer or cruiser, this may be a destroyer squadron commander, while an amphibious ship may embark an amphibious squadron commander. Larger ships, such as carriers, may embark a flag officer with a rather large staff.

In each case, the duties of the CICWO are usually laid out in an instruction published by the senior officer of the embarked staff. He or she will spell out the necessary support from the flagship. Normally, this will consist of several consoles in the CIC, a chart or plot table, a large screen display, one or two status boards, and a few watchstanders to augment the staff. In the case of a larger staff on a carrier or large amphibious ship, there will normally be a dedicated space to support the embarked commander. You will also be required to keep the embarked staff informed of the ship's activity, as well as assist in maintaining the situational awareness of the staff as they execute their larger, force-wide responsibilities.

You should endeavor to make the time the embarked staff spends on your ship a very pleasant and tactically successful experience for them. By helping them succeed, your ship will succeed in its mission. As you stand your watches, take the time to stop by the embarked staff module prior to assuming the watch. Try to consider tactical events from the perspective of the embarked staff. For example, if you are steaming in formation with a group of ships, the embarked staff will be interested in an accurate plot of all ships in the force. You should support their requirements with the flagship's sensors and ensure they can keep track of their entire force. Check in with them every hour or so and inquire as to their general sense of how everything is going and satisfaction with their support from your ship.

## A FEW PRINCIPLES FOR CIC WATCH OFFICERS

Here are ten good watchstander rules for CICWOs:

***Be in charge.*** If you are getting overwhelmed, call for help early. You will know if events are overtaking your ability to sort them out and provide quality support to the officer of the deck. The first call to make is to the senior watch officer. He or she will be able to provide some additional support to your watch team as required.

***Never lose your temper.*** It clouds your judgment and increases chaos. Your fundamental job is to bring order out of chaos, not to add more chaos with loud or angry comments or questions. There will be many frustrating moments in the course of some watches you stand in a CIC, and there will be many factors over which you have no control. But you always have the opportunity to keep control of yourself. Remember that your watch team will look at you for their cue when things get hectic. Your reactions will count a great deal. Stay calm and cool on the outside, no matter how high the frustration gets on the inside.

***Constantly seek to match problem to resource to plan.*** You will face many problems, and your first instinct should be to think, "What resources can I bring to bear to solve this problem?" Next you should consider a plan that will permit you to use the resources to solve the problem. Here is one possible scenario: There is an Iranian Kaman patrol boat operating somewhere to the east of your ship. You know this because of electronic intercepts from your ship's SLQ-32. Your problem is to refine the location of this potential threat to your ship. Immediately consider where you can obtain resources to work the problem. You need aircraft, which can move rapidly and triangulate the electronic signal. Work to get control of a helicopter from your own ship, a land-based aircraft such as a P-3, or an aircraft from the carrier's air wing if you are operating with a CV or CVN. Once you have control of an aircraft, you need a plan. Fly the aircraft off-axis a sufficient distance from the ship to establish triangulation with the electronic line of bearing from the ship. Your cross fix should establish the position of the Kaman. Think "problem to resource to plan" and you will usually resolve whatever issue you face.

**Adjust warning condition and weapons posture as required.** It is very easy to forget about making changes to warning conditions and weapons posture. As the CICWO, you must remain attuned to changes to these extremely important aspects of your ship's operations. While you will not be in a position to direct warning condition and weapons posture without approval from the commanding officer, you should remain informed of the tactical situation and ready to make appropriate recommendations, especially in the absence of a posted TAO.

**Keep your status boards updated.** This seems so simple yet is often overlooked or forgotten in the bustle of standing watch in a CIC. Your watch team will need to ensure information of general use is posted and available. Keeping the boards updated will also force your team to stay on top of the entire tactical picture.

**Keep your watch station notebooks updated.** Each watch station should have a three-ring binder or notebook in which general tactical updates and messages can be filed, pass-down information can be posted, and standing direction from the CO can be kept. As CICWO you should take a look at each watch station notebook at least once during each watch.

**Minimize communications over the circuits.** The key is ensuring you don't pass superfluous information. Never use a "double call up," wherein you call another unit and await confirmation from them before passing information. You should simply call up the unit and immediately pass your traffic. Always have a good sense of what you will say whenever you pick up a radio handset, and never transmit in haste.

**Be confident, polite, professional, and "can do" on the circuits.** Your tone will translate directly and quickly into your ship's reputation. Be upbeat and try to solve problems for other units, not add to the general confusion of a situation. If you are frustrated or angry, don't pick up a handset. Carefully monitor your more junior watchstanders as well, trying to encourage them to be assertive but pleasant when discussing issues with their opposite numbers on other ships.

**Always have a plan, especially when using airplanes.** Don't simply turn fuel into noise without purpose. Brief pilots clearly and with energy. Take their debriefs with enthusiasm and interest. One of the key things you must do in a CIC is to provide pilots with the information they need to have a tactically successful flight. They will stop through on their way to preflight the aircraft and get the information you provide. Likewise, they will stop through the CIC after the flight and conduct a debrief with you. If you come across as too busy to take their debrief, or provide inadequate information to them before their flight, they will quickly lose interest in coming back.

**Remember to study the rules of engagement.** It is critically important to fully understand all the issues related to rules of engagement. In the real world, when ordnance is released, everything changes forever. Remember that.

## PUBLICATIONS

As the CICWO, you are essentially the "keeper of the library" for the ship during tactical operations. The bridge watch team is focused on looking out of the bridge windows and will count on you and your watchstanders to constantly review the publications to ensure the ship is in tactical and operational compliance with the rules.

Be sure to familiarize yourself with the ship's tactical library before you find yourself in the middle of a busy watch. You should have a working knowledge of the most frequently used publications, as well as a general sense of where to find key information. At the end of this book you will find a fairly complete list of current publications with which a competent CICWO should be familiar. The key types of publications and some of the best-known individual titles are annotated below.

### Fleet Exercise Publications

These publications contain the general guidance for conducted exercises. They list the "how to" aspect of putting together the day-to-day evolutions for watchstanders. Some of the key FXPs with which you should be very familiar are FXP-1, Antisubmarine Warfare Exercises; FXP-2, Antiair Warfare Exercises; and FXP-3, which includes guidance on strike warfare, antisurface ship warfare, intelligence, and electronic warfare.

### Allied Publications

These are the publications that the North Atlantic Treaty Organization (NATO) uses for the conduct of exercises involving all the allied nations ascribing to that treaty. They are also used as the basis for exercises with other nations allied to the United States but not in NATO, for example, Australia, Japan, and South Korea. Some of the particularly important or frequently used allied publications include: ATP-1, Volumes 1 and 2, Allied Maritime Tactical Instructions and Procedures and the accompanying Signal and Maneuvering Book; ATP-3 and 3(B), Antisubmarine Evasive Steering; AXP-1, Allied Submarine and Antisubmarine Exercise Manual; and ATP-8, Doctrine for Amphibious Operations.

### Naval Doctrine Publications

These important publications talk about the role of the Navy and Marine Corps in joint operations. These publications are growing in number and importance. Some of the key ones that the CICWO should have perused include NDP-1, Naval Warfare; NDP-5, Naval Planning; and NDP-6, Naval Command and Control.

### Joint Doctrine Publications

This is the fastest growing area of publications in the U.S. military and constitutes the emerging joint doctrine that binds the services together. Joint doctrine is emerging every year and is accessible on the World Wide Web at both the unclassified and classified levels.

Your ship's operations officer will know how to access these important publications. They are divided into several groups, including personnel and administration, intelligence operations, logistics, plans, and C4 systems. As CICWO, you should have at least a basic familiarity with the operational joint doctrine publications (the 3.0 series) that bear on maritime affairs.

### Naval Warfare Publications

Long the backbone of the tactical library, the naval warfare publications are—in effect—written Navy doctrine for the day-to-day conduct of operations at sea. Some of the key ones you should be familiar with as the CICWO include: NWP 1-03, Joint Reporting System and the associated series of reporting system publications; NWP 1-10.1, the Tactical Action Officer Handbook; NWP 1-14, Commander's Handbook on the Law of Naval Operations; NWP 3-01 series on antiair warfare; NWP 3-20 series on surface ship operations, with a close look at the tactical manual for your specific ship class; and NWP 3-21, the antisubmarine series. You might also find a need for a couple of others for reference, including NWP 3-50 on search and rescue; NWP 3-56 on tactical communications, and NWP 4-01.4 on underway replenishment. Finally, the NWP 3-2 series on aircraft tactical manuals will also provide valuable reference when working with specific aircraft.

### MINE WARFARE AND MINE AVOIDANCE

One area of watchstanding that may involve the watch officer both on the bridge and in the CIC is the potentially critical activity of avoiding mines. In the course of qualifying both as an officer of the deck and as a CIC watch officer, you will be involved in the study of how to avoid mines.

It is important to realize that many nations have the ability to lay mines. Several U.S. ships have struck mines over the past decades, including the USS *Samuel B. Roberts* (FFG-58), the USS *Tripoli* (LPH-10), and the USS *Princeton* (CG-59)—as well as the tanker *Bridgeton* while she was under U.S. escort. All of these mine strikes occurred in the dangerous waters of the Arabian Gulf.

Mines constitute a psychological deterrent. They are inexpensive and easy to deliver, and they are very time consuming to remove.

They are, in effect, a very valuable force multiplier for poor countries. Worldwide, since 1982, thirty-eight ships of various nations have been sunk or damaged by mines.

While a thorough discussion of types and placement of mines is outside the scope of this work, you should take the time to review applicable references occasionally. Review the various types of mines: bottom, moored, drifting, propelled warhead, and very shallow water.

In terms of mine avoidance, as a watch officer—either on the bridge or in the CIC—you should be aware of the basic material and tactical measures involved in finding and avoiding mines. Some of the key elements of mine avoidance include degaussing, acoustic measures, cathodic protection, sonar (particularly the increasingly available Kingfisher), visual aids, readiness conditions, and plant operations.

Most ships have a standard checklist that should be executed when nearing or entering a suspected mine field. If your ship does not have one, the basic steps include the following:

> Transit during daylight hours where visual detection is possible.
> Energize degaussing, which will protect against magnetic mines.
> Set and maintain watertight integrity (that is, set material condition Zebra).
> Impose silent routine and quiet ship conditions.
> Maintain constant engine rpm.
> Keep speed slow (six knots or below).
> Pass mined area at high tide and deepest point.
> Be ready to maneuver or anchor.
> Post mine lookouts.
> Alter course if necessary.
> Minimize below-deck personnel.
> All hands use head protection and life jackets.
> Use helo flying down the intended track to sweep visually.

If you encounter a mine ahead, attempt to pass no closer than three hundred yards and submit an immediate report of the mine's location, maintaining visual contact if possible while marking and plotting the location. You may want to consider exiting a mine field by backing out along the course you made good entering.

As a last resort, consider small arms fire, but the preferred method is to contact a higher authority to obtain explosive ordnance disposal (EOD) assistance. These professionals can be flown to your ship, parachute into the surrounding water, and destroy the mine.

# Appendix A

# SAMPLE STANDING ORDERS

USS FISKE (DDG XX) INSTRUCTIONS 3121.1C

Subj:   COMMANDING OFFICER'S STANDING ORDERS

Ref.    (a)  U.S. Navy Regulations, 1990
        (b)  OPNAVINST 3120.1 (Series) SORM
        (c)  Navigational Rules COMDTINST M16672.2C
        (d)  ATP-1(C) Volume I, Allied Maritime Tactical Instructions
             and Procedures
        (e)  ATP-1(C) Volume II, Allied Maritime Tactical Signal and
             Maneuvering Book
        (f)  Watch Officer's Guide

Encl:   (1)  Standing Orders

1. *Purpose.* To promulgate my Standing Orders to the Officer of the
Deck (OOD) while FISKE is under way or at anchor. Supplemental
Night Orders will be issued daily when under way or as required.
This instruction amplifies references (a) through (f), which contain
information basic to OOD responsibilities.

2. *Discussion.*

a. Reference (a) formalizes the time-honored tradition of the Commanding Officer's absolute responsibility for the safety of his or her ship and the ship's crew.

b. As an OOD in FISKE, your responsibilities are clear: do not collide or ground. You will not go wrong if, in peacetime, you act to keep the ship safe, and in battle, you carry out the mission.

c. I will never criticize the OOD who maneuvers FISKE into open sea room because he or she is uncertain of navigation or concerned about maneuvering safety.

3. *Responsibility.* As the Commanding Officer, I am completely and inescapably responsible for this ship, its equipment, and the lives of all personnel on board. I depend upon and trust you to assist me in this responsibility with forehandedness and action, and by informing me promptly and fully of any event or occurrence which bears upon the safety and operability of FISKE.

4. *Action.*

a. These orders are permanent. If there is ever a conflict between these Standing Orders and my supplemental Night Orders, the Night Orders take precedence. However, bring the conflict to my immediate attention.

b. The Navigator will maintain FISKE's Night Order Book and keep a copy of these Standing Orders in front of that book along with a "Record of Acknowledgment" sheet. Each Officer of the Deck, Junior Officer of the Deck, Tactical Action Officer, Combat Systems Coordinator, Combat Systems Officer of the Watch, CIC Watch Officer, CIC Watch Supervisor, Engineering Officer of the Watch, Quartermaster of the Watch, and Boatswain's Mate of the Watch will read and signify they understand these orders monthly, by signing the "Record of Acknowledgment" sheet. Supplemental Night Orders prepared by the Navigator for my signature will be reviewed by the Operations Officer (who will make appropriate operational entries as well as verify the correctness of the Navigator's entries) and the Executive Officer prior to my review.

c. All officers or chief petty officers standing on operational underway watch between 2000 and 0800 shall initial the Night Orders prior to relieving the watch.

d. Recommendations for changes or additions to this instruction may be made at any time. Forward them to the Senior Watch Officer or the Navigator.

e. The Navigator is responsible for the proper maintenance of this instruction and will maintain the Night Order Book, consisting of a copy of this instruction and my supplemental Night Orders, as a permanent record.

J. Barry

*Distribution* (via LAN):
   All Officers
   All Chief Petty Officers
   All First Class Petty Officers
   All Quartermasters

*LIST OF EFFECTIVE ORDERS*

| Order Number | Title |
|---|---|
| 1. | Responsibility and Authority |
| 2. | Required Reports |
| 3. | Conduct of the Watch |
| 4. | Relieving the Watch |
| 5. | Restricted Maneuvering Doctrine |
| 6. | Man Overboard Procedures |
| 7. | Navigation |
| 8. | Formation Steaming |
| 9. | Planeguard Operations |
| 10. | Communications |
| 11. | Helicopter Operations |
| 12. | Ship Anchored |
| 13. | Towed Array Operations |
| 14. | Embarked Staff |

### STANDING ORDER NUMBER ONE

### RESPONSIBILITY AND AUTHORITY

1. *Command Responsibility.*

a. I am completely and inescapably responsible for FISKE and all lives, equipment, and property onboard at all times. Your designation as an Officer of the Deck (OOD) means you have earned my trust and confidence in both your watchstanding abilities and your mature judgment.

b. Never hesitate to call me. I am always on duty. When reports are required, make certain I understand your report. I will never criticize an OOD for reporting any situation deemed important. If you have any doubt whether I understand your report, or if you would just feel better if I were on the Bridge, request my presence. In an emergency, concentrate on the safety of the ship and have the BMOW pass "Captain to the Bridge" on the 1MC. Should my immediate presence be required in CIC, modify the above word to "Captain to Combat."

2. *Officer of the Deck (OOD).*

a. The Officer of the Deck is responsible for the conduct of the watch and for compliance with these Standing Orders. Under way, the OOD is the officer on watch charged with the safety of the ship. During the period of the watch, the Officer of the Deck has authority from me over all other officers and crewmen except the Executive Officer. When I am absent from the Bridge the Executive Officer and the Senior Watch Officer have the authority to relieve the Officer of the Deck when, in their judgment, such urgent action is considered necessary for the safety of the ship. The Officer of the Deck has the authority to take immediate action without waiting for my arrival on the Bridge when, in his or her judgment, that action is necessary to ensure the safety of the ship or crew. As OOD you have the responsibility of keeping me promptly and completely informed on the action you do take.

b. When in Condition III or a higher state of readiness, the Tactical Action Officer (TAO) will direct the employment of weapons systems subject to my negation. The OOD will follow direction from the

TAO unless such direction or maneuvers will cause imminent danger to the ship. Call me in either case.

c. You are required to be rested, alert, and, at night, with your eyes adapted to darkness upon taking the watch. If you do not feel fit to take the watch, notify me of the circumstances. If you become ill while on watch, call a relief and notify me. You will remain on the Bridge and in charge until properly relieved. These principles apply to each member of your watch team.

d. The use of standard phraseology and repeat back is of utmost importance to clear understanding of order. Use standard phraseology and repeat back and ensure that all members of the watch team do likewise.

e. Although "control" in the sense of positive speed or course orders may be passed to the TAO, USWE, ASUWC, or EWC under certain circumstances, Conn in the accepted sense, and the responsibility it entails, never leaves the Bridge. The relief of the watch and of the Conn shall be distinct and separate actions on the part of the relieving OOD. The officer relieving the Conn shall in every case inform the watch that he or she has the Conn so that no doubt will exist as to the control of the rudder and engines. Should I give a direct order to the Helm or Lee Helm at any time, it will be understood that I have assumed the Conn. The officer having the Conn will announce that I have assumed the Conn to preclude any misunderstanding. The relieving officer shall require the Helmsman to report the helm and engine status immediately after he assumes the Conn. The fact that the Conn has been taken by myself or the Executive Officer does not relieve the OOD from his or her responsibility to keep the whole situation in hand, to carry out the normal routine, and to state positively and forcefully opinions and recommendations for the safe operation of the ship.

f. Relationship with the Senior Watch Officer. Immediately notify the Senior Watch Officer if any of your assigned watchstanders are incapable of performing their duties. This order applies to all watchstations, including the OOD and other key watchstanders. The Senior Watch Officer has the authority to assume the Deck or Conn whenever such action is deemed necessary.

g. Relationship with the Navigator. The OOD shares responsibility for the safe navigation of FISKE with the Navigator. The Navigator shall advise the OOD of safe courses and speeds to steer; however, I do not expect the OOD to blindly follow all recommendations provided. The OOD must evaluate each maneuvering recommendation against the actual situation.

(1) Provided the OOD evaluates the Navigator's maneuvering recommendation as sound, such advice is sufficient authority to change course. Report the change to me after it has been taken if insufficient time exists to obtain my concurrence in advance.

(2) Before assuming your watch, review the chart actually in use and observe FISKE's present position and predicted track. Satisfy yourself that the methods being used to fix our position are valid and sufficient. Bear in mind all available information must be considered.

(3) Never hesitate to call the Navigator at any time to check FISKE's position or projected track during your watch. The Navigator—like the Captain—is on watch 24 hours a day.

(4) The Navigator is authorized to summon me to the bridge by any means necessary (including the 1MC) when, in his or her opinion, the OOD is not taking sufficient action necessary to preserve FISKE's safety.

## STANDING ORDER NUMBER TWO

### REQUIRED REPORTS

1. The following is a list of reports you, as OOD, are required to make to me when they occur:

a. General

(1) Relief of the deck when I am on the Bridge.

(2) In the event you are relieved by the Executive Officer or Senior Watch Officer or feel it is unsafe to follow the direction of the TAO.

(3) All occurrences the OOD feels are worthy of note by me, especially those which bear on the safety and operability of FISKE.

(4) Conflicting instructions from higher authority or orders from an embarked staff contrary to these standing orders or standard procedure.

(5) Conflicting interpretations of tactical signals, maneuvers, or situations between yourself and the TAO or CICWO.

(6) Any deviation from these Standing Orders or my Night Orders.

(7) Anytime you decline to relieve the watch, whatever the reason.

b. Formal Reports

(1) 12 O'clock Reports. The hour of 1200 with the following required reports. This report may be made by the Messenger if I am not on the Bridge and it will contain:

(a) Muster Report.

(b) Combat Systems 12 O'clock Report (Magazine Temps).

(c) Fuel and Water Report.

(d) Draft Report.

(e) Boat Report.

(f) Chronometer Report.

(g) Position Report.

(2) Position reports at 0800 and 2000 when under way. These reports may be made by the messenger if I am not on the Bridge. This report is also made to an embarked commander at 0800, 1200, and 2000.

c. Schedule

(1) Commencement and completion of significant evolutions.

(2) Inability to complete check-off lists or steps for:

(a) Getting Under Way.

(b) Entering Port.

(c) Helicopter Operations.

(d) Underway Replenishment.

(3) Expected arrival and departure times of VIP and Senior officers.

d. Emergencies

(1) Whenever in doubt or when a possible emergency is developing.

(2) When you take necessary action in an emergency to avoid collision, grounding, or other danger.

(3) Planes and vessels in distress.

(4) Any accidents or injuries to personnel.

(5) Any potentially dangerous, unusual, or important sighting such as breakers, unlighted or derelict vessels or flotsam, discolored water, audible or visible emergency/distress signals, waterspouts, and any other occurrence you deem out of the ordinary.

e. Weather

(1) Marked changes in the weather, specifically:

(a) Sustained true wind of 20 knots or greater.

(b) Wind speed changes of 10 knots or veer of 20 degrees in one hour.

(c) Increase in seas of 2 feet in a two-hour period.

(d) Barometric pressure at or below 29.5 inches *or* a change in barometric pressure of 0.04 inches in one hour *or* 0.10 inches in a four-hour period.

(e) When temperature drops to 45 degrees Fahrenheit.

(f) If visibility changes significantly or reduces to 5 miles or less.

f. Navigation

(1) When any navigational sensor indicates FISKE is standing into danger.

(2) When crossing the 50 fathom curve.

(3) If fathometer depth and charted depth differ by more than 20%, or when the fathometer unexpectedly reads less than 100 feet.

(4) When the ship's position is in doubt.

(5) When fixes plot outside the drag circle at anchor, or when there is an indication of dragging.

(6) When navigational sightings are not sighted within 15 minutes of expected time, 15 degrees of expected bearing, or radar landfall is not made within 10% of expected range. Call the Navigator too.

(7) Unexpected deviation in the magnetic compass.

(8) When turning on lights during a period when FISKE is fully darkened or has lights dimmed.

(9) When encountering any unexpected buoys, navigation lights, or hazards to navigation.

(10) Whenever fixes deviate from the Navigator's track by 5 miles or 10% of the distance to the nearest unsafe water, whichever is less.

(11) Upon entering inland/international waters as determined by COLREGS Demarcation Line.

g. Contacts. Maintain a maneuvering board plot of all contacts that will have a CPA of 10,000 yards or less. Do not delay required action for want of information. Maintain a scopehead plot on all contacts within 20 nautical miles.

(1) Call me for any surface contact with a CPA less than 10,000 yards giving:

(a) Present position (relative).

(b) Target angle.

(c) Bearing drift.

(d) CPA.

(e) Appropriate Rule(s) of the Road.

(f) Maneuvering intentions.

(2)  Contact Reports should be clear and succinct. Make the report as follows: "Captain, this is (name), OOD. I have a (type of vessel, if known), off my (port/stbd bow/beam/quarter) with a target angle of ____. The vessel has (left/right) bearing drift and has a CPA off my (port/stbd bow/beam/quarter) at a range of ____ yards. This is a (meeting/crossing/overtaking) situation. I am the (stand on/give way vessel). My intentions are to ____."

(3)  Any difference in contact between Bridge and CIC.

(4)  When a contact is identified as a naval vessel, inform me of the Commanding Officer's identity and relative seniority. Promptly request or grant permission to proceed on duty assigned, as appropriate, then advise me.

(5)  When other naval vessels or auxiliaries are operating in the vicinity.

(6)  Presence of a potentially hostile ship, submarine, or aircraft.

(7)  Prior to calling away the SNOOPIE (Shipping, Naval or Otherwise Photographic Intelligence and Evaluation) Team to gather information on a vessel with intelligence value or significance.

h.  Communications

(1)  Tactical signals, including changes in formation, course, or speed of this or any other ship in company.

(2)  Any changes in the EMCON condition in effect.

(3)  Loss of communications on any maneuvering or warfare commander circuit for a period of 10 minutes.

i.  Maneuvering

(1)  Inform me of unplanned course and speed changes prior to their execution except as follows:

(a)  When you are required to take immediate action to avoid risk of collision in accordance with the Navigation Rules.

(b)  To avoid objects in the water ahead which may be hazardous to the sonar dome or screws.

(c) Course and speed adjustments required to maintain PIM or assigned station.

(d) Course and speed changes required to patrol an assigned screen sector.

(e) "Immediate Execute" signals from the OTC, which alter our course or speed. Inform me as soon thereafter as practical.

j. Formation steaming

(1) Whenever a ship joins or departs the formation.

(2) All sonar contacts held by FISKE or by other units in our formation/exercise.

(3) Breakdown of ship(s) in company.

(4) When station limits are exceeded by 2 degrees in bearing or 5% of range.

(5) When unable to maintain station, when other ships in company are significantly out of station, or when other ships in company change course or speed unexpectedly.

(6) If any unit questions your movements or actions, or issues a reprimand.

(7) If unable to comply with a tactical signal.

k. Material

(1) Fresh water drops below 70% and every 10% change below that.

(2) Any degradation to steering system or inability to conduct daily equipment shifts or drills.

(3) All degradations of equipment which may affect FISKE's safety or could have an adverse impact on current or planned operations.

l. Environmental. Prior to using the main drain system, regardless of the ship's distance from land.

2. Do not assume that because I am on the Bridge I see and/or hear all contacts, signals, voice transmissions, etc. Make reports on the as-

sumption that I have not. Do not be reticent about reporting any unusual circumstance or events, whether internal or external to FISKE, even if only a matter of interest. Keep me fully informed at all times. I will do the same for you in order to permit you to discharge your duties most effectively.

3. Minimize multiple reports to me on the same event. The most appropriate watchstander should make a report to me (e.g., the TAO should report a loss of the AN/SPI-1D and the OOD should call regarding HELO OPS). The same report from multiple watchstanders is an indication of poor internal coordination. Department Heads may, as appropriate, call me with amplifying information.

4. On occasion, I may direct that all reports be made to the Executive Officer. When I do so, the Executive Officer will decide if a report is critical enough to warrant my immediate attention. I will be very specific with watchstanders when I exercise this option.

### STANDING ORDER NUMBER THREE

### CONDUCT OF THE WATCH

1. *General.* As Officer of the Deck, you are in full charge of everyone standing watch in FISKE. As such, you are responsible for continuous improvement of your watch team. You are also responsible for the watchstanding standards of all crew members assigned to your watch section.

2. *Safety.*

a. Whenever you consider it dangerous for personnel to go topside (e.g., the weatherdecks, mast, etc.), restrict such access or traffic by passing appropriate word over the 1MC. When it is imperative to visit such locations, take all required and prudent precautions such as:

(1) Obtain my permission.

(2) Get the best person for the job.

(3) Ensure the "buddy system" is used.

(4) Insist on life preservers and tended safety lines.

(5) Alter course and/or speed if such action provides more favorable conditions.

(6) Ensure competent supervision.

(7) Ensure you are included in the specially tailored Safety Brief that must be conducted prior to beginning any such visit.

b. Remember to give warnings over all 1MC circuits when you anticipate heavy rolls or heels.

c. Always ensure the After Lookout is properly equipped and posted where best suited to prevailing weather conditions and upcoming operations. The After Lookout must always have binoculars, a life ring, light, and smoke float immediately available. Ensure he or she knows what is expected in the event of a man overboard.

3. *Required Permission.* Obtain my permission prior to:

a. Sending sailors aloft.

b. Sending sailors over the side.

c. Setting special details.

d. Allowing work on any energized circuits or equipment containing a component with more than 30 volts potential.

e. Allowing anyone to enter a fuel tank, void, or sump.

f. Transferring or handling live ammunition.

g. Testing main engines.

h. Turning shafts.

4. *Watch Administration.*

a. The Executive Officer runs the ship. Carry out the daily routine as published in the Plan of the Day and keep the Executive Officer advised of any changes you feel are necessary.

b. Control the proper use of the general announcing system and the General, Chemical, Collision, and Flight Crash alarms and the ship's whistle.

c. Keep tactical publications and CMS handy and be prepared to use them.

d. Render honors to passing ships as required by custom and regulations.

e. Ensure the Executive Officer and Department Heads are promptly informed of changes to the tactical situation, operational schedule or the approach of heavy weather and any other circumstance which will require action on their part or a change in routine.

5. *CIC Relationship.* Insist CIC employ its full range of capabilities to keep you informed of the surface and air pictures. CIC is required to scopehead track and report to you all surface contacts within 20 miles. For contacts with a CPA < 10,000 yards, maneuvering board and DDRT will be used to provide course, speed, CPA, and time of CPA, until you authorize CIC to cease reporting. Ensure this information is provided to you promptly.

a. Exchange information with CIC. Information between the Bridge and CIC must flow in both directions. Always keep CIC informed of your course and speed, prevailing weather conditions, and any changes that occur. Stay attuned to the requirement to provide CIC with visual information they may not have. Most importantly, always keep CIC apprised of your intentions in sufficient time to permit them to utilize the information.

b. Instruct your CIC Watch Officer to contact you directly whenever he or she feels a danger exists or your actions are not understood. Make certain you convey your intentions clearly and directly to the CIC Watch Officer whenever necessary. Take advantage of opportunities to discuss possible courses of action with your CIC Watch Officer for mutual support and more effective watch section coordination. The general principles outlined below provide additional guidance:

(1) When maneuvering to avoid other ships, or recommending a maneuver, always use sufficient rudder to ensure your intentions are clearly apparent to the other vessel.

(2) Insist CIC keep track of the identity and position of other ships in company at all times when they are within radar range.

(3) In situations where risk of collision exists (CPA < 10,000 yards), require CIC utilize both a record geographic plot (DRT) as well as the maneuvering board relative plot.

c. If you and CIC ever disagree regarding an impending situation, notify me immediately.

6. *Relationship with the Engineering Officer of the Watch (EOOW).*

a. The Engineering Officer of the Watch (EOOW) is responsible for the safe and proper operation of FISKE's propulsion, electrical, and auxiliary systems. I require him or her to operate the engineering plant in accordance with good engineering practices, and strict adherence to approved specific operating and casualty procedures (EOP and EOCC).

b. The OOD shall normally limit his or her orders for control of the engineering plant to:

(1) Orders to start or secure main engines after first obtaining my permission.

(2) Speed changes by use of the throttle controls, engine revolution indicators, IVCS Net 83, or the 21MC. In an emergency where none of the primary means of communication are available, the 1MC may be used.

c. The EOOW is required to report any changes, conditions, or casualties to machinery or equipment which may limit ship's operation.

d. The EOOW is required to request permission from the OOD for the following:

(1) Start Main Engines and Gas Turbine Generators (except as noted in the Restricted Maneuvering Doctrine).

(2) Pump bilges.

(3) Place any vital machinery or equipment out of commission for preventive maintenance.

(4) Refueling boats.

e. The OOD shall inform the EOOW of the following:

(1) Anticipated upcoming speed and/or power requirements (as early as practicable).

(2) Anticipated and actual times of:

(a) Setting or entering Restricted Maneuvering Conditions.

(b) Arriving at or departing from all pollution discharge restriction zones.

(3) Whenever FISKE enters or passes through areas containing debris or vegetation which might clog sea chests/suctions or cooling water systems.

(4) Any other operations affecting the engineering plant.

(5) Abnormal stack smoke emission.

(6) Unexpected liquid discharge overboard.

(7) Whenever FISKE is within 12 miles of land or within 2,000 yards directly astern of another vessel (distilling plant operations).

## STANDING ORDER NUMBER FOUR

### RELIEVING THE WATCH

1. *Prior to Relieving the Watch.* The Officer of the Deck (under way) shall:

a. Ensure you are physically fit, appropriately clothed, equipped, and (for night watches) have adequate night vision to stand an alert watch.

(1) You will avail yourself of sufficient rest before relieving the watch. You will not relieve when feeling sick or overly tired, or if you judge yourself unable to fulfill your responsibilities as a watch-stander. Any watchstander who has not had a total of five hours of sleep in the previous 24 hours must notify his or her immediate supervisor who will specifically evaluate the relief's ability to stand a proper watch. The OOD must report this "lack of sleep" condition to the Senior Watch Officer. In the event the watch is not relieved under these circumstances, I shall be immediately notified.

(2) If you become ill, you shall call a relief and notify the Senior Watch Officer and myself.

(3) Upon watch relief, both the oncoming and off-going watchstanders shall satisfy themselves that the relieving watchstander is fit to relieve the watch. If not, that watch shall not be relieved.

(4) Any changes to assignments on any underway watch bill must be submitted to the Senior Watch Officer, recommended by the Executive Officer, and specifically approved by me before that change goes into effect.

b. Ensure you have a thorough knowledge and clear understanding of FISKE's material and operational status and any changes expected during your watch. To this end, you shall:

(1) Visit CIC and get briefed by the CICWO or TAO. Inspect radar and EW displays and status boards.

(2) Read and be familiar with the schedule of events in the Plan of the Day, PRE-EX messages, and any special instructions. Read and initial my Night Order Book and seek verbal amplification from myself, the Executive Officer, the Operations Officer, and/or the Navigator if you have any doubts or confusion regarding FISKE's status, upcoming evolutions, or any other aspect of your watch.

(3) Study the navigation chart. Note our present position, planned track, all possible navigation hazards, and available navigation aids.

c. Ensure a complete exchange of information with the previous Officer of the Deck, including as a minimum data with regard to:

(1) The Night Orders. Review and carry out my Night Orders. Check the data contained in the Night Orders against the navigation plot, OPORDER, and any special orders. If there is any discrepancy or doubt concerning FISKE's position, situation, or the intent of the Night Orders, do not relieve the watch. Call me immediately.

(2) The accuracy of the ship's position. Make yourself aware of all navigation aids in use or expected. Check the chart and bearing book for completeness, accuracy, and neatness. If any questions con-

cerning FISKE's position exist, notify the OOD and call the Navigator prior to relieving.

(3) Set and Drift experienced or expected.

(4) OPORDERS, Plans, and SOEs in effect including events scheduled during your watch.

(5) Tactical formation and organization, including FISKE's station and any unexpected signals.

(6) Gyrocompass in use and all compass errors.

(7) Status of communications circuits and stations responsible for guarding those circuits.

(8) The surface radar picture, the location, identity, and voice calls of the guide, OTC, OCE, Screen Commander, other ships in company, and all surface contacts.

(9) Status of all contacts, to include relative position, course and speed, CPA, and time of CPA, and whether or not I have been notified.

(10) Existing and forecasted weather.

(11) Our course, speed, and propulsion plant status, to include major equipment out of commission and the resultant impact on FISKE's mobility.

(12) Steering pumps and units in use.

(13) Material condition set, condition of readiness, and EMCON status.

(14) Status of weapons systems and navigational equipment.

(15) Any major equipment out of commission and the estimated time of repair (ETR).

(16) Any special work or evolution, such as weapons handling in progress, scheduled that may occur during your watch. In the case of planned evolutions, ascertain the status of their preparations.

(17) Lighting measures in effect. Ensure proper navigation lights are displayed. When, in your opinion, running lights are essential to safety USE THEM, even during darkened ship.

(18)  Status of your watch section (relief, qualification, appearance, night adaptation, and rest). Neither the OOD nor the BMOW shall be relieved until all watch reliefs are on deck.

(19)  All FISKE guard ship assignments.

(20)  Any unexecuted orders, either external or internal.

(21)  My location.

d.  Ensure an inventory of Bridge publications and CRYPTO materials is made by the JOOD and initialed in the Bridge inventory folder.

2. *Pattern of Relieving.*

a.  Promptness in reporting to relieve a watch is required as a matter of simple courtesy. The actual time required to relieve will vary and be circumstance dependent, and reliefs should plan to be on deck and complete their relieving process to conform with the times listed in sub-paragraph (g), below. However, officers must never allow themselves to feel pressured to relieve by a certain time. Never accept a watch until you are comfortable with the situation and have all information you require.

b.  Whenever an oncoming watch officer feels he or she cannot relieve the watch, notify me.

c.  Oncoming OODs will not normally be relieved until all signals have been executed.

d.  The watch shall not be relieved during complex maneuvers which require the undivided attention of the OOD. At such times, the oncoming watch team should remain in the after portion of the Bridge or on the wings until the specific maneuver(s) is (are) completed.

e.  Relieving watch officers will be on the Bridge 15 minutes prior to actually relieving, in order to be thoroughly prepared to relieve and if not able to be there shall contact the Senior Watch Officer as far in advance as possible to arrange for a relief.

f.  The actual change of the OOD watch shall be made with meticulous care and formality as the relieving OOD is completely responsible for FISKE once he or she has relieved. The OOD will not be relieved until the rest of the watch is relieved and settled, normally on the hour.

g. Watches will be relieved in accordance with the following schedule:

    (1) JOOD—1/2 hour before the hour

    (2) CICWO/TAO—15 minutes before the hour

    (3) OOD—on the hour

h. Be particularly alert during the change of the watch. Keep the noise level down. Remember, watches in ships around you are probably being changed at the same time. Additionally, any knowledgeable "adversary" will probably time his attacks to coincide with customary watch rotation times.

3. *Upon Relief.* The off-going Officer of the Deck (under way) shall:

a. Review the Deck Log for accuracy and completeness, then sign it. Initial all corrections in the margin.

b. Debrief the BMOW and specific watchstanders, if appropriate, concerning the watch team's performance. "Continuous Improvement" must always be your guiding goal in these debriefs.

4. *Declining to Relieve.*

a. An officer may decline to relieve the deck when he or she:

    (1) Considers FISKE to be in peril.

    (2) Finds we are appreciably out of station.

    (3) Does not feel physically capable of relieving the watch.

    (4) Is not satisfied with the completeness of the tactical picture being turned over.

b. Any officer who declines to relieve the deck, shall immediately notify me of this fact and state his or her reasons.

5. *Relieving the OOD Under Way.*

a. I may assume the Deck or Conn at any time. Normally, I will make the announcement, "This is the Captain. I have the Conn." However, should I ever give a direct order to the Helm or Lee Helm without such previous announcement, or should the Helmsmen or

Lee Helmsman respond as though I had issued them a direct order, the Conning Officer shall immediately announce, "The Captain has the Conn." I will continue to exercise the Conn until it has been properly and positively turned over to another Conning Officer or OOD.

b. There must never be any misunderstanding as to the identity of the Conning Officer. In case of doubt, it is the OOD's responsibility to immediately clarify who has the Conn. The question, "Captain, do you have the Conn?" is proper in this situation. Upon all such occasions, the OOD shall continue to perform those functions of which he or she has not been relieved. Specifically, the OOD shall continue to forcefully express recommendations regarding the safe and proper operation of FISKE.

c. The Executive Officer, when on the Bridge at sea, may relieve the OOD in any situation when I am not on the Bridge when such action is necessary for FISKE's safety.

d. The Executive Officer, when in CIC at sea, may also relieve the TAO or CIC Watch Officer in any situation when I am not in CIC when such action is necessary for FISKE's safety.

e. The Senior Watch Officer has the authority to assume the Deck or Conn whenever such action is deemed necessary and I am not on the Bridge.

## STANDING ORDER NUMBER FIVE

### RESTRICTED MANEUVERING DOCTRINE

1. *Purpose.* This instruction provides guidance to operate FISKE during "Restricted Maneuvering Conditions."

2. *Background.* EOCC consists of technically correct, logically sequenced procedures for responding to and controlling commonly occurring casualties. When properly followed, these procedures place the plant in a safe, stable condition while the cause is determined. However, these procedures do not consider the impact that controlling or immediate actions might have during operations in close proximity to danger. Therefore, this order specifies FISKE policy

and procedures to be followed whenever ship safety takes precedence over propulsion plant protection.

3. *Restricted Maneuvering Doctrine.* "Restricted Maneuvering Conditions" exist whenever FISKE is:

a. Operating in restricted waters.

b. Steaming in close formation at reduced standard distance or interval.

c. Engaged in replenishment at sea operations alongside any other vessel (UNREP).

d. Whenever "Restricted Maneuvering Casualty Control Procedures are now in effect" is passed over the 1MC.

4. *Maximum Reliability Lineup.* This is a specific propulsion and electrical plant configuration which provides FISKE maximum plant reliability. Maximum Reliability Lineup will be directed by me, the Executive Officer, or the Officer of the Deck, prior to entering a restricted maneuvering condition. Maximum Plant Reliability will be automatically set by the Engineering Officer of the Watch (EOOW) when:

a. General Quarters is sounded.

b. The Underway Replenishment Detail is set.

c. The Sea Detail is stationed for returning to port. In the foregoing circumstances, the EOOW will notify the OOD the plant is being configured for Maximum Reliability. When the Sea Detail is set for getting under way, the OOD may grant the EOOW permission to bring the plant to Maximum Reliability configuration once the Sea Detail is stationed, the OOD is on the Bridge, communications are established with the fantail (to ensure vicinity around screws are clear), and communications are established between the OOD and EOOW.

FISKE will never knowingly enter a Restricted Maneuvering Condition without first establishing the Maximum Reliability Lineup configuration. "Manned and Ready" reports from Central Control Station (CCS) and After Steering during the above details will *not* be made until all provisions of Maximum Reliability Lineup have been satisfied. I will be personally advised of any inability to achieve "Maximum Reliability Lineup."

Whenever a "Maximum Reliability Lineup" is ordered, the engineering plant will be configured as follows:

    a.   Main Propulsion

        — Full Power Mode.

        — GTM 16th stage bleed air valves CLOSED.

        — Oil Distribution (OD) Boxes manned.

    b.   Electrical Plant

        — Two Generators aligned to a ring bus; a third GTG will be "on" with its generator breaker open.

        — 14th stage bleed air valves CLOSED.

        — 60 HZ Switchboards manned.

    c.   Steering Gear

        — After Steering manned by a qualified after steersman, engineman, electrician, and safety officer (normally AUXO).

        — Computer assisted manual mode of control.

Once established, no changes to the "Maximum Reliability Lineup" plant configurations are authorized unless expressly approved by me, the Executive Officer, or the OOD. No preventive or corrective maintenance or testing will be accomplished that might cause loss of electrical power or ship control. When "Maximum Reliability Lineup" is no longer required, "Secure from Restricted Maneuvering Casualty Control Procedures" will be passed over the 1MC.

5. *Restricted Maneuvering Casualty Control Procedures.* Restricted Maneuvering Casualty Control Procedures are only authorized when the following word is passed over the 1MC:

"Restricted Maneuvering Casualty Control Procedures are now in effect."

Passing of this word must be logged in both the Deck and Engineering Logs. Central Control Station will repeat back "Restricted Maneuvering Casualty Control Procedures are in effect" to the Bridge via NET 83.

I will limit the time FISKE operates under "Restricted Maneuvering Casualty Control Procedures" to only those times I feel engineering casualties would compound the potential for immediate danger due to maneuvering restrictions.

A verbal order to the EOOW from me, the Executive Officer, or OOD, in that hierarchy, takes precedence over any other means of transmitting propulsion orders from the Bridge to CCS, the SCU, or OD Box operator (e.g., a verbal order from me over the 1MC takes precedence over orders received via the EOT.)

The Restricted Maneuvering Casualty Control Procedures specified below are to be followed by all Bridge and Engineering watchstanders whenever FISKE is restricted in her ability to maneuver. Generally, these provisions do not differ from standard EOCC, except that:

*EOCC casualty procedures will NOT be peremptorily taken if such actions will take shaft control or electrical power away without expressed permission from me, the Executive Officer, or OOD except as specifically outlined below.*

*All ship control stations will always be in communication and aware of ordered course and speed.* All throttle control station Manual or Programmed Control Levers will precisely match ordered speed. After Steering personnel will always maintain a clear picture of the maneuvering situation.

    a.  *GTM CASUALTY.* Carry out EOCC procedures except:

        (1)  Do not stop the last GTM on the affected shaft.

        (2)  Do not transfer thrust control.

        (3)  Do not move program control levers to idle.

Until so directed by me, the Executive Officer, or the OOD. For a post-shutdown fire, the PACC operator shall motor the affected GTM using high-pressure air.

    b.  *LOSS OF LUBE/FUEL/CRP OIL SYSTEM PRESSURE/MAJOR OIL LEAK.* Carry out the EOCC procedures except:

        (1)  Do not stop the last GTM on the affected shaft.

        (2)  Do not transfer thrust control.

(3) Do not order the affected shaft slowed, stopped, or locked.

(4) Do not stop the affected lube/fuel/CRP oil service pumps unless a major leak in that system has been identified as the cause of the casualty.

Until so directed by me, the Executive Officer, or the OOD.

c. *REDUCTION GEAR/SHAFTING CASUALTY.* The EOOW shall report the casualty to the OOD and recommend slowing the ship or stopping the affected shaft. The OOD will acknowledge the report and direct the EOOW to postpone EOCC actions if the ship's safety is in jeopardy. Once the ship is clear of hazards and safe to maneuver, the OOD shall order full EOCC procedures.

d. *LOSS OF CONTROLLABLE REVERSIBLE PITCH PROPELLER (CRP) CONTROL.* Carry out EOCC procedures except:

(1) Do not transfer thrust control to PACC.

The EOOW shall order the affected system OD Box operator to take local pitch control. Conning orders shall be passed by the Lee Helm via NET 83 to the OD Box operator who will acknowledge and answer desired pitch commands. If pitch is not controllable at the OD Box, the manual control valves will be placed in the "off" position, and treated as a loss of CRP hydraulic pressure.

e. *CLASS BRAVO FIRE IN A MAIN SPACE.* Carry out EOCC and Main Space Fire Doctrine procedures except:

(1) Propulsion shafts *originating in an unaffected* space will not be slowed or stopped.

(2) A propulsion shaft *originating in the space containing the fire* will be trailed vice locked until so directed by me, the Executive Officer, or the OOD.

(3) Do not stop the lube oil service pump on the affected shaft, unless lube oil leak is the source of the fire.

If the fire becomes uncontrollable, full EOOC and Main Space Fire Doctrine procedures commence except the transfer of thrust control on the unaffected shaft, which will remain with the Helm.

f. *INADVERTENT SPACE HALON RELEASE.* The affected space shall be immediately evacuated and online equipment will remain in operation. Ventilation will commence and the space will be manned by watchstanders in Oxygen Breathing Apparatus (OBA) until the Gas Free Engineer certifies the space "safe for personnel."

6. *Battle Override.* Battle Override will be employed only with my permission except that the EOOW shall apply Battle Override to the last GTM on the last shaft during use of Restricted Maneuvering Casualty Control Procedures.

7. *Restricted Maneuvering Doctrine at General Quarters.* When GQ is sounded, configure the plant for Maximum Plant Reliability in accordance with the guidance contained on this Standing Order. When at General Quarters and the need to ensure propulsion and electrical continuity prudent, the Executive Officer, OOD, or I will order the setting of "Restricted Maneuvering Casualty Control Procedures." In this instance, the provisions of this order will be followed, except that OD Boxes will not be manned unless a casualty affecting CRP Control is experienced.

STANDING ORDER NUMBER SIX

MAN OVERBOARD PROCEDURES

1. *General.* Historical data compiled by the Naval Safety Center indicates that any person falling over the side only has a 70% chance of survival. I will probably not be on the Bridge when a person falls over the side. Both I and the person in the water are completely dependent upon the judgment and initial responses of the OOD. Accordingly, should a shipmate fall over the side, prompt and correct action on the part of the entire watch team will make the difference between life and death.

a. During a shipboard recovery, initially maneuver to "try to run over" the individual.

b. When you get close, fall off upwind and position him forward of the bridgewing, ideally beneath the J-Bar Davit.

2. *Procedures.* A basic, safe man overboard recovery will entail these fundamental steps:

a. MANEUVER FISKE

(1) Swing the stern away from the side the person fell over, using full rudder.

(2) Normally, use a tight direct full-circle recovery (Anderson Turn), Williamson Turn, or Racetrack Turn or based on sighting, visibility, maneuvering limitations, speed, and anticipated recovery method. At very slow speeds and when the AN/SQR-19B Towed Array is deployed, it is best to use the RHIB.

b. PASS THE WORD—TWICE—On all circuits

(1) Three basic segments.

(a) The words "Man overboard."

(b) The "side."

(c) Type "recovery" planned (ship, boat, or helo [if a helo is airborne in the area]).

c. NOTIFY OTHER SHIPS

(1) Sound SIX short blasts on ship's whistle.

(2) Break OSCAR by day and two pulsating lights (red over red) by night.

(3) Deploy smoke floats and a life ring.

(4) Radio/telephone transmission.

d. MARK POSITION

(1) All Lookouts (port, starboard) will deploy a smoke float. Additionally, the aft lookout will deploy a life ring with strobe light.

(2) Keep the person in sight. Everyone topside who can see the person must point to the individual. During reduced visibility and at night, ensure people topside remain quiet—we may hear the person in the water before he or she can actually be seen.

(3) On the Bridge, use the ARPA trackball to position the cursor close aboard astern to mark the approximate position of the person. Then depress the "TRUE MARKS" button to "freeze" a geographic point

at the spot marked. This point will be helpful in verifying CIC's bearing and range to the individual.

(4) Shift the DRT plot scale in CIC to the 200 yards per inch scale.

e. ESTABLISH COMMUNICATION WITH RECOVERY DECK STATIONS (Foc'sle or Boat Deck)

(1) Monitor progress, readiness, and status of rescue detail.

(2) Keep all stations informed of your intentions on IVCS nets and/or 1MC.

f. RIG/POSITION LIFESAVING EQUIPMENT

(1) Search lights.

(2) Heaving lines.

(3) Swimmer's gear.

(4) Debarkation nets.

(5) J-bar davits/rescue collar.

g. POSITION PERSON IN WATER. Downwind forward of the weather break with all way off.

3. The above guidance is general in nature and will vary with the particular circumstances of each "man overboard" emergency. Before you label the situation as a classic maneuver, consider who else is out there. For instance, is there a ship astern? Is a helo airborne and nearby? If our ability to maneuver is limited (proximity of other ships, TACTAS deployed, etc.) do not maneuver into a collision or a cascading casualty.

4. Preplanning, training, and practice are the only ways to recover a man overboard safely. You must always be ready for a man overboard emergency.

## STANDING ORDER NUMBER SEVEN

### NAVIGATION

1. *Requirements.* Keep yourself continually advised of FISKE's position, course, speed, and intended track. Personally supervise the nav-

igation plot maintained by your QMOW and ensure an accurate, up-to-date DR plot is always maintained.

a. Dependent upon EMCON in effect, you are directed to make free use of CIC, radar, sonar, fathometer, Global Positioning System (GPS), lookouts' visual bearings, and other means available to establish and/or verify FISKE's position. Do not blindly depend upon one NAV AID; use all sensors available. However, if even one sensor or means of navigating indicates FISKE is standing into danger, believe it, take appropriate precautionary action, and inform me.

b. Positive knowledge of our position is never more imperative than when making landfall or in waters whose depth is 50 fathoms or less. In addition to charts in CIC and on the Bridge, separate charts will be prepared for me and the Conning Officer indicating the track, courses, and speeds FISKE is to follow.

c. If you are ever in doubt of FISKE's position, or believe it could be substantially different than plotted, slow or stop the ship to remain in known good water. Immediately call me and the Navigator to the Bridge.

d. Ensure FISKE's navigational position is fixed at least as often as indicated in the following matrix:

| Area | Distance from Nearest Land | Fix Frequency |
| --- | --- | --- |
| Restricted waters | Less than 2 nautical miles | 2 minutes |
| Piloting waters | 2–10 nautical miles | 3–15 minutes as conditions warrant |
| Coastal waters | 10–30 nautical miles | 15 minutes |
| Enroute navigation (open ocean) | Over 30 nautical miles | 30 minutes |

(1) A good rule of thumb for fix intervals is "if hazard to navigation falls within a circle whose radius is that of two DR intervals," then either the fix interval or ship's speed requires adjusting.

(2) The Bridge and CIC will each maintain an independent plot which will be compared after each fix. Set and Drift will be computed

after every fix and shall be applied to subsequent DR positions to determine an EP in the event that planned fixes are not obtained.

(3)  A DR position will be plotted on the Bridge and in CIC at least:

(a)  Every hour on the hour.

(b)  At the time of every course change.

(c)  At the time of every speed change.

(d)  For the time at which a fix was obtained.

(e)  For the time at which a running fix was obtained.

(f)  For the time at which a single LOP was obtained.

(4)  Before entering restricted waters, the Navigation Detail will be set in sufficient time to avoid danger.

(5)  All other navigational information available, e.g., GPS, soundings, DR track, visual navigational aids, shall be compared to the fix taken to ensure proper correlation. Should the various data not match with the fix taken, steps shall immediately be taken to determine the source of the error. Never place blind reliance on any single source of information. Should the position be in doubt, the OOD will first ensure that he or she is not standing into danger (immediately take all way off the ship if necessary), then notify the Navigator and me.

(6)  The Navigator is responsible for ensuring that both the Bridge and CIC are using the same track. I will sign all charts (Bridge and CIC) used in conjunction with entering/leaving port after satisfying myself with the information presented.

(7)  Record all Navigational Sightings. Ensure positive identification of all navigational lights using a stopwatch. Call me and the Navigator promptly if an aid is not sighted within 15 minutes after the predicted time of sighting.

(8)  Approach to Land or Shoal Water. Approach land no closer than 12 NM and enter water no shallower than 50 fathoms without my permission. Never take the ship into less than 10 fathoms of water unless I am on the Bridge or I otherwise direct such action.

2. *Sounds.* The following general procedures are in effect for the use of the fathometer, subject to modification by me. Depth readings will be taken and recorded:

a. Whenever a fix is taken.

b. When in water over 100 fathoms: at least hourly.

c. When in water over 100 feet but less than 100 fathoms: at least every 15 minutes.

d. When in water less than 100 feet: at least every 3 minutes.

e. Continuously during Sea and Anchor Detail and other times when maneuvering in restricted waters.

f. Use the fathometer at all times and compare the indicated depth with the chart, except as otherwise dictated by the EMCON conditions or other operational considerations.

g. *Shoaling.* The fathometer is normally the best indicator of shoaling water. Ensure its reading is compared with charted depth whenever a fix is obtained. The scale in use (i.e., fathoms or feet) must be proper for the anticipated charted depth. If FISKE is ever in a shoaling situation (fathometer depth is dangerously decreasing continuously), your first reaction should be to take all way off, verify position and fathometer accuracy, and call the Navigator and me.

3. *Navigational Running Lights.* Display required navigational running lights and shapes. Navigational running lights will be checked one-half hour prior to sunset and burned between the hours of sunset and sunrise or during reduced visibility unless otherwise ordered. Require the Boatswain's Mate of the Watch to report "All navigation lights are bright lights" hourly while navigation lights are burning. Remember that DIM lights do not comply with Navigation Rules and will not be used without my approval.

4. *Relationship with Navigator.*

a. The Officer of the Deck shares responsibility with the Navigator for the safe navigation of the ship. In this regard OODs are not to blindly steer recommended courses, but are to make their own evaluations on each recommended action based on their knowledge of the tactical situation. Before relieving, you will have reviewed the chart actually in use, observed the present and predicted position of the ship during your watch, and satisfied yourself on the validity of the methods being employed to fix the ship's position. Do not hesitate to call the Navigator at any time to check the ship's position or its projected track during your watch.

b. The Navigator shall advise the Officer of the Deck of a safe course to be steered, and the OOD shall regard such advice as sufficient authority to change course if timeliness requires such a course change, but the change will be reported to me immediately thereafter.

5. *Rules of the Road.*

a. You are expected to know and comply with the Rules of the Road. This requires study and frequent review.

b. You are expected to take all appropriate measures to avoid embarrassment to other vessels. If required to maneuver in accordance with the Rules of the Road, do so early. It is normally most appropriate to change course rather than speed, since this meticulously shows the other ship your actions. Whether you change course or speed, make the change large enough that it is readily observable on the other ship. *TAKE ACTION EARLY.* The least desirable of many correct solutions, taken early, is preferable to the best solution taken too late.

c. Small craft operators are often ignorant of the Rules of the Road. Never assume that a small craft or sailboat will act lawfully, or even intelligently, in any given situation. Always anticipate the unexpected and leave yourself a way out. Do not hesitate to use the VHF Bridge to Bridge radio or whistle signals to alert the other vessel to the danger of the situation.

6. *General.*

a. The OOD will ensure the ARPA's plot is maintained in a condition appropriate to the existing conditions. At a minimum, auto tracking will be initiated on all surface tracks within 20 NM. While the OOD may adjust the ARPA as deemed best, it will normally be kept in "true" to assist me in rapidly assimilating the surface picture. The ARPA is an outstanding safety tool and I expect it to be used by Bridge watchstanders.

b. Maneuvering boards will be used on the Bridge and in CIC for surface tracks with CPAs < 10,000 yards. The DDRT will also be used for surface tracks with CPAs < 10,000 yards. The OOD will compare Bridge and CIC results, comparing these also with the ARPA.

c. When in piloting waters, ensure the gyro error is determined at least once each watch and posted on the bridge. It should be determined daily in the open sea.

d. Determine surface radar and/or repeater range and bearing errors and ensure they are posted on the Bridge.

e. Report to me and the Navigator radar landfall and the sighting of all land, shoals, rocks, lighthouses, beacons, discolored water, aids to navigation, and the like.

## STANDING ORDER NUMBER EIGHT

### FORMATION STEAMING

***I will never criticize an OOD who maneuvers FISKE out of a station, sector, or screen and into open sea room because he or she is uncertain of navigation or maneuvering safety.***

1. Anticipate maneuvers and events. Think ahead and formulate a plan. When joining a formation, have its disposition plotted well in advance and keep current positions of each ship. Report to me whenever a ship is joining or leaving the formation.

2. Be vigilant. You are your own best lookout. Use mechanical and electronic sensors and navigation aids, but do not become solely dependent on them. LOOK where you are going, step onto the open bridge wing on the side toward which you are about to turn. Learn to recognize aspects and determine approximate ranges with binoculars, particularly at night.

3. You are required to maintain an accurate up-to-date formation diagram including all ships with which we are in company.

4. Whenever you take emergency action, keep other ships in formation informed using radio circuits and visual signals.

5. See that the ship is skillfully steered and kept on course and that the assigned station is maintained within plus or minus 2 degrees and plus or minus 5% of range; report to me if these limits are ever exceeded.

6. Except in cases of patrolling an area station or conforming to a signaled zigzag, course changes of 5 degrees or more, or speed changes of 2 knots or more required to maintain station are not minor changes and you must inform me.

7. No change in course should be made unless an officer on watch has been stationed on the side to which the ship is turning and has checked astern in that direction. Never turn toward a ship abaft your beam—even with what appears to be safe maneuvering space—if it can be avoided.

8. Upon receipt of an IMMEDIATE EXECUTE signal, I expect you to take the required action (put over rudder, increase speed, etc.) before or as you inform me of the signal. In this case do not delay action to make the required report. A change in speed of not less than 4 knots or a change in course of not less than 20 degrees, or both, generally is considered appropriate. Review your solutions for possible course and/or speed adjustments. Advise me when any ship(s) is (are) seriously off station.

9. Notify me immediately if:

a. you are unable to maintain station or if other ships in company are significantly out of their assigned station.

b. you suddenly find you need an unexpected speed or course change to maintain station, or you do not understand the movements of the Guide or any other ship in the formation.

10. You are not authorized to cross ahead of another combatant or vessel closer than 3,000 yards, pass abeam less than 2,000 yards or astern less than 1,000 yards unless in an emergency, without first discussing such a course of action with me. The above-mentioned areas are to be construed as stay out zones. Always have in the back of

your mind a clear area into which the ship may be safely headed to avoid danger. Constantly run over in your mind emergency procedures, "What do I do if . . . ," so that if the situation arises, the action is second nature. These ranges are doubled if the vessel in proximity is an aircraft carrier or large-deck amphib.

11. When range permits, utilize the stadimeter to maintain station. Practice estimating visual ranges to specific ships so as to permit accurate ranging when in EMCON.

12. The fact that the ship is in formation does not relieve you from responsibility for avoiding contacts and ensuring safe navigation. Make timely recommendations or raise questions concerning contemplated OTC actions with regard to contacts or navigational hazards. Do not hesitate to maneuver independently if necessary to avoid contacts, or ships in formation having difficulty, or to give a wide berth to a navigation hazard. Keep me informed.

13. Always keep other ships in mind and try to assist them if in any difficulty. For example, when at the head of a column and contacts or hazards are spotted, or avoiding maneuvers are necessary, inform ships astern.

14. Signals received by radio or via the signal bridge will be simultaneously broken by the Bridge and the CIC. Once broken, CIC will pass their interpretation of the signal to the Bridge, which will either concur or nonconcur with CIC's interpretation. The OOD will ensure concurrence between CIC and the Bridge before acting on a signal. Advise me if concurrence is not reached promptly.

15. Use the ARPA's auto track capability to monitor the movements of all units in the formation. Compare ARPA information to the SRC's presentation for units in proximity to FISKE.

16. Ensure a Bridge ASTAB is configured for "Surface Friend" and that the call signal ASTAB indicates Link PUs for easy cross reference. Remember for Link participants, the course/speed indication on the "Surface Friend" ASTAB is the course/speed that unit is reporting itself on over Link 11, so it, along with ARPA information, is a good corroborative source of a friend's course/speed.

STANDING ORDER NUMBER NINE

PLANEGUARD OPERATIONS

\*\*\*I will never criticize an OOD who maneuvers FISKE out of plane-guard station and into open sea room because he or she is uncertain of the carrier's aspect, movement, or intentions.\*\*\*

1. *CV Operations.* Operations in close proximity to an aircraft carrier landing and launching aircraft require extraordinary vigilance and adherence to prudent seamanship to ensure the safety of the ship. When assigned as a planeguard, FISKE must be ready to recover a downed aviator or man overboard at a moment's notice. Nothing must be permitted to delay execution of this critical mission. Prior preparation is required, as well as frequent rehearsal of planned emergency actions.

2. When operating with CVs, stay out of a moving envelope 6,000 yards ahead, 4,000 yards abeam, and 2,000 yards astern unless directed to a station within this envelope by competent authority and I am on the bridge. Never turn toward a CV during maneuvers. If in doubt about a carrier's aspect or course during maneuvers, turn away to open range and call me immediately.

3. *Preparations.* The Officer of the Deck is fully responsible for making the ship ready to rapidly recover a downed aviator, and taking and maintaining assigned stations. In preparing for planeguard operations the following guidelines, though not all-inclusive, should be considered:

a. Upon notification of impending planeguard operations, or 2 hours prior to the start of land/launch operations, inform me of your intentions and begin timely preparations.

b. Review the standard operating procedures for the specific carrier involved and note specific actions required by you or your watch team.

c. Muster the lifeboat crew and ensure they are instructed on specific procedures and your intentions with regard to type of pickup, maneuvering, etc. Personally instruct the Petty Officer in charge and Boat Officer on their duties. Ensure portable radios are ready and tested and sound-powered phones have been connected and checked. At night, provide and test necessary lighting.

d. Research the appropriate lighting measure. Unless otherwise directed by a specific carrier's SOP, lighting measure GREEN will normally be set during actual flight operations. This includes side lights set on dim, aircraft warning lights, a blue stern light, and no masthead lights. Ensure normal running lights are displayed on bright except when actually conducting flight operations, and especially when the carrier is reversing course or otherwise maneuvering. Follow the motions of the carrier in this regard by observing shifts between white and blue stern lights, but do not hesitate to turn normal running lights on bright if the carrier begins to maneuver unexpectedly or you otherwise are uncertain as to the carrier's intentions or your position. In such circumstances, inform me immediately.

e. Be forehanded in bringing up required communication circuits such as CCA, land launch, departure, marshall, the primary maneuvering circuit, and the designated Bridge-to-Bridge channel. Obtain radio checks as operations and the situation permit, but do not fill the airwaves with repeated call ups.

f. Know the station you are to be assigned, or query the carrier early enough to enable you to proceed to station so as to be in position at the appointed time or 30 minutes prior to sunset. Anticipate carrier maneuvers up or downwind to ensure you are not grossly out of position and end up in a long tail chase.

4. *Stationing.* Normally carriers will assign a station 170 degrees relative, 1,000–2,000 yards astern. 170 degrees relative at 2,000 yards is typical.

a. Station limits in bearing remain 2 degrees. If in 170 degrees relative position, simply position yourself in line with angled deck line up lights and you should be well within limits.

b. Since the carrier can be expected to make frequent speed changes, station limits in range will normally be extended from 200 yards short to 500 yards long in range. Make speed changes boldly to remain within limits set by me. Remember, the carrier's reported and actual speed may be several knots different. Do not stop adjusting speed until the measured range rate is zero.

c. I expect you to stay on station. Continue to aggressively drive the ship toward the exact point station. Do not be an incrementalist. Maneuver boldly. Change course by 5 or 10 degrees or more, and speed by 5 or more knots until you see the relative motion required to get you to station. Watch bearing drift and range rate carefully. Keep checking and rechecking. Do not assume a specific course and speed for the carrier until you have verified her actual course over several minutes and can control your closing and opening rate at will.

d. The best estimate of the carrier's course and speed is the data reported over Link 11 tempered by your own observations and judgment. Ensure the carrier's PU is present on a surface contact ASTAB. Also ensure an ARPA track is initiated on the carrier. Note tactical signals and flashing light messages and obtain the best possible data from the DRT or maneuvering board, but do not rely on these aids alone. Watch the carrier's aspect, bearing drift, and range closely to obtain course and speed.

e. Ensure you anticipate carrier movements and react in a timely manner. If the carrier turns toward your side, turn away. If the carrier turns away from you, you can usually safely parallel the carrier's movements. Be alert for the unexpected.

5. *Maneuvering.* Expect the carrier to do the unexpected. Never assume it will turn or slow until you actually see a change in aspect, bearing drift, or range. Anticipate the carrier's next turn, especially during cyclic operations.

a. The objective is to remain astern, or off the quarter of a maneuvering carrier. Do not allow yourself to get ahead of the carrier's beam; take action to preclude the carrier turning inside of you when it reverses course. Remember, the carrier may turn greater than 180 degrees, or even 360 degrees, to reduce angle of heel or find a better wind.

b. If you are on the carrier's starboard quarter (e.g., 170 degrees relative, 2,000 yards) and the carrier turns to port away from you, simply maintain your original course and follow around outside the carrier's wake. Increase speed markedly if necessary to close the turning point, and/or turn outboard to prevent the carrier from closing your projected course when coming all the way around. Do not turn too early or slow. Watch the carrier's wake and follow around. At night, use the 3-minute rule to calculate time to turn and start a stop watch when the carrier signals its rudder is over or when the turn is detected first by Bridge personnel.

c. If you are on the carrier's starboard quarter (e.g., 170 degrees relative, 2,000 yards) and the carrier turns to starboard toward you, immediately put on left standard rudder and come 40 degrees left of original course. Cross through the carrier's wake and then come back right, following the carrier through the turn just outside the carrier's wake as above. Remember, the OOD on the carrier will be looking for your starboard running light so he or she knows you have turned toward the carrier's wake and will be well clear. Show your sidelight smartly.

d. If the carrier increases speed, as determined by an opening range or tactical signal, increase speed markedly so you will not get left behind. It is always easier to slow than regain lost ground. However, do not close inside your inner station limits without my permission.

e. If the carrier slows, as detected by a decreasing range or tactical signal, decrease speed slowly as we will tend to slow more quickly than the much larger carrier. If range decreases noticeably, slow 5 or 10 knots to regain control of your range rate. If you reach the inner edge of your station, slow to 5 knots or bare steerage way until range begins to open again, then quickly resume ordered course. Do not hesitate to stop, sheer out, or back down to preclude closing dangerously close. Keep me fully informed.

f. Ensure regular running lights are displayed on bright whenever the carrier and/or we are maneuvering.

g. Do not hesitate to use the radio to resolve a developing emergency situation. If you take such action, immediately inform me and:

(1) Use plain language and ships' names vice tactical signals and call signs; e.g., "AMERICA this is FISKE, my rudder is right. My speed is 12. I do not understand your intentions."

(2) Always give your course, speed, and intentions.

(3) Use any circuit on which you have good communications with the carrier's bridge. Usually this will be the tactical circuit in use or designated Bridge-to-Bridge channel.

(4) Use the whistle to signal your actions.

h. Do not hesitate to take action to resolve an emergency situation. Inform me immediately, but do not let this reporting requirement detract from your primary responsibility for ship safety. If circumstances warrant, simply direct the Boatswain's Mate to pass "Captain to the Bridge" on the 1MC or sound the collision alarm.

i. If the situation warrants, or the carrier's maneuvers are unclear, turn away smartly, increase speed, and place the carrier astern to open your range. In all situations you should have an escape course in mind to use if the situation becomes unclear.

6. *Man Overboard.* In the event of an aircraft crash or man overboard, the objective is to recover the person as quickly as possible.

a. If a helo is assigned planeguard, it will normally be the primary recovery vehicle. However, be alert, especially at night, to assume this role if the helo becomes disoriented or two or more people are positioned in the water a good ways apart from each other.

b. Close the area to within about 500 yards and stand by to assist. Remain well clear of the area upwind of the man if a helo is making the recovery.

c. Primary concern is to mark the area with a light/ring buoy and/or smoke afloat. If need be, order the carrier or helo to drop a marker.

d. Rehearse in your mind the myriad of specific procedures to take in various scenarios. Discuss the merits of a shipboard or boat recovery with me and get my concurrence with your intentions.

e. Use the best radio circuit to coordinate initial operations. Usually this will be the CCA, departure, or Land Launch in use. Emergency/SAR forces will not shift frequencies. Instead, forces involved in continuing operations should shift to an alternate frequency. Use plain language and any other means to facilitate a timely rescue.

f. At night, immediately break out lights and begin preparations for a lengthy search.

g. Ensure the best possible location of the crash or person in the water is plotted on the DRT and logged in the deck log.

## STANDING ORDER NUMBER TEN

### COMMUNICATIONS

1. *General.*

a. Ensure the ship is maintaining a proper communications guard on those tactical circuits specified in the approved communications plan.

b. In consonance with the TAO/CICWO, direct whether the Bridge or CIC will guard specific circuits. The primary maneuvering circuit in use will always be guarded on the Bridge. Answer all transmissions promptly, in proper order, but only when required.

c. Do not permit changes in equipment or circuits unless the tactical situation permits and the TAO or Operation Officer has approved the modification. All changes in equipment or circuits will be coordinated through the CIC Watch Supervisor who directs the Radio Watch Supervisor in the performance of his or her duties.

d. Be alert to access applicable SAS channels on the Bridge when necessary for specific operations (Helo land/launch, Carrier Marshal, ASW C&R, etc.).

e. Ensure call signs, authentication aids, and other communications software are ready for instant use.

f. Ensure that you are fully aware of all recognition signals, voice radio and visual codes and call signs, both administrative and tactical, that are in effect and in use in the particular area, formation, or operation in which this ship is engaged. Guard Channel 16 on Bridge-to-Bridge, or other channel specified for the area.

g. Require the assignment of a qualified radio telephone talker to the Bridge whenever the volume of traffic on the Bridge-to-Bridge radio is too great to permit monitoring by the normal steaming watch.

h. Keep a correct up-to-date tactical signal log on the Bridge so as to permit reconstruction. Scraps of paper, grease pencil notes, etc., are not acceptable.

i. Be alert to the possibility that some ships in formation may not have received a signal, especially in immediate execute situations. On turning, always look carefully to both sides and watch ships in company to ensure they move in a safe direction.

j. Use your signalmen. They are experts at tactical signals.

k. Require the timely change of daily codes and verify their successful insertion as EMCON permits.

2. *Record Message Traffic.* During Condition IV steaming, and such other times as message traffic shall be routed to the OOD, the OOD shall screen such message traffic and have routed to me:

a. All messages addressed action to the ship, by name, of immediate precedence or higher.

b. Weather messages which indicate a deterioration in conditions.

c. Any other such messages he or she deems are appropriate for me to see immediately.

3. *Visual and Radio Signals.* The following guidelines are set forth to ensure prompt and correct action on all signals transmitted and received:

a. Time permitting, have CIC break and interpret signals before they are hoisted and/or transmitted to ensure that there is not part of the signal that is confusing or incorrect.

b. Ensure that the Signal Bridge reports visual signals to the Bridge and CIC concurrently.

c. CIC will break and interpret *all* incoming tactical signals and have the Signal Bridge do the same on visual signals before execution of the signal in order to compare their decoding to that of the Bridge.

d. Control of the primary maneuvering circuit will remain on the Bridge. CIC will normally cover this circuit at all times.

4. *Radiotelephone Procedures.* Insist upon professional, seamanlike procedures over all radiotelephone circuits. Sharp, short responses should be routine.

a. Do not pass long, rambling administrative messages over R/T circuits.

b. Do not conduct repeated radio checks—assume our equipment is faulty and get it fixed/changed.

c. Keep transmissions short. The best transmission on an R/T circuit is "Roger, Out." Use it frequently.

d. Do not get involved in repeated relays for other units.

e. If given a reprimand, the only proper response is "Roger, Out." Then inform me.

5. *Operation of Bridge-to-Bridge Radio.* Operation of the Bridge-to-Bridge radio must conform to the United States Public Laws cited in USCG Manual CG-439.

a. No person shall operate the Bridge-to-Bridge radio except myself and the OOD, unless I direct otherwise.

b. A log required by USCG Manual CG-439 shall be maintained on the Bridge near the transceiver.

c. Specific attention is directed to USCG Manual CG-439 and OPNAVINST 2400.24A for proper procedures and limitations on the use of the high power mode of the transmitter.

d. When under way in, or entering U.S. territorial waters, Channel 13 must be guarded by the OOD, JOOD, or other officer under the control of the OOD.

e. References are to be maintained by the Navigator in the charthouse.

6. *Exchanging Calls with Unidentified Contacts.*

a. I do not desire to routinely discuss maneuvering intentions with other vessels on Bridge-to-Bridge radio, during open ocean steaming unless the OOD is concerned about the intentions of another vessel. This in no way restricts the OOD from answering calls of other vessels, subject to the EMCON constraints under which we may be operating.

b. Flashing light can be used to alert other ships, particularly "give-way" vessels if a constant bearing, or near constant bearing, decreasing range short CPA time (less than 10 minutes) exists. Bridge-to-Bridge radio shall be used at night and during daylight if there is no response by another ship to our flashing light. Make appropriate entries in the VHF Bridge-to-Bridge log.

c. Advise me if the ship is challenged by any ship not part of our task organization. Unless otherwise directed, do not delay in answering a challenge.

## STANDING ORDER NUMBER ELEVEN

## HELICOPTER OPERATIONS

1. *General.* Helicopter operations shall be conducted in accordance with FISKEINST 3710.1 series (AVIATION STANDARD OPERATING PROCEDURES).

a. Anticipate the setting of Flight Quarters well in advance to permit thorough preparations and safety checks. Be aware of alert conditions established. Advise me when ready to launch, recover, or hover an aircraft and I will give "Green Deck."

b. Ensure proper communications are established among the Bridge, CIC, Helo Control Station, the crash detail, and the helo.

c. Verify the helo pilot is in possession of the latest navigational data.

d. Position the ship for desired wind conditions prior to engaging rotors. Do not request a green deck unless you are within the NWP-42 wind and roll/pitch envelopes for the type helo you are receiving. If you cannot obtain satisfactory winds and roll/pitch, ensure you apprise me.

e. Control the following specific actions from the Bridge, after obtaining my permission:

(1) Green Deck: Helo operations authorized.

(2) Amber Deck: Engaging and Disengaging rotors authorized.

(3) Red Deck: Helo operations not authorized.

2. *Emergencies.* In the case of an emergency involving a helicopter under our control, set emergency Flight Quarters, close the helicopter's position at maximum speed (including coming to Full Power), determine the helicopter's problem, determine if we are the best platform to recover the helicopter and, if not, immediately contact the platform which may be, and notify our immediate Operational Commander. In the case of an emergency recovery the OOD may give a green deck. Should a helicopter not under our control declare an emergency and FISKE's TAO or OOD determines we are in a position to provide an emergency recovery, immediately contact the helicopter's controlling unit and offer FISKE's assistance. If appropriate to the circumstances (i.e., we are in the best position to provide assistance), simultaneously with offering our assistance to the helicopter's control unit, close the helicopter's position at maximum speed and set emergency Flight Quarters. In the case of such a recovery, the OOD may give a green deck.

3. *Wind and Sea Considerations.* NWP-42, Shipboard Helicopter Operating Procedures, provides guidance, operational procedures, and training requirements for the shipboard employment of helicopters. The Officer of the Deck shall be thoroughly familiar with all the requirements of this publication. In addition he or she shall:

a. Ensure the helicopter check-off list located in the Bridge OOD folder is completed prior to helicopter operations.

b. Maneuver the ship only during a "Red Deck" condition to obtain optimum wind, pitch, and roll conditions. The OOD must be cognizant of the tactical situation and maneuver the ship for minimum disruption of the formation or speed of advance while obtaining true wind from forward of the beam for all launch or recovery operations.

STANDING ORDER NUMBER TWELVE

SHIP ANCHORED

1. *General.* As Officer of the Deck while the ship is anchored, your primary attentions should be directed toward the safety of the ship and its personnel.

2. *Navigation.* When at anchor, have visual anchor bearings and radar ranges taken and logged and the ship's position plotted at least

every 15 minutes. Report to the CDO immediately if the fix plots outside the drag circle as specified by the Navigator, or if you have any indication that the ship is dragging anchor. If two fixes plot outside the drag circle, or you feel the ship is actually dragging anchor, take immediate action to station the sea anchor detail, veer chain, bring main engines on line on one or both shafts or radio for tug assist. Do not delay action to enhance the readiness and safety of the ship while you are further assessing the situation.

a. Station an anchor watch who is qualified to determine how the anchor is tending, strain of the anchor chain, and if the anchor is dragging. Establish continuous sound-powered phone communications between the foc'sle and the Bridge and require frequent reports on the anchor.

b. Ensure the QMOW is qualified and instructed as to the specified visual bearings and radar ranges specified by the Navigator to record and plot.

c. As OOD, personally take a fix at least every 2 hours to verify the position of the ship yourself.

d. At night, show proper anchor lights, aircraft warning lights, and standing deck lights as directed.

3. *Weather.* Be alert for changes in the weather, make reports to the CDO regarding changes in weather as specified in these Standing Orders. Be specifically alert for unusual wind shift, approach of a thunderstorm or squall line, and increasing waves or swells. In event of reduced visibility or fog, sound appropriate signals on the bell and gong as required by the Navigation Rules. Ensure the ship is brightly lighted.

4. *Approaching Ships/Contacts.* Inform the CDO of all ships that enter, leave, or pass nearby the vicinity of the anchorage. Report if a ship is anchoring or weighing anchor, appears to be dragging, or otherwise could become a hazard to the ship.

a. Record the range and bearing of ships anchored nearby and report any significant changes or unusual activity.

b. Allow no small craft, water taxis, or barges to approach the ship without your permission. Use radio loud hailer, the 1MC, or other means to warn them away if situations require, launch the RHIB to direct other boats to keep clear. Keep the CDO informed.

5. *Propulsion Status.* Whenever the ship is at anchor, propulsion plant readiness will be such as to permit reducing the strain on the anchor and getting under way on at least one shaft within 10 minutes. The steering system will be aligned for starting on the Bridge.

6. *Boats.* As OOD, you control the dispatch of and are responsible for the safety of the ship's boats. You may exercise your authority through the Quarterdeck Watch, but the responsibility remains with the Officer of the Deck.

a. Be especially alert to deteriorating weather. Make recommendations to the CDO concerning implementation of heavy weather precautions or cessation of boating if circumstances dictate.

b. Ensure boats are manned by fully qualified crews, are operated in a seamanlike manner, maintain positive communications with the ship, and are refueled regularly.

c. Hoist boats aboard during the night or when no longer required.

7. *Communications.* Maintain guard on the Bridge on all required inport circuits specified by SOPA.

a. Ensure you have voice communications with any ship's boat before you permit it to cast off.

b. Maintain a listening watch on the specified Bridge-to-Bridge channel for the port in which anchored.

c. Have the harbor operations or administrative net ready for use.

d. If established, maintain positive communications with ship's beach guard and be prepared to provide assistance as required.

e. If stationed, ensure the visual signaling watch is alert and carrying out their duties. If a signal watch is not posted, assume their duties yourself.

8. *Security.* Take all necessary precautions to protect the ship and

its boats from theft, terrorist attack, intrusion, or other untoward event.

a. Station an anchor watch and other such lookouts as may be required to warn you of the approach of boats or swimmers.

b. Station sentries as necessary to warn off boats or provide topside security. Arm them as required by the situation.

c. At night, ensure the water adjacent to the ship, the waterline, itself, and any ladders, boats' booms, or other fixtures/lines over the side are well illuminated.

9. *Watches.* In addition to a normal Quarterdeck watch and specified inport engineering security watches, the following watches will be established as a minimum while at anchor:

a. Bridge:

(1) QMOW/OS; qualified as Anchor Watch.

b. Topside:

(1) Anchor Watch/Phone Talker.

(2) Sentries as required.

c. CIC:

(1) 2 qualified OSs.

d. Other:

(1) Qualified Duty Boat Crew.

(2) Boat Officer in foreign ports, when appropriate.

10. *Emergency Actions.* In the event you suspect the ship is dragging anchor, or another ship is approaching or dragging anchor dangerously close, consider the following actions:

a. Establish communications with CCS.

b. Light off steering on the Bridge.

c. Veer additional anchor chain.

d. Station the Special Sea and Anchor Detail.

e. Direct CCS to light off at least one engine and order ahead turns to ease the strain on the anchor, move away from shoal water, or permit weighing anchor and proceeding to sea.

f. Radio for tugs or other assistance.

g. Inform nearby ships.

11. Do not delay taking any or all of the above actions while you assess the situation further. It is better to start an engine and station the sea detail needlessly based on early/false indications of dragging, than to jeopardize the safety of the ship while "confirming" the ship is dragging anchor. Act on the first indication that something is wrong.

12. *Reports.* Make the following reports to the CDO:

a. If any fix plots outside the drag circle of the Bridge as specified by the Navigator.

b. Inability to obtain a fix or confusion with navigational aids. Any doubt whatsoever.

c. Veering of chain, starting of steering units or main engines, stationing the sea detail, or any other emergency actions you take or recommend.

d. Evidence of the ship dragging anchor. A bumping or grinding of the anchor chain. Heavy strain on the anchor, or a "walking" anchor.

e. Changes in the weather.

f. Reduced visibility.

g. Cessation of boating.

h. Ships entering, departing, or nearing the anchorage, or those out of position or appearing to drag anchor.

i. Approach of small craft, burn boats, etc.

j. Any change in propulsion status or readiness.

k. Disposition of boats and any difficulties encountered.

l. Noteworthy communications from other ships or harbor authorities.

m. Security precautions taken or recommended.

n. The presence or absence of the CO and XO.

## STANDING ORDER NUMBER THIRTEEN

## TOWED ARRAY OPERATIONS

1. *General.* While the towed array is deployed, there are important speed and maneuvering considerations which apply.

2. *Maneuvering Restrictions.*

|  | Launch[2] | Recovery[2] | Array Imminent (on deck or within 200 ft of skin) | Towing |
|---|---|---|---|---|
| Speed | 5–15 knots | 10–15 knots | Maintain speed | Steerage Way to 30 knots |
| Sea state | 5 or Less | 5 or Less | 5 | 6[1] |
| Rudder restriction | 5° Rudder max | 5° Rudder max | Maintain CSE | None |
| Course change restriction | 180° max | 180° max | Maintain CSE | 180° max |

[1] For Sea States of 6 or above, if array is already streamed, full scope is recommended. Maintain forward motion and avoid following seas.

[2] Avoid following seas when launching and recovering the array.

3. *Emergency Situations.*

a. Man Overboard. The recommended recovery of a man overboard with TACTAS deployed is a Racetrack Turn. Launch the RHIB at the earliest acceptable opportunity (i.e., when you have a good lee). Also, take the winds into account. If the course you are on will establish a lee for launching the RHIB, then slow, maintain course, launch the RHIB. Once RHIB is in the water, increase speed and complete

Racetrack Turn to take a position near the person in the water. Use your best judgment in establishing a lee for launching the RHIB, and maintaining a visual on the person in the water. Maintain speed above that which would ground the array. I will make the decision to ground the array should it ever become necessary.

b. Propulsion System Failure

(1) Immediately begin emergency recovery of the array. Pass the following over the 1MC twice: "Engineering Casualty. Commence emergency retrieval of the towed array. SONAR division man TACTAS room."

(2) If propulsion is not restored prior to losing all way through the water, order the EOOW to lock the shafts. Continue to recover the array. When the array is on deck, unlock the shafts and start main engines to get under way.

## STANDING ORDER NUMBER FOURTEEN

### EMBARKED STAFF

1. If a staff is embarked in FISKE, one of our primary missions is to support that staff in the execution of their responsibilities. You are directed to take such action as will enhance our performance as flagship.

2. When a staff watch is posted, establish a cooperative, supportive environment, providing all possible assistance.

3. When a staff watch is not posted, the TAO (if posted) or CICWO will assume duties as the Staff Watch Officer. Ensure all provisions of the Embarked Commander's Standing Orders are carried out and all reports made as required.

4. As flagship, one of our primary functions is to provide rapid, reliable communications. Ensure the staff communications plan is in effect and that circuit restoration priorities are posted, completely understood, and enforced. Do not permit routinely shifting frequencies or equipment on important circuits without the prior knowledge and approval of the Operations Officer and/or the Staff Watch Officer.

a. Supervise the Signalmen in the performance of their duties as staff watchstanders. Specifically, ensure the Embarked Commander's call sign and seniority are used in replies to standard call ups and exchanges, whenever appropriate.

b. Be alert to answer all radio circuits for the staff if they are otherwise occupied. Know their proper call sign(s) and ensure you immediately inform them of the message received.

c. Never assume it is not necessary to make formal or routine reports to the staff simply because they are onboard, or in the space when a report is received or an incident occurs. Remember, other units are trying to keep the big picture and rely on information they copy on the nets. You can assist the staff in the accomplishment of their mission by making a judicious, timely report or request. The CIC watch must establish suitable divisions of labor with staff personnel for guarding circuits, controlling aircraft, plotting contacts of interest, etc.

5. Maintain the best possible connectivity on all circuits (including the link picture) for the staff as conditions permit.

6. Cooperation is critical to a smooth-running ship and staff team. However, you are expressly charged to bring all cases of conflicting instructions or interpretation to my personal attention immediately when such instructions affect the safety of FISKE. If you are ever confronted by a situation where the Embarked Commander or a member of his staff has directed or requested you to act contrary to these Standing Orders or any other orders or regulations in effect, you are directed to request my immediate presence to resolve the uncertainty.

# Appendix B

# MATERIAL CONDITIONS OF READINESS

The three standard conditions of material readiness that apply to U.S. Navy surface ships are the following:

X-ray     Set only in secure harbors and naval facilities. All fittings marked X-ray (X) are closed at all times except when in use.

Yoke     Normal peacetime in-port and underway cruising condition. All fittings marked X-ray (X) and Yoke (Y) are closed at all times except when in use. When open, the fittings should be so logged in the D.C. closure log.

Zebra     Set during peacetime emergency evolutions and wartime battle situations. All fittings marked X-ray (X), Yoke (Y), and Zebra (Z) are closed and may be opened only on receipt of permission from D.C. Central.

The following classifications of fittings are found on board U.S. Navy surface ships:

X-ray     Closed at all times when not in use.
X

| | |
|---|---|
| Yoke<br>Y | Fittings for which alternate Zebra accesses exist. Normally closed when not in use, the only exception being when condition X-ray is set. |
| Zebra<br>Z | Normally open for operation of the ship, habitability, and access. Closed during battle or emergency evolutions and conditions. |
| William<br>W | Ventilation and plumbing fittings normally open during all conditions of readiness. |
| Circle<br>X-ray<br>Ⓧ | Fittings that may be opened without special authority to allow the transfer of ammunition and the operation of vital systems. |
| Circle<br>Yoke<br>Ⓨ | |
| Circle<br>Zebra<br>Ⓩ | May be opened during condition Zebra on authority of the commanding officer to allow the distribution of food, access to sanitary facilities, or the ventilation of battle stations and other vital areas. When open, must be guarded for immediate closure if necessary. |
| Black D<br>Zebra<br>Ⓩ | Closed for darkening ship at night. |
| Circle<br>William<br>Ⓦ | Nonvital ventilation and plumbing fittings normally open during condition Zebra but may be closed in the event of a nuclear, biological, or chemical attack. |

# Appendix C

# TYPICAL SCHEDULE FOR GETTING UNDER WAY

| Time | Event | Responsibility |
|------|-------|----------------|
| 48 to 6 hours | Verify schedule for lighting off boilers (steam ships). | Engineering officer/ EOOW |
| Within 24 hours of getting under way | Conduct navigation brief.- Compare CIC and bridge charts and track. Conduct steering checks. Return checklist to navigator for filing. | Navigator |
| 8 hours | Start gyros. | Combat Systems Officer |
| 4 hours | 1. Ascertain from the executive officer the following:<br>  a. Any variation in standard time of setting special sea detail | OOD or CDO |

| Time | Event | Responsibility |
|------|-------|----------------|
| | b. Time of heaving in to short stay | |
| | c. Disposition of boats | |
| | d. Instructions concerning U.S. and guard mail | |
| | e. Number of passengers, if any, and expected time of arrival | |
| | 2. After obtaining permission from the executive officer, start hoisting in boats and vehicles no longer required. | OOD or CDO |
| | 3. After obtaining permission from the executive officer, rig in booms and ac-commodation ladders not in use and secure them for sea. | OOD or CDO |
| | 4. Have the word passed giving the time the ship will get under way and the uniform. | OOD or CDO |
| | 5. Energize and check all CIC equipment. | CIC officer |
| | 6. Conduct radio checks. | Communications officer |
| 1 hour | 1. Set material condi-tion Yoke (mate- | Division officers |

| Time | Event | Responsibility |
|------|-------|----------------|
| | rial condition Zebra in low visibility). | |
| | 2. Clear ship of visitors and inspect for stowaways. | Chief master-at-arms |
| 45 minutes | 1. Pass the word "All hands shift into uniform for getting under way. The uniform for getting under way is _____." | OOD |
| | 2. Muster crew on station. | Division officers |
| | 3. Man after steering and pilothouse, test steering engine, controls, communications, and emergency steering alarm. Do a time check. | Navigator |
| | 4. Test engine-order telegraph and revolution indicator. | Engineer |
| | 5. Test anchor windlass. | Engineer |
| | 6. Test running lights. | Engineer |
| 30 minutes | 1. Pass the word "Station the special sea detail." | OOD |
| | 2. Test fathometer and sonar equipment. | Navigator/ASW officer |
| | 3. Adjust bridge radarscope. | CIC officer |

| Time | Event | Responsibility |
| --- | --- | --- |
| | 4. Check navigation equipment on bridge. Check gyro repeaters against master gyro. | Navigator |
| | 5. Test sound-powered communications circuits. | OOD |
| | 6. Receive departmental reports of readiness to get under way, including material condition Yoke/Zebra set. | OOD/Executive officer |
| | 7. Make report of inspection for stowaways. | Chief master-at-arms |
| | 8. Record fore and aft draft of ship. | Damage-control assistant |
| | 9. Direct central control to report when main engines are ready for testing. Upon receiving this report, obtain from the CO permission to test main engines, and direct engineering control accordingly. A qualified OOD must be on the bridge when engines are tested. | OOD |
| | 10. Disconnect utility | Engineer |

| Time | Event | Responsibility |
| --- | --- | --- |
| | lines to pier and stow. | |
| | 11. Pass the word "The OOD is shifting his (her) watch to the bridge." | OOD |
| | 12. Light off gas turbine (if applicable). | |
| 15 minutes | 1. Report ready for getting under way to the executive officer, who will report to the CO. | OOD |
| | 2. If the ship is moored to a buoy, take in chain or wire, and ride to manila lines when ordered. | OOD |
| | 3. When directed, test the ship's whistle. | OOD |
| | 4. When directed, rig in brow. | First lieutenant |
| | 5. As boats are hoisted or cleared away, rig in booms and davits. | First lieutenant |
| | 6. Check ship for smartness. | OOD |
| | 7. Obtain permission to get under way from SOPA or whoever is designated. | OOD |
| 10 minutes | Pass the word "All hands not on watch, fall in at quarters for leaving port." | OOD |

| Time | Event | Responsibility |
|---|---|---|
| Immediately before getting under way | Warn central control to stand by and answer all bells. | OOD |

# Appendix D

# TYPICAL SCHEDULE FOR ENTERING PORT

| Time | Event | Responsibility |
|---|---|---|
| Within 24 hours of entering port | Conduct navigation brief. Compare CIC and bridge charts and tracks. Conduct steering checks. Return checklist to navigator for filing. | Navigator |
| Before entering restricted waters | 1. Deballast as required. | Engineering officer |
| | 2. Pump bilges when conditions permit. | Engineer |
| | 3. Dump trash and garbage when conditions permit. | First lieutenant |
| 1 hour | 1. Ascertain time of anchoring (mooring) from the navigator, and notify department heads and central control. | OOD |

| Time | Event | Responsibility |
|------|-------|----------------|
| | 2. Pass the word "Make all preparations for entering port. Ship will anchor (moor _____side to) at about _____." | OOD |
| | 3. Ascertain time for quarters for entering port from the executive officer. | OOD |
| | 4. Check smartness of ship. | OOD |
| | 5. Obtain information on boating from executive officer, and inform the first lieutenant. | OOD |
| | 6. Lay out mooring lines if they are required. | First lieutenant |
| | 7. Prepare anchors for letting go. | |
| | 8. Pass the word "All hands shift into the uniform for entering port. The uniform for entering port is _____." | OOD |
| | 9. Set material condition Yoke (material condition Zebra in restricted visibility). | OOD |
| | 10. Station the special sea and anchor details. Do a time check. | OOD |
| | 11. Obtain from the navigator information on depth of water at an- | OOD |

| Time | Event | Responsibility |
|------|-------|----------------|
| | chorage, and from the CO what anchor and scope of chain are to be used, and inform the first lieutenant. When the ship is being moored to a pier, inform the first lieutenant of range of tide and time of high water. | |
| 30 minutes | 1. Complete setting of special sea detail. | OOD |
| | 2. Recheck appearance of ship. | OOD |
| | 3. Direct the chief master-at-arms to see that personnel on upper decks are in proper uniform. | OOD |
| | 4. Swing lifeboat in or out as necessary. | First lieutenant |
| | 5. Request permission to enter port from proper authority before anchoring or mooring. | OOD |
| | 6. Pass the word "All hands to quarters for entering port." | OOD |
| 15 minutes before mooring or anchoring | 1. Station quarterdeck watch. | Senior watch officer |
| | 2. Assemble on the quarterdeck the guard mail petty officer, mail clerk, disbursing or supply officer, shore patrol, or other details leaving the ship in the first boat. | Oncoming OOD |

| Time | Event | Responsibility |
|------|-------|----------------|
| | 3. If the ship is going to a buoy, lower boat with buoy detail as directed. | First lieutenant |
| | 4. Stand by to receive tugs if requested and if required in going alongside. | First lieutenant |
| Upon anchoring or mooring | 1. Rig out boat booms and lower accommodation ladders. | First lieutenant |
| | 2. Lower boat as directed. | First lieutenant |
| | 3. Record draft of ship fore and aft. | Damage-control assistant |
| | 4. Secure main engines as directed by the CO. | Engineer officer |
| | 5. Secure the special sea detail. Set in-port watches. | OOD |
| | 6. Secure gyros only if permission is obtained from the CO. | Executive officer/ navigator |
| | 7. Pass the word "The OOD is shifting his (her) watch to the quarterdeck." | OOD |

# Suggested Readings and References

This is not an inclusive list, but here are some of the major publications you will encounter in the standing of watches both on the bridge and in the CIC.

## JOINT DOCTRINE

Joint Publication 0-2, "Unified Actions Armed Forces"
Joint Publication 1-0, "Joint Warfare of the Armed Forces of the United States"
Joint Publication 1-02, "DOD Dictionary of Military and Associated Terms"
Joint Publication 1-01, "Joint Publication System"
Joint Publication 3-0, "Doctrine for Joint Operations"
Joint Publication 5-0, "Doctrine for Planning Joint Operations"

## NAVAL DOCTRINE PUBLICATION

Naval Doctrine Publication 1, "Naval Warfare"
Naval Doctrine Publication 2, "Naval Intelligence"
Naval Doctrine Publication 3, "Naval Operations"
Naval Doctrine Publication 4, "Naval Logistics"

Naval Doctrine Publication 5, "Naval Planning"
Naval Doctrine Publication 6, "Naval Command and Control"

## FLEET EXERCISE PUBLICATION

Fleet Exercise Publication 1, "Antisubmarine Warfare Exercises"
Fleet Exercise Publication 2, "Antiair Warfare Exercises"
Fleet Exercise Publication 3, "Strike Warfare, Antisurface Ship Warfare, Intelligence, Electronic Warfare"
Fleet Exercise Publication 5, "Amphibious Warfare and Mine Warfare"

## ALLIED PUBLICATION

Allied Communications Publication 113, "Call Sign Book for Ships"
Allied Exercise Publication 1, "Allied Submarine and Antisubmarine Exercise Manual"
Allied Exercise Publication 2, "Allied Maritime Above Water Warfare Exercise Manual"
Allied Tactical Publication 1, Volume 1 and 2, "Allied Maritime Tactical Instructions and Procedures" and "Allied Maritime Tactical Signal and Maneuvering Book"
Allied Tactical Publication 3 and 3(B), "Antisubmarine Evasive Steering"
Allied Tactical Publication 4, "Allied Naval Gunfire Support"
Allied Tactical Publication 8, "Doctrine for Amphibious Operations"
Allied Tactical Publication 28, "Allied Antisubmarine Warfare Manual"
Allied Tactical Publication 31, "NATO Above Water Warfare Manual"
Allied Tactical Publication 33, "NATO Tactical Air Doctrine"
Allied Tactical Publication 43, "Ship-to-Ship Towing"
Also, the Exercise Tactic (EXTAC) series and the Inter-American Navy (IAN) series of publications provides information for operations with Pacific Rim and South American navies.

## NAVAL WARFARE PUBLICATION

Naval Warfare Publication 1-01, "The Naval Warfare Publication System"
Naval Warfare Publication 1-02, "Naval Terminology"
Naval Warfare Publication 1-03, "Joint Reporting System"
Naval Warfare Publication 1-03.1, "Operational Reports"

Naval Warfare Publication 1-10.1, "Tactical Action Officer Handbook"

Naval Warfare Publication 1-11.1, "Characteristics and Capabilities of U.S Navy Combatant Ships"

Naval Warfare Publication 1-14, "Commander's Handbook on the Law of Naval Operations"

Naval Warfare Publication 3-01.01, "Antiair Warfare"

Naval Warfare Publication 3-01.10, "Antiair Warfare Commander's Manual"

Naval Warfare Publication 3-03.1, "Tomahawk Land Attack Missile Employment"

Naval Warfare Publication 3-04.1, "Helicopter Operating Procedures"

Naval Warfare Publication 3-20.1, "Antisurface Warfare Commander's Manual"

Naval Warfare Publication 3-20.3, "Surface Ship Antisurface Warfare Tactics"

Naval Warfare Publication 3-20.6 Series, "Class Tactical Manuals"

Naval Warfare Publication 3-21.0, "Coordinated Submarine/Task Group Ops"

Naval Warfare Publication 3-21.3, "Surface Ship Antisubmarine Warfare Principles"

Naval Warfare Publication 3-22 Series, "Aircraft Tactical Manuals"

Naval Warfare Publication 4-01.4, "Underway Replenishment"

Naval Warfare Publication 6-00.1, "Command and Control"

## ALLIED AND NAVY COMMUNICATIONS PUBLICATIONS

Allied Communications Publication 113, "International Call Signs"

Allied Communications Publication 125, "Procedures for Radiotelephone Communications"

Naval Tactical Publication 13, "Flags and Pennants for the OOD"

## DEPARTMENT OF THE NAVY

Manual of the Judge Advocate General (JAGMAN)

Standard Organization and Regulation of the U.S. Navy (OPNAVINST 3120.32C)

U.S. Navy Regulations

Uniform Code of Military Justice

## DEPARTMENT OF TRANSPORTATION, COAST GUARD

Navigation Rules, International-Inland (COMDTINST M16672.2C), 30 Sept 95

## BOOKS

Brittin, Burdick H. *International Law for Seagoing Officers.* 5th ed. Annapolis, Md.: Naval Institute Press, 1986.

Bruhn, Lt. Cdr. David D., USN, with Capt. Steven C. Saulnier, USN (Ret.), and Lt. Cdr. James L. Whittington, USN. *Ready to Answer All Bells: A Blueprint for Successful Naval Engineering.* Annapolis, Md.: Naval Institute Press, 1997.

Crenshaw, Capt. R. S., Jr., USN (Ret.). *Naval Shiphandling.* 4th ed. Annapolis, Md.: Naval Institute Press, 1975.

Kotsch, Rear Adm. William J., USN (Ret.). *Weather for the Mariner.* 3d ed. Annapolis, Md.: Naval Institute Press, 1983.

Kotsch, Rear Adm. William J., USN (Ret.), and Richard Henderson. *Heavy Weather Guide.* 2d ed. Annapolis, Md.: Naval Institute Press, 1984.

Maloney, Elbert S. *Dutton's Navigation and Piloting.* 14th ed. Annapolis, Md.: Naval Institute Press, 1985.

Noel, Capt. John V., Jr., USN (Ret.). *Knight's Modern Seamanship.* 16th ed. New York: Van Nostrand Reinhold, 1977.

Smith, Capt. Richard A., RN (Ret.). *Farwell's Rules of the Nautical Road.* 7th ed. Annapolis, Md.: Naval Institute Press, 1993.

Winters, Lt. Cdr. David D., USN. *Boat Officer's Handbook.* 2d ed. Annapolis, Md.: Naval Institute Press, 1991.

# Index

# About the Author

Captain Jim Stavridis is a 1976 graduate of the U.S. Naval Academy. He commanded Destroyer Squadron 21 and USS *Barry* (DDG 52) and has served in destroyers, cruisers, and aircraft carriers. He is editor of *Division Officer's Guide, Watch Officer's Guide,* and *Command at Sea.*